American Soldiers in Iraq

American Soldiers in Iraq offers a unique snapshot of American soldiers in Iraq, analyzing their collective narratives in relation to the military sociology tradition.

Grounded in a century-long tradition of sociology offering a window into the world of American soldiers, this volume serves as a voice for their experience. It provides the reader with both a generalized and a deep view into a major social institution in American society and its relative constituents—the military and soldiers—during a war. In so doing, the book gives a backstage insight into the U.S. military and into the experiences and attitudes of soldiers during their most extreme undertaking—a forward deployment in Iraq while hostilities are intense.

The author triangulates qualitative and quantitative field data collected while residing with soldiers in Iraq and compares and contrasts various groups, from officers and enlisted soldiers, as well as topics such as boredom, morale, preparation for war, day-to-day life in Iraq, attitudes, women soldiers, communication with the home-front, "McDonaldization" of the force, civil-military fusion, the long-term impact of war, and, finally, the socio-demographics of fatalities. The heart of *American Soldiers in Iraq* captures the experiences of American soldiers deployed to Operation Iraqi Freedom at the height of the conflict in a way unprecedented in the literature to date.

Essential reading for students of sociology, military studies, and political science, as well as being of much interest to informed general readers.

Morten G. Ender is Professor of Sociology at the United States Military Academy at West Point, New York. His research in military sociology has appeared in *Journal of Adolescence, Military Psychology, Journal of Political and Military Sociology*, and *Armed Forces & Society*.

Cass Military Studies

American Soldiers in Iraq
McSoldiers or Innovative Professionals?

Morten G. Ender

Routledge
Taylor & Francis Group

NEW YORK AND LONDON

First published 2009 in the USA and Canada
by Routledge
270 Madison Avenue, New York, NY 10016

Simultaneously published
by Routledge
2 Park Square, Milton Park, Abingdon, Oxon, OX14 4RN

Routledge is an imprint of the Taylor & Francis Group, an informa business

Typeset in Times New Roman by
HWA Text and Data Management, London
Printed and bound in the United States of American on acid-free paper by
Edward Brothers, Inc

British Library Cataloguing in Publication Data
A catalogue record for this book is available from the British Library

Library of Congress Cataloging-in-Publication Data
Ender, Morten., 1960–
    American Soldiers in Iraq: McSoldiers or innovative professionals/
    Morten G. Ender.
       p. cm
    Summary: "American Soldiers in Iraq offers a unique sociological
    snapshot of American soldiers in Iraq, analyzing their collective
    narritives in relation to the military sociology tradition"–Provided by
    publisher.
    1. Iraq Warm 2003– 2. UNited States–Armed Forces–Iraq. 3.
    Americans–Iraq. 4.Sociology, Military–Iraq. I. Title.
DS79.76.=E526 2009
956.7044´3420973–dc22   2008 043557

ISBN10: 0–415–77788–7 (hbk)
ISBN10: 0–415–77789–5 (pbk)
ISBN10: 0–203–87937–6 (ebk)

ISBN13: 978–0–415–77788–9 (hbk)
ISBN13: 978–0–415–77789–6 (pbk)
ISBN13: 978–0–203–87937–5 (ebk)

Dedicated to my mom
SGM(R) Ilka M. Brown (*née* Ender)

In Memory of
2LT Emily J.T. Perez

Contents

11 Conclusion: soldiers, minds, and American society   151

Tables

Charts

Acknowledgments

No person is an island, and no book goes to press without the assistance and encouragement of others. A book about soldiers, especially during war, is no exception. Data sources for this book date back to the mid-1990s. A whole range of folks contributed in unique and exceptional ways across the years to make this book possible.

In the fall of 1994, Professor David Segal popped into my office in graduate school and announced a research trip to Haiti to study American soldiers deployed to Operation Uphold Democracy. I asked, "Can I go?" As we prepared for Haiti, then-President Bill Clinton brought the troops home early and rather than venturing to Haiti, we instead visited with them at their garrison at Fort Drum, New York in February 1995—2 months after they returned to the United States and after the division's block leave (a collective vacation for 4 to 8 weeks). I want to acknowledge and thank members of that particular research team for including and mentoring me on that trip: particularly David Segal, Lenny Wong, and Angela Manos provided instrumental insights to military issues. I also want to thank the 10th Mountain Division leaders—especially Dave Mead—for their hospitality and support during our research visit and the thousands of 10th Mountain troops and spouses for sharing their experiences during focus group interviews and on questionnaires.

A special shout-out and thanks go to my student Stephen Ruggiero, aka Mr. Sociology. Steve recognized the need for some military sociology in the early stages of the war in Iraq. He encouraged me to survey American soldiers at the end of their Kuwait deployment in support of Operation Iraqi Freedom, and he coordinated and administered the survey on the ground in Kuwait. Thanks to Steve and LTC Thompson for proctoring the questionnaires and the battalion of soldiers for taking time out to complete the surveys.

I would like to extend my sincerest appreciation and gratitude to the 1CD leadership—Peter Chiarelli, Keith Walker, and Paul Funk—for providing the encouragement and support to conduct this research while I was in Iraq. Further, a thousand thank yous to the many soldiers of the 1st Cavalry Division—both officer and enlisted who provided research assistance and support. Special recognition is reserved for those anonymous enlisted soldiers who selflessly stepped up and helped prepare 22,000 pages of survey questions all through the night the day before distribution (who knew Iraqis don't collate) and the small cadre of soldiers who assisted with some data entry while in Iraq. I am especially grateful to my diligent and thoughtful colleagues and battle buddies in Iraq who literally had my back and assisted me in situations that can only be described as simultaneously perilous, exhilarating, and productive. They include in no particular order Patrick Michaelis, Everett Spain, Diane Ryan, Patrick Buckley, Chris Talcott, James Merlo, Steve Smith, and Dave Meyer. I want to extend a special acknowledgment and much gratitude to my friend and colleague Scott Efflandt for taking me out and showing me Baghdad. A shout-out as well to Justin Powell for being the best driver in Iraq—I hope all your dreams are coming true. Jim Gallup, you are the best fieldworker and research associate I have ever met. Powder bags full of credit to you for your unbridled energy, commitment, and integrity. You pushed me beyond my own expectations. You are my ideal for how I prepare my cadets—I want them to all to be like you. A small but noteworthy recognition to Brian Reed for the pep-talk in Texas prior to my departure for Baghdad—you were right and to Debra, Ethan, and Garth Weaver and the Cole family for their gracious and supportive hospitality in Texas. Finally, I am extremely grateful to the thousands of soldiers in Iraq who took the time to complete the surveys and share their views responding to the open-ended questions. I have tried to give you a voice in this book. Some soldiers expressed cynicism and criticism as to whether such research would ever see the light of day and, if so, whether it would represent them honorably and confidentially. Well, here it is.

Back in the United States, Katie Hauserman, Mike Shrout, Remi Hajjar, Todd Woodruff, Anita Howington, Brian and April Tribus, Steve Ruth from Texas, Jan Piatt, Carl LaCasia, Gretchen Matthews, and Kathleen Plourd provided important and vital administrative and research assistance at various stages on this project. Tom Kolditz, Barney Forsythe, and Dan Kaufman believed in me and trusted I could manage myself in Iraq. In Germany, Oliver Walter provided valuable and practical insight in the latter stages of the book.

It is necessary for military sociologists to go where soldiers go. However, Baghdad, Iraq was not a safe place in the summer of 2004—it was downright dangerous. While my son Axel and wife Corina are ruggedly individualistic, highly resilient, and hardy beyond measure, a number of people did look out and support them in my absence. That backing in our little community of friends and neighbors helped us and gave me the peace of mind to focus on the work at hand. I want to thank the Endres Family—Taylor, Cheryl, and Mike, the Ruths—Bettina and Stevie, Michelle Michaelis, and Kay Kolditz. Additionally, we have some terrific and supportive neighbors, and they showed concern in small but meaningful ways while I was away in Iraq. They include the Brennans—Joan and Fred, the Pitts—Hannah, Katie, Courtney, Mary Jane, and Tom, and the girl next door, Vanessa.

Peter Wissoker, Jessica Galan, Jay Williams, and an anonymous reviewer provided thoughtful and valuable feedback on previous drafts of the book. Thank you to the Population Reference Bureau for permission to reprint an important table that compares military positions and occupations open to women. Similarly, thank you to Ellis Paul for reprint permission of a lyric from his song *Kiss the Sun.* Rebecca Schiff you are awesome for turning me on to Routledge. At Routledge, Andrew Humphrys believed in this project immediately. He, Rebecca Brennan, and Alexa Richardson have been magnificent in working with me across the many miles.

I dedicate this book to my mother. My sister and I owe her special thanks for an Army career that showed us all that is America and Europe. All my remaining thanks and praises to the two most important people in my life— Axel and Corina. You both intuitively knew when and where I needed time and space to work this book. I appreciate all your support, attention, and patience with me.

Lest I forget, the reader should know that the views expressed here are solely my own and do not purport to reflect the position of the United States Military Academy, the Department of the Army, or the Department of Defense.

Acronyms

1CD	1st Cavalry Division
A/C	Air-conditioned or air conditioning
ACFT	Aircraft
AO	area of operation(s)
AOR	area of responsibility
ASB	aviation support battalion
AVF	all-volunteer force
BDA	battle damage assessment
BDE	brigade
BFT	Blue Force Tracker (GPS driven, situational-awareness display)
BN	battalion
CA	civil affairs (a branch or MOS)
CAO	casualty assistance officer
CDR	commander
CMO	Civil-military operations
CO	company commander or commander
COIN	Counterinsurgency Field Manual
CPA	Coalition Provisional Authority (Iraq)
CSM	command sergeant major
DCU	desert camouflage uniform
DEROS	date eligible for return from overseas
DFAC	dining facility
DNVT	digital network (non-secure) voice telephone
DoD/DOD	Department of Defense
DOT	Dictionary of Occupational Titles
ECP	entry control point (like the FOB gate)
EO	equal opportunity
FA	field artillery
FBCB	Force XXI Battle Command Brigade
FBCB2	Force XXI Battle Command, Brigade-and-Below
FBCBL	Similar to a FBCB2 or a variant thereof
FOB	forward operating base

GAO	Government Accountability Office
GPA	grade point average
GWOT	Global War on Terror(ism)
HQ	headquarters
HMMWV	High Mobility Multipurpose Wheeled Vehicle
ICDC	Iraqi Civil Defense Corp (now Iraqi National Guard)
IED	improvised explosive device
ING	Iraqi National Guard
I/O	institutional/occupational model or thesis
KBR	(formerly) Kellogg Brown & Root
KIA	killed in action
MARS	Military Affiliate Radio System
MCS	maneuver control system
MFO	multinational force and observers
MGB	medium girder bridge
MI	military intelligence
MIA	missing in action
MIPR	military interagency procurement (or purchase) request
MNF	multinational force
MOOTW	military operations other than war
MOS	military occupational specialty
MP	military police
MR	monitor room
NCO	non-commissioned officer
NGO	non-governmental organization
ODS/S	Operation Desert Shield/Storm (Persian Gulf)
OEF	Operation Enduring Freedom (Afghanistan)
OIF	Operation Iraqi Freedom (Iraq)
OPTEMPO	operational tempo
OR	operational readiness rate
ORH	Operation Restore Hope (Somalia)
OUD	Operation Uphold Democracy (Haiti)
QAQC	quality assurance/quality control
PAC Clerk	personnel clerk (usually at the battalion level)
PCC	pre-combat checks
PCI	pre-combat inspection
PMCS	preventive maintenance checks and services
PMS	professor of military science
POC	point of contact
POSH	prevention of sexual harassment
POW	prisoner of war
PSG	platoon sergeant
PT	physical training

PTSD	posttraumatic stress disorder
PX	post exchange (on-base store)
R&R	rest and relaxation
REMFs	rear echelon mother fuckers
ROE	rules of engagement
ROTC	Reserved Officer Training Corp
RPG	rocket propelled grenade
SAT	Standard Academic Test
SF	Special Forces
SSA	supply support area
SUV	sport utility vehicle
TOC	tactical operation(s) center
TCP	traffic control point
TMP	transportation motor pool
ToS	Transfer of Sovereignty
TPI	Third Party Independents
TTPs	techniques, tactics, and procedures
UCMJ	Uniformed Code of Military Justice
USMC	United States Marine Corp
VBIED	vehicle-born improved explosive device
VEH	vehicle
VTC	video teleconference
WAC	Women's Army Corps (U.S. Army)
WAAC	Women's Auxiliary Army Corps (U.S. Army)
WASPs	Women's Air Service Pilots (Army Air Corps)
WAVES	Women Accepted for Voluntary Emergency Service (U.S. Navy)
WWI	World War I
WWII	World War II
XO	executive officer

Military ranks and pay grades by branch of service

Military grade	Abbr.	Army	Marines	Air Force	Navy and Coast Guard
Officers					
O10	GEN	General	General	General	Admiral
O9	LTG	Lieutenant General	Lieutenant General	Lieutenant General	Vice Admiral
O8	MG	Major General	Major General	Major General	Rear Admiral-Upper H
O7	BG	Brigadier General	Brigadier General	Brigadier General	Rear Admiral-Lower H
O6	COL	Colonel	Colonel	Colonel	Captain
O5	LTC	Lieutenant Colonel	Lieutenant Colonel	Lieutenant Colonel	Commander
O4	MAJ	Major	Major	Major	Lieutenant Commander
O3	CPT	Captain	Captain	Captain	Lieutenant
O2	1LT	1st Lieutenant	1st Lieutenant	1st Lieutenant	Lieutenant Junior Grade
O1	2LT	2nd Lieutenant	2nd Lieutenant	2nd Lieutenant	Ensign
Warrant Officers					
W5	CW5	Chief Warrant Officer 5	Chief Warrant Officer 5	n/a	n/a
W4	CW4	Chief Warrant Officer 4	Chief Warrant Officer 4	n/a	Chief Warrant Officer 4
W3	CW3	Chief Warrant Officer 3	Chief Warrant Officer 3	n/a	Chief Warrant Officer 3
W2	CW2	Chief Warrant Officer 2	Chief Warrant Officer 3	n/a	Chief Warrant Officer 2
W1	WO	Warrant Officer 1	Warrant Officer 1	n/a	n/a
Enlisted ranks					
E9	SGM	Sergeant Major	Sergeant Major	Chief Master Sergeant	Master Chief Petty Officer
E8	MSG	Master Sergeant	Master Sergeant	Senior Master Sergeant	Sen. Chief Petty Officer
E7	SFC	Sergeant First Class	Gunnary Sergeant	Master Sergeant	Chief Petty Officer
E6	SSG	Staff Sergeant	Staff Sergeant	Technical Sergeant	Petty Officer 1st Class
E5	SGT	Sergeant	Sergeant	Staff Sergeant	Petty Officer 2nd Class
E4	SPC	Specialist	Corporal	Senior Airman	Petty Officer 3rd Class
E3	PFC	Private 1st Class	Lance Corporal	Airman 1st Class	Seaman
E2	PVT2	Private E2	Private 1st Class	Airman	Seaman Apprentice
E1	PVT	Private	Private	Airman Basic	Seaman Recruit

U.S. Army units, number of personnel, composition, and the typical rank of the commander

Unit	Approximate number of personnel	Composition	Typical rank of the commander
Army	100,000	2+ corps and a HQ	General
Corps	30,000+	2+ divisions	Lieutenant General
Division	15,000+	3 brigades, HQ, support units	Major General
Brigade	4,500+	3+ regiments, HQ	Brigadier General
Regiment	1,500+	2+ battalions, HQ	Colonel
Battalion	700	4+ companies, HQ	Lieutenant Colonel
Company	175	4 platoons, HQ	Captain
Platoon	40	4 squads	Lieutenant
Squad	10	1 squad	Staff Sergeant

1 Introduction

American soldiers

Who cares?

(American soldier in Iraq)

I feel this survey was the biggest waste of my time since I was deployed, simply because it will probably not make anything better.

(23-year-old, white male E-3, married for the first time with one child)

Thanks for wasting my time by having me fill out this survey just like all other surveys I have filled out in the Army—it will be read and then forgotten.

(26-year-old, white male E-4, married for the first time)

I feel that these damn surveys are a waste of time that somebody with too much time on their hands has nothing better to do.

(25-year-old, Hispanic male junior officer, married for the first time with one child)

I would love it if we could get the results of this survey. I will contact Dr. Ender.

(25-year-old, white male junior officer, married for the first time)

I would like to be contacted about the results of this survey.

(23-year-old white female junior officer, never married)

A suggestion: Send results of this survey to those who participated. I know I would like to have some idea on what the results are.

(27-year-old white male E-5, married for the first time with one child)

I would be very interested in getting a copy of the completed study if one is planned.

(28-year-old unknown race male junior, married for the first time with two children)

So why do we give this survey? Is this going to change the way I live, NO! All this is, is a way to see how people think.

(23-year-old white male E-4, never married)

Introduction

War in Iraq for Americans continues at this writing. Despite the length, no common tag for the war has emerged. Some leading labels given to the U.S.-led invasion of Iraq that began in earnest in March 2003 include "Operation Iraqi Freedom," "War in Iraq," "The Long War," "Global War on Terror," and "War against Al' Qaeda." Similar to the U.S. experiences in Germany and Japan after WWII and in Korea and Vietnam, the ongoing belligerency in Southwest Asia is experiencing a tyranny of time—U.S. presence is ongoing, intense, and dangerous. Similar to earlier American wars, American soldiers appear to be remaining in Iraq in various capacities for a number of years. Because of the ongoing deployments, this book is certainly not the last word on American soldiers in Iraq. Yet, few to no books exist about the American soldier experience in Iraq from a sociological perspective. There are certainly many macro-level opinionated and strategic treaties on the wars in Iraq and Afghanistan. Likewise many micro-level, personal accounts from individual soldiers, spouses, key leaders, and reporters provide asymmetrical perspectives on the Iraq experience. These works take either political or anecdotal perspectives. This book carves a new niche between case studies and the political and provides a systematic sociological snapshot of American soldiers in Iraq.

The book has a threefold purpose grounded in a century tradition of sociology[1]—offering a window to the world of American soldiers in Iraq, serving as a voice for their experience, and describing elements of diversity in the all-volunteer force that is the American armed forces. First, sociology introduces and exposes people to a world beyond their lived experience. It depicts the others of the social world both domestically and internationally to include subcultures, groups, and populations. A window is important in overcoming the lack of worldliness found among populations. This book aspires to provide the reader with both a generalized and a deep view to a social institution in American society and the relative constituents that few have access to—the military and soldiers. It provides the reader an atypical view, a backstage insight into the U.S. military and experiences and attitudes of soldiers during their most extreme undertaking—during a forward deployment in a foreign land far from home while hostilities are intense.

Second, the book provides a voice for soldiers—it tells their story—not through one personal account but through a collective narrative. It represents their interests by examining their social life as lived and experienced while in Iraq. Their story unfolds empirically through their words, their responses to surveys, and through my observations in Iraq.

Finally, the book focuses on diversity and similarity among American soldiers with specificity to the context of the all-volunteer force. It does so by comparing and contrasting various groups and topics that have long been of keen interest to military sociologists who have studied members of the armed forces from a sociological vantage point. Here, assortments of soldiers' demographics couple with their miscellany of attitudes, perspectives, and experiences.

The heart of this book captures the experiences of American soldiers deployed to Operation Iraqi Freedom in Iraq in the summer of 2004. In late May of 2004, former military colleagues at West Point requested my assistance in Iraq to help work with local Iraqi researchers interested in broadening some already established systematic, comprehensive, and longitudinal public research of the Iraqi population.[2] I agreed to assist under the condition I would have enough time and resources available to access and study soldiers in Iraq as well. Thus, I deployed a few weeks later. First to Fort Hood, Texas for 10 days of pre-deployment preparation and readiness that all Americans—military or civilian—participate in prior to going into a battle-space such as Iraq. Next, it was on to Kuwait and then Iraq with a small team of five Army officers, all of whom had similar, short-term projects that summer. Once in Iraq, I attached to the Division Headquarters of the 1st Cavalry Division based out of Fort Hood, Texas. I completed my primary project with the Iraqis rather easily and quickly found, as I had anticipated, that I had freedom, support, and encouragement to study American soldiers in Iraq.

The quotes that open this chapter come directly from American soldiers deployed in Iraq in the summer of 2004. The quotes come from comments written in at the end of a survey I distributed to the troops. Emblematic of most pencil-and-paper questionnaires, the last section thanks respondents and offers them an opportunity to add anything else in their own words related to their experience. Normally, people in general provide few to no comments here. However, soldiers in Iraq are not in a run-of-the-mill social situation and they are expressive about their opinions. I include these personal standout comments here for emphasis for one of the many audiences that I hope will find this book of special interest—that is past, present, and future American soldiers. I also hope to reach the educated public, university and college students, military policy makers and leaders, and social and behavioral scientists.

Americans have certainly learned to differentiate between the war and the warrior. They have become comfortable with the contradiction of supporting the service member and having less or more support for a particular war. This cultural value dichotomy emerged during the first Persian Gulf War in 1990 and 1991 and now weaves through our national fabric. The goal in this book is to get to know the American soldier. Who are these service members? What is their individual and collective experience? What is on their collective minds? What attitudes do they hold? How has the war in Iraq shaped them? These and other questions receive attention in the following chapters with a range of readers in mind.

I can now return to the soldiers quoted earlier and respond to the collective themes. First, throngs of us certainly care about American soldiers. Next, you did not waste your time responding to my survey. Stuffing results away in a drawer in a basement somewhere is not an option for me. I have the privilege—and frankly, there is nothing better to do to bring these words and numbers out into the light of day. Third, consider this my delivery of the findings to you and others. Finally, I certainly hope the results and discussion make people think, and think hard and long, about war, those who experience war, and what war does to people.

Stories about American soldiers in Iraq and their families on the home-front have proliferated in the print media and appear in the pages of *The Christian Science Monitor*, *New York Times, Washington Post*, and *Newsweek* and *Time* (2003/2004), among many others. They are accessible by Googling the newspaper or magazine of your choice with the key words "American soldiers" and "Iraq." Likewise, journalists write personal stories from afar or on their experiences embedded in units in Iraq. Scholarly social science publications are appearing, and many more are likely to follow as the slow journalism of social and behavioral science takes the time necessary to produce scholarship (Musheno and Ross, 2008; Wong and Gerras, 2006; Wong et al., 2003). One example is a two-volume special issue on the sociology of the Iraq war in the journal *Sociological Focus*.[3] Notably, by the end of 2005, after 38 months into the war in Iraq, roughly 300 books existed about the war (American Association of University Professors, 2006; Greene, 2006; Inskeep, 2006; Memmott, 2005). Many more will certainly appear in the years and decades to follow. Few to none center on the collective social experiences and thoughts of American soldiers in Iraq, particularly while in Iraq.

It is peculiar yet somewhat understandable that the military is of primary sociological interest during times of relative war, only to quietly recede back into public and scholarly oblivion during times of relative peace. It is certainly the largest single organization in America—the largest "company" in the United States that in 2004 comprised roughly 2,230,872 uniformed service members in the four services including the active duty, reserve, and National Guard component as of December 31, 2004 (and not including the millions of civilians working within and governing it) (United States Government Accountability Office, 2005). The active duty military component comprised the largest majority with 63 percent (1,405,449 people). Of the four active components, the U.S. Army was the largest, with 488,143 (35 percent) service members. The military is compelling simply for its hefty socio-demographic composition. There is tremendous potential here in applying sociology to the study of the military, and it deserves a place alongside the study of other social institutions in American society such as the family, medicine, and religion (see Cockerham, 2003). Similarly, the military and the array of constituent members comprising it require continuous empirical scrutiny.

Diversity in the U.S. military

"Military diversity" appears oxymoronic. Like the ubiquitous term *military intelligence*, many might find military diversity a contradiction in terms. Indeed, the social history of the American soldier in the minds of Americans shows them to be of fairly typical and homogenous social characteristics. He was a "he," white, young, a U.S. citizen, Christian, fit, and heterosexual. This overgeneralization does reflect the social reality. American soldiers have been predominately male, white, young, full citizens, physically fit, Christian, and straight. The U.S. military has traditionally inducted people lucky enough to possess these seven hegemonic characteristics. Those "unlucky" enough to possess one or more social characteristics other than these face relative exclusion from service to the nation. Relative means either an outright ban from military service or, if in the military, lacking full membership status. For example, African-Americans have consistently served in the service of the U.S. military dating back to the American Revolution, including official segregation up through the early 1950s and even later in Vietnam, where they unofficially experienced exclusion from whites in the combat arms—essentially warranting second-class military citizenship. The less one conformed to the lucky seven historical social characteristics, the less their luck through both official and unofficial sanctions to fulfill service in the U.S. military and gain full citizenship.[4]

The stereotype of the American soldier is of political conservative, violent, traditional, authoritarian, obedient, rigid, macho, bureaucratic, and inflexible—a stereotype perpetuated by American film (Suid, 2002). These attitudes and beliefs comprise a view of a "military mind" that dates far back into American history (Lyons, 1963). This one-sided perspective periodically returns as it did in the 1990s following a series of popular positions that a civilian-military gap emerged in U.S. society (Dunlap, 1992; Ricks, 1993; 1997) with officers collectively possessing the foregoing characteristics and diverging from their more liberal, passive, progressive, authoritative, disobedient, lax, effeminate, impractical, and flexible civilian peers. A barrage of subsequent systematic research did not bear this dichotomy out (see Feaver and Kohn, 2001a).

The American military, much like American society, shifts socio-demographically. American society influences the military, but it does not necessarily reflect the larger societal change. The demographic shift in the armed forces is greatly influenced by the military's (wo)manpower policies increasingly moving toward a military that reflects the larger society more than at any point in her history (Dansby et al., 2001; D.R. Segal, 1989; Soeters and van der Meulen, 1999; Zweigenhaft and Domhoff, 2006). The history of filling the ranks of the American military dominates with obligatory service (with some occasional suspensions of conscription) primarily through the conscription of young males. In 1973, the shift to the all-volunteer force (AVF) replaced obligatory service with a market-model, volunteer military. While members of many minority groups (e.g., racial/ethnic minorities, women, non-Christians, and homosexuals) had distinguished service across American history, the change to the AVF marked a major turning point toward increased proportional representation of some groups in the U.S. military to that of U.S. society.

Following the change in socio-demographics is a similar diversity in mind among service members. While the U.S. military certainly continues to systematically discriminate in institutionalized policy and practice against select populations such as homosexuals, women, and people with physical anomalies, including the aged, there has been increased inclusion in recent years. This increased inclusion has fostered diversity in mind among American soldiers that transcends a typical, singular view about the world—essentially subverting stereotypical views of the way soldiers perceive social reality. This book highlights both the diversity in social characteristics as well as diversity in mind and experience of American soldiers—specifically among the forward deployed in recent years. Further, it offers the reader unique access to their experiences during a major military deployment.

American soldiers: Haiti, Kuwait, and Iraq

The major focus of this book is on American soldiers who served in Iraq. For perspective on the experiences of soldiers in Iraq, I use two additional samples to provide comparison groups: a sample of American soldiers who served in Kuwait in 2003 and a sample of American soldiers who served in Haiti in 1994. Most of the topics addressed in the present study follow up general studies of soldiers dating back to WWII. More than half of the questions asked of soldiers in Iraq came from questions asked of soldiers deployed to Kuwait and Haiti. These latter two data sources provide benchmarks on significant topics both generally and specifically, examining similarity and divergence. The specific topics comparing recent deployments to Kuwait and Haiti to deployments to Iraq include a host of social psychological dimensions from soldier morale to representing the military to others. Chapter Ten, the last chapter featuring data, examines all American service member fatalities from Iraq between March 2003 and October 2007 based on individual casualty data reports provided through the Department of Defense.

The vast majority of the American soldiers in this study are from a deployment to Iraq. These American soldiers mostly represented the 1st Cavalry Division out of Fort Hood, Texas. The "1st Cav," as it is affectionately referred to, deployed to Iraq for a 12 to 16-month deployment beginning in late 2003 and early 2004. The 1st Cav data reported on here originate from a broad range of methods including participant observations, both informal and in-depth interviews, and an open- and closed-ended survey instrument. I sought to survey 1,000 soldiers while in Iraq, and ultimately I obtained 968 surveys from soldiers and saw and interacted with hundreds more both on and off the Forward Operation Bases in Iraq.

The research accounted for here channels traditional military sociological topics from past wars. Topics include soldier demographics, preparation for deployment, the tempo of the work day, soldier morale, job satisfaction, reenlistment intentions, representing the military to others, reenlistment options, civilian job options, support of others during the deployment, communication with the home-front, attitudes toward domestic, social, and foreign policy issues, attitudes toward women in the military, and the personal impact of the deployment on the soldiers. In addition to closed-ended survey questions representing the foregoing, 19 open-ended questions solicited feedback from soldiers in their own words on a range of exploratory topics, including creativity, efficiency, quantification, control, predictability, micromanagement, and mission perception, in their daily activities.

The Iraq sample of soldiers represents an availability sample of soldiers deployed to Iraq at the time of the survey. I had the good fortune on one occasion to have all five brigade-level U.S. Army active duty commanders available at one place. With the approval and support of the division commander, I gave them a brief history of the sociology of war and the purpose of the study and I requested they return to their units with 200 surveys each and distribute them to 15 percent of the officers and 85 percent of the enlisted troops in their brigades all over Iraq. About 800 surveys were completed and returned while I was in Iraq. An additional 200 surveys went to a unit in Taji, Iraq approximately 1 month later. I eventually received those surveys through snail mail back in the United States in late August 2004. Of 1,200 distributed surveys, 968 were usable—an 81 percent response rate—an exceptional feat in an active war zone.

In addition to the Iraq study, two other surveys of soldiers and one set of archived data of service members provide some benchmarking comparisons to place the Iraq data in social perspective. The first of these are American soldiers who deployed to Haiti ($n = 522$). I assisted in the collection of survey and interview data from members of the 10th Mountain Division at Fort Drum, New York in February 1995, who 2 months earlier had returned from a mission labeled as Operation Uphold Democracy (OUD) (Ender, 1996; Reed and Segal, 2000). OUD was an intervention/nation-building effort in Haiti organized to ensure restoration of democracy following the peaceful departure of a military ruler. U.S. soldiers from the 10th Mountain Division went ashore on 19 September 1994 following political negotiations. They had a twofold mission: "be a presence" during the political transition and restore civil order. A multinational force went in to carry out the United Nations mandate to remove the military and restore a constitutional government and the majority-elected, Catholic priest named Jean-Bertrand Aristide. The U.S. sought to cultivate democratic institutions but also to stem the flow of illegal immigrants that were pouring into the United States at the time. American 10th Mountain Division soldiers comprised the majority of members from a coalition of nations known as the Multinational Force Haiti. The mission officially ended in December 1994.

The Department of the Army sponsored a study including questionnaires of American soldiers with Operational Personnel Tempo, referring to multiple and successive forward deployments by the same soldiers and their units, as the main focal point of the study. Most of these particular soldiers had three previous deployments: Saudi Arabia and Kuwait for Operations Desert Shield and Storm (August 1990–June 1991), Somalia for Operation Restore Hope (December 1992–May 1993), and Florida for hurricane relief following Hurricane Andrew (September 1992–October 1992). In late February 1995, we visited Fort Drum and secured an availability sample of soldiers representing just over five percent ($n = 522$) of the division of roughly 10,000 active duty soldiers.[5]

The second project provided another data source to benchmark the Iraq soldier data. It is an availability sample of a group of American soldiers ($n = 185$), who comprised a combined U.S. Army National Guard and active duty transportation battalion returning from 6 months in Kuwait in July 2003 following support of the initial Operation Iraqi Freedom. A former sociology student and a platoon leader in the battalion worked with me to administer the survey in Kuwait as the unit prepared to return home at the conclusion of their deployment. The Kuwait veterans received questions identical to those asked of the 10th Mountain Division veterans of Haiti years earlier. American soldiers in Iraq received the same questions. Comparisons and contrasts between these three groups provide an historical anchor, sociological perspective, and contemporary context in which to place the soldiers in Iraq. These findings should allow for associations with future generations of American soldiers as well.

Finally, the last quantitative source examined for this book is a secondary data analysis of archived demographic data of all American service member fatalities (3,807) serving Operation Iraqi Freedom in Iraq between March 21, 2003 and October 6, 2007. These data originate from official individual casualty reports released by the Department of Defense.

In addition to the quantitative data sources, two major qualitative data sources are used. First, a number of open-ended questions were included on the Iraq veteran survey to explore new and novel topics specific to the war in Iraq. Second, I also served as a participant observer and maintained a journal during my stay in Iraq. I refer to this "deep hanging out"[6] wherein I used my knowledge, intuition, and skills as a military sociologist to interpret the context and culture of Americans, Coalition Forces, Iraqis, and a host of international others living, soldiering, and working in Iraq. I grounded my observations in the previous work of sociologists and other social and behavioral scientists conducting qualitative research in forward-deployed military contexts dating back to WWII including the work of Robin Williams, Roger Little, Charles Moskos, David Segal, John Wattendorf, Laura Miller, Lenny Wong, and Tom Kolditz among others. References to the work of these scholars appear throughout this volume. Last, I am cognizant of my privileged position and status as an insider and my role in negotiating and gaining access to these unique military samples and the contexts in which they were working (Higate and Cameron, 2006). I am diligent in accounting for these advantages and make efforts not to overstate my observations. I conclude the book with some discussions of the limits of the findings, a sociologically imaginative discussion of the generation serving in the military today coupled with a personal statement about the war in Iraq, and some concluding remarks on inclusiveness at the intersection of the armed forces and society.

Who Are They? American soldier sample demographics

The distributions in Table 1.1 provide the sample demographics of the three surveys of soldiers who served in Iraq, Kuwait, and Haiti and a comparison to overall active U.S. Army demographics from 2004 (U.S. Army G-1 Human Resource Policy, 2007). The samples are representative of the U.S. Army in 2004 (recognizing Haiti veterans are from 1995). The exception was significant underrepresentation of Haiti veteran female soldiers.

The ranks of the soldiers are distributed across four rank groups—E1 to E3, E4, NCO, and all officers. The officer-to-enlisted ratio for the sample is consistent with the Army at 1 officer to 5.2 non-commissioned officers (enlisted soldiers). Again, a noticeable underrepresentation of officers and an overrepresentation of NCOs resulted in the surveys of Haiti soldiers. Some of the socio-demographics diverge more from group to group and from Army demographics overall. In terms of race and ethnicity, Iraq soldiers of African, Asian, Native, and Hispanic-American descent were within a few percentage points of their overall U.S. Army representations. Bi-racials and Others among Iraq veterans tripled their Army percent and white-American underrepresentation. The Haiti veterans are overall closer to Army demographics with some slight percent increases in Native-Americans. The ages of the soldiers in the samples from Iraq and Kuwait look to be older than the overall Army but—the breakdown in data management misconstrue the percentages—a closer examination shows the numbers to be closer. Yet, the somewhat older age among the National Guard soldiers would explain the higher levels of education of the deployed soldiers compared to the overall U.S. Army in 2004. Similarly, the soldiers who deployed to Haiti were more likely to be infantry- and armor-branched compared to the combat service support of soldiers deployed to Kuwait. The percentage of Iraq veterans combat-branched fell in the middle of the other two data sources, showing the diversity of specialties of soldiers in Iraq. Finally, Kuwait and Iraq veterans had more deployment experience than their Haiti peers, despite the latter group' having multiple deployments in the late 1980s and early 1990s.

Officer branches traversed the spectrum of branches including infantry, Armor, field artillery, other combat arms, combat support, and combat service

Table 1.1 Sample demographics of three surveys of American soldier veterans of Iraq, Kuwait, and Haiti and U.S. Army active duty soldiers

Demographics	Iraq soldiers Summer 2004 (n = 968)	Kuwait soldiers February 2003 (n = 185)	Haiti soldiers February 1995 (n = 522)	Active army demographics, 2004 (n = 494,291)
Gender				
Male	87.6	86.8	93.9	85.3
Female	12.4	13.2	6.1	14.7
Rank				
Junior enlisted	46.9	52.9	66.1	40.6
NCO	34.8	33.2	29.5	44.7
Officers	18.3	14.0	4.5	14.8
Race				
African-American	19.6	17.7	16.9	22.7
Asian-American	1.1	.6	—	—
Whites	55.7	55.4	62.5	60.1
East Indian-American	.1	—	—	—
Hispanic-American	11.7	7.4	8.1	10.3
Middle Eastern-American	.3	—	—	—
Native American	1.1	2.2	—	—
Pacific American	1.7	.6	—	—
Bi-Ethnic-American	2.7	8.6	—	—
Others	6.1	7.4	16.8**	6.9 **
Age				**Age**
17–19	3.5	7.8	—	17–19 7.0
20–22	23.1	23.5	—	20–24 34.0
23–25	23.1	25.1	—	25–34 35.0
26+	49.7	43.6	—	35–44+ 24.0
Religious affiliation				
Christian	67.3	68.6	—	—
Others	22.7	15.2	—	—
None/Atheist/Agnostic	9.9	15.1	—	—
Married status				
Yes	51.4	51.5	55.0	51.0
No	48.6	48.5	45.0	49.0
Significant other (married, fiancé, dating, etc)				
Yes	74.8	79.8	75.2	—
No	25.2	20.2	24.8	—
Children				
Yes	43.6	45.3	43.6	46.0
No	56.4	54.7	56.4	54.0

Demographics	Iraq soldiers Summer 2004 (n = 968)	Kuwait soldiers February 2003 (n = 185)	Haiti soldiers February 1995 (n = 522)	Active army demographics, 2004 (n = 494,291)
Political affiliation				
Democrat	25.3	21.6	—	—
Republican	31.1	34.7	—	—
Other/None	43.6	43.7	—	—
Military branch (Officers Only)				—
Combat	43.5	6.7	67.2	—
Combat Support	12.9	16.7	18.6	—
Combat Service Support	23.6	76.7	14.2	
Education				
Some high school/ diploma	37.7	47.8	52.6	76.0
Some college	40.0	38.6	41.6	7.0
4 Year college degree	16.9	9.2	3.9	11.0
Some graduate School/ degree	5.4	4.3	2.0	6.0
Previous military deployments				—
Yes	59.6	66.6	39.3	—
No	40.4	33.4	60.7	

Notes
1 Columns may not equal 100 percent due to rounding error.
2 **Includes all except African-Americans, Whites, and Hispanics.
3 A dash ("—") implies the question was not asked or no data are available.

support. Understandably, the veterans of Haiti were underrepresented in armor and combat service support and overrepresented in field artillery. Most of the soldiers in Iraq had been with the unit for 2 years or more (data not shown) and were comparable to the Haiti veterans. Similarly, both Iraq and Haiti veterans had been together with the majority of people in their unit during the deployment. All three sample groups had deployment experience. Some of the demographics appear representative of the Army overall. Religious affiliations, marital status, significant others (combining marital status with fiancés, dating, etc), number of children, and political affiliations, where data were available, paralleled with the U.S. Army. Despite a handful of inconsistencies, the samples of active duty deployed soldiers in Iraq and Haiti and the active duty and National Guard mix of soldiers deployed to Kuwait are solid representations of the U.S. Army. Yet, any generalizations to the military overall should be cautionary and applied primarily to the U.S. Army and not necessarily the other services especially the U.S. Marines who had a significant presence in Iraq at the time.

The chapters

The remainder of the book now turns to the American soldiers in Iraq with some comparisons to Kuwait and Haiti. Again, the purpose of the book is to provide a window to the world of deployed soldiers and give them a say-so in what they experienced. Variety is an additional purpose and provides a perspective for framing today's American soldiers. Despite uniformity, American soldiers today appear rather diverse in mind and experience.

The book opens with an interpretation of everyday life in Iraq for American soldiers by examining a long-studied topic in war—boredom—and the five dimensions that comprise it—underutilization, cultural deprivation, lack of privacy, isolation, and the relativity of time and space. I compare and contrast these dimensions to previous experiences of American soldiers, finding both convergence and divergence of experiences with past deployments.

In the next set of chapters, I provide more quantitative and social psychological evidence from the surveys of the soldiers comparing Iraq, Kuwait, and Haiti. Using similar studies dating back to WWII from military sociologists and psychologists around the world, Chapter Three presents results from topics including morale, perceptions of preparation, satisfaction with work, and everyday experiences in the war zone. Chapter Four continues with the social psychology of American soldiers with a focus on attitudes and how American soldiers both reflect and deflect one another along broader social issues that transcend the boundary between civilian life and working for Uncle Sam. In Chapter Five, I expand the social psychological attitudinal research from the domestic to more global topics and focus on attitudes toward foreign policy issues and the varied roles the U.S. military may perform following national and international decisions.

Chapter Six returns to the varied, day-to-day experiences of American soldiers in Iraq. The focus is on the major elements of the McDonaldization thesis. These dimensions include efficiency, quantification, control, predictability, and the irrationality of rationality. I contrast these five dimensions with some significant niche experiences of soldiers in Iraq, including opportunities for innovation, adaptation, and creativity afforded in the difficult, ambiguous, changing, and dangerous work and leisure world that was Iraq in 2004.

In Chapter Seven, I leverage the experiences of women veterans in uniform and re-present some of the topics from previous chapters. Notably, female service members are consistently more similar than different from male peers who they served alongside in Iraq, Kuwait, and Haiti. The chapter concludes with a new topic not covered in the previous chapters—contemporary attitudes toward the roles of women in the military.

In Chapter Eight, I turn to the uses and gratifications of communication media among soldiers. The U.S. war in Iraq and Afghanistan are the most communicated wars in U.S. history for American soldiers. The chapter spotlights communication media use and satisfaction and provides a brief social history of media for interpersonal communication during military forward deployments.

Chapter Nine relies on both qualitative and quantitative data to highlight future orientations of soldiers and explores the legacy of both a major military deployment and military service in general on the lives of American soldiers. Specifically, whether military service and a deployment are a turning point in their lives, what their reenlistment intentions and options are, and how, given their veteran status, they will represent the military to future generations.

In Chapter Ten, I turn to the ultimate demand of military life—death in the ranks. I analyze the social backgrounds of 3,807 U.S. service member fatalities between the first deaths in Iraq on March 21, 2003 and through October 6, 2007—the beginning of the so-called surge of American forces in Iraq in the fall of 2007. The analysis is anchored in the social history of U.S. service member deaths showing that in many ways, once in Iraq, death is a random, indeed a relatively equal-opportunity matter for service members, across a number of socio-demographic characteristics. Even in death, there is inclusiveness across the mosaic of American soldiers. This finding helps demystify who dies and who does not among American soldiers in war.

The concluding chapter returns to the major findings of the study—both the homogeneity and diversity of mind and experience among American soldiers in the U.S. Army. Further, the conclusion highlights some limitations and delimitations of the present study. I further take some literary liberty of offering my perspectives on this generation of service members as a great subgeneration of Americans and a personal statement on the war in Iraq. I end with a discussion of the civil-military fusion.

2 Creeping banality

The boredom factor and American soldiers

We are mostly bored.

U.S. Army Captain in Iraq

Introduction

Soldier life in Iraq lacked progression by the summer of 2004. Below I provide a panorama of boredom and the dimensions of boredom found in previous U.S. military interventions compared to experiences in Iraq. Five elements of boredom are discussed—underutilization, cultural deprivation, lack of privacy, isolation, and time and space—as I observed them relative to the experience of soldiers in Iraq. Next, two studies are highlighted that systematically compare boredom among U.S. peacekeeping troops in the Sinai with those in the prewar desert preparing for the first Persian Gulf War. Finally, the chapter concludes with a discussion of boredom in war and the implications of the findings for soldiers in Iraq. The bottom-line, up-front conclusion is that boredom in Iraq for American soldiers is both similar and dissimilar to that in past wars.

Elements of boredom

Boredom correlates with the social psychological notion of alienation. In his reflections on boredom from a sociological perspective, Peter Conrad (1997) finds the social history of boredom emerging alongside the Western emergence of the new self and increased leisure. Today, an absence of flow of human experience, no future, and unmet social expectations capture boredom—a socially constructed four-walled padded room. It is clearly something negative. For example, under-stimulation and disconnection characterize boredom for American undergraduates (Conrad, 1997). Other dimensions include repetition, lack of interaction, and minimal variation. Boredom constructs in time and space. Most significantly, the conclusion to draw is that a feeling of entrapment may intensify the feelings and context of the boredom experience.[1]

Boredom can also result from overload of information. Sociologist Orrin Klapp (1986) locates boredom and overload on a continuum with no stimulation on one extreme and overstimulation on the other. In a similar and more recent vein, Thomas Friedman (2006) recently argued that the world had flattened as a sense of sameness is overcoming the world. Speed of information around the world is creating a "creeping banality" wherein cultural banality is the norm rather than the exception. This creates cultural homogenization and, ultimately, may lead to cultural ethnocide.

Boredom has long been a feature of the military. A classic line from a no-less classic study of American soldiers in WWII states: "…combat as actually experienced consisted of periods of intense activity and excitement punctuating the periods of routine and boredom" (Williams and Smith, 1949:87–88). It captures the essence of the war experience for soldiers and many since. Likewise, military duty fosters contexts for boredom to emerge—even during peacetime. Elements of military "contingent work" features:

> long periods of inactivity interrupted only and punctuated occasionally by the exercise of valued skills; is focused on objects, not people, and on landscapes that rarely change; and finally, it often reveals an inconsistency between the skills and the status that workers value and the activities they are expected to perform in between episodes of "real work"
>
> (Charlton and Hertz, 1989:300–301).

Research on the military has thus come to define and refine elements of boredom (see Harris and Segal, 1985; Segal et al., 1984; Segal and Segal, 1993). The question asked "To what degree are the elements of the boredom factor, specifically, underutilization, cultural deprivation, lack of privacy, isolation, and time and space continuations, experienced by American soldiers in Iraq." Stories recounted below from Iraq both confirm and confound earlier findings of boredom elements.

Boredom in the Army: The Sinai and Saudi Arabia in the late twentieth century

Peacekeeping in the Sinai

In the mid-1980s, military sociologist David Segal and associates conducted some of the first focused studies on boredom in a military context. Military leaders and early observers of active duty soldiers participating in the Multinational Force and Observers in the Sinai found boredom to be a problem—paramount of which was underutilization. Underutilization referred to routinization and monotony of activities. Underutilization dates back to peacekeeping missions in the 1970s wherein combat-oriented soldiers more often reported boredom than their combat support and combat service support peers—although, medics were likely to report some boredom (Moskos, 1975; Rikhye et al., 1974).

Research on cultural deprivation in the Sinai connected perceived restrictions rather than actual rules or physical ones—the restrictions linked to the desert environment and a lack of peoples and towns, a few fellow service members, and a handful of Bedouin tribesmen who spoke no English. Essentially, the soldiers merely had their sparse military compound, limited accoutrements, and the surrounding desert for stimulations. The lack of privacy felt by troops in the Sinai was prevalent. They worked, slept, and played collectively and in close proximity. Portable stereos and headphones provided the only source of individual privacy.

Isolation referred to contact with the home-front. Mail and telephones were not readily available in the Sinai. Mail was nonexistent initially and took weeks when it finally was. Telephonic communication proved to be rare and expensive when available. Communication with home was the most highly valued element of the deployment—and it was poor. The early researchers also noted that isolation further manifested by a temporal and spatial element—a sensory deprivation. Time of day, week, and even month reoriented soldiers. Known as "Creeping Bedouin Syndrome," it eventually led to a disregard for clock time and a new preoccupation with event time—mostly the events of eating and sleeping.

Over time, Army leaders brought in many resources and accoutrements to deal directly with boredom. However, research showed that it never quite got any less boring than when the peacekeepers first arrived (Applewhite et al., 1993). Indeed, some attempts to overcome boredom created new problems. For example, a new enlisted club for after-hours drinking facilitated alcohol-related health problems. Improved communications with family actually magnified rather than reduced the isolation felt by the soldiers from their families and loved ones.

The first Persian Gulf War

During Operation Desert Shield, the military title for the first Persian Gulf War (1990–1991), the U.S.-led coalition placed U.S. forces in Saudi Arabia prior to the onset of belligerent hostilities between coalition and Iraq military forces. Sociologist John Wattendorf (1992) conducted in-depth interviews with American soldiers in this prewar desert situation. He is the closest to date at replicating the classic and important military sociological work of Harvard sociologist Samuel Stouffer and his associates in World War II (Stouffer et al., 1949, 2 vols). Wattendorf built upon the work of previous studies of peacekeeping troops and boredom in the Sinai. He found evidence for the four elements of boredom. The caveat, however, for the American soldier in the prewar environment of Saudi Arabia was her anticipation of an attack on or by the Iraqis in Kuwait (which notably never came). The heightened sense of readiness ameliorated some boredom but not all of it. Cultural deprivation manifested and developed as well. There was certainly more intermixing with local nationals and a few Saudis in the early 1990s than peacekeepers had been doing in the Sinai desert in the 1980s—but physical movement was somewhat more restricted in Saudi Arabia. While some restrictions existed (more so for female soldiers), few complaints emerged. The one area that created the greatest consternation was the prohibition of alcohol—soldiers desired it, despite the absolute prohibition.

Like their brothers in arms in the Sinai, American combat soldiers in Saudi Arabia felt the most underutilized and ultimately were bored. They trained for two types of missions: first, defending Saudi Arabia and, second, preparing to fight an invading Army of Iraq in Kuwait. Both precipitated tedious training but provided significant downtime. Concomitantly, support troops on the other hand worked long and rigorous hours during the buildup with limited downtime.

Privacy in the prewar desert was nonexistent. Compounds and camps provided very small and warehoused sleeping arrangements in open bays. Like NCOs in the Sinai, prewar Saudi-deployed American soldiers had very few opportunities to segregate from their subordinates. Gender and rank commingled to create problems for both genders in the prewar desert environment.

Finally, isolation in Saudi Arabia and the Sinai were similar. Mail as a one-way communication mode took 1 month to receive word back. Notably, mail to "Any Soldier" via public support proved somewhat successful. Ironically, there was a backlash. Soldiers later learned that the overwhelming abundance of such public mail support actually contributed to the delay of their more personal mail. Telephonic access was similar to the Sinai, with access limited and expensive. Soldiers and families accrued excessive telephone bills. What emerged are the first elements of actual and perceived inequity in the use communication media—wherein leaders and those in the rear areas had greater access.

In terms of the loss of spatiotemporal reality, like the Sinai, temporal elements of the deployment played a considerable role in the American soldiers' lived experience in Saudi Arabia. Sinai soldiers knew their tour lasted only 6 months and, consequently, their day morphed to evolve around event rather than clock time. Their sense of what day it was, and eventually month, became lost on soldiers. As the first Persian Gulf War actually loomed on the horizon, an uncertainty and "fragile morale" existed among American soldiers regarding the length of the tours, rotation policies, and the degree of danger allied with one's location in the war. Unlike the "Creeping Bedouin Syndrome" in the Sinai, American soldiers in Saudi Arabia, waiting anxiously for the battle of Operation Desert Storm to begin, were preoccupied with the uncertainty of the deployment, when the war would begin and end, and when they would be able to return home. Boredom permeated their experiences.

The boredom factor revisited: experiences in Iraq

Underutilization

Underutilization implies some noticeable level of routinization and monotony of activities. As noted earlier, underutilization has long been an element of peacekeeping in missions and was evident among mostly combat troops and medics in the prewar desert of Saudi Arabia in the months leading up to the first Persian Gulf War in 1990 to 1991.

Combat troops and medics were fully engaged in Iraq in the summer of 2004. Underutilization lacked in terms of amount of time spent doing military-related activities. Medical personnel in Iraq were fully working 12- to 16-hour daily shifts, 7 days a week. As of November 16, 2004, 10,726 U.S. service members had been killed or wounded—13 percent of whom died. This does not include the Iraqi civilian, military, and insurgent wounded attended to and served by the U.S. military as well. Indeed, the U.S. forces suffered severe shortages of qualified medical personnel to support the large military force alone, and the American medical personnel reached out to attend the local populations (Gawande, 2004).

For combat troops, they too felt overutilized for a range of missions. Known as "Full Spectrum Operations," American soldiers in Iraq in the summer of 2004 had five major areas of concern (Chiarelli and Michaelis, 2005). The areas included somewhat traditional combat operations, training and employing Iraqi security forces (both military and police), establishing essential services (e.g., electricity, running water, solid waste pickup, and disposal of raw sewage); governance; and creating economic pluralism.

For American soldiers on the ground in Iraq, the context of Full-Spectrum socially structured their Rules of Engagement (ROE). ROE prescribe for soldiers how they can use force. While commanders up and down the military chain of command normally define the use of force, such definitions can also vary from mission to mission for the same unit of soldiers. For example, it was common for a patrol in the morning to conduct a humanitarian mission taking soccer balls to middle school students and that evening conduct a neighborhood raid. Or, as British Admiral Sandy Woodward, the Commander of the Task Force in the Falkland Islands in 1982 is oft quoted as saying:

> I shall have to amplify the ROE so that all commanding officers can know what I am thinking, rather than apply their own interpretation, which might range from "ask them for lunch to 'Nuke' em for breakfast"
>
> (quoted in Department of the Army, 1994).

However, there was considerable concern among American soldiers in Iraq with whom I talked regarding the ROE. The three Ps guided their collective mission and individual behavior while off the Forward Operating Base (FOB) among the Iraqis—polite, professional, and prepared (to kill). Every off-post mission was exceptionally dangerous where soldier convoys of typically three vehicles meticulously planned their missions, based on recent and historical knowledge about the area. They also planned contingency efforts in case of attacks and other likelihoods. Every soldier in the convoy had a particular role based on various contingencies. Thus, for example, I participated in a few 10-mile drives from Camp Victory (a FOB) to the Green Zone and back to Victory that involved an entire morning to undertake. Convoys were targets of improvised explosives planted either on the road or in parked or rolling vehicles with or without a suicidal driver, mortars, rocket-propelled grenades, and small arms fire, killing and wounding soldiers and civilians indiscriminately. Medics and evacuation personnel were rarely wanting for activity. Indeed, inactivity was preferred. Contrary to boredom, combat soldiers specifically, as well as any soldiers going outside the FOB, and the medics on the FOB, experienced ongoing overload in terms of the amount of time and degree to which they responded to a host of others.[2]

I did observe considerable boredom on the part of specific American soldiers confined to the FOB for their responsibilities. Enlisted support personnel working in service support of the FOB such as administrative people and signal personnel incurred a great deal of underutilization. Soldiers conducting guard duty on the FOB, especially those in seemingly no-risk/low-risk positions, such as identification card checkers for buildings, watched movies on portable DVD players, read, and listened to music on portable music stereos. This boredom factor was not lost on their leaders. To overcome the experiences of underutilized troops, one inventive brigade level leader began an equilibrium system. Essentially, he "grounded" some of his individual combat personnel on the FOB and mandated a system sending support personnel out on convoys in their place. This both rested his overutilized people and more fully employed the underutilized; both groups appeared to appreciate the opportunities afforded by this practice.

I also observed incidents of such behavior in the more dangerous guard positions such as towers and gates leading unto the FOB but mostly with Iraqis. There was some concern that Iraqi soldiers provided questionable security on the perimeter outside the gate area guarded by Americans and they might be bored and slack in their responsibilities. I overheard concerns of this and saw some evidence of relaxed watchfulness on the part of the Iraqis. For example, during the hottest part of the day, many Iraqi soldiers took refuge in shaded underpasses along the highway or near tree lines, essentially forsaking guard posts nearest the road and in sun-drenched open areas.

Many combat soldiers referred to their convoy missions as *Groundhog Day*— referring to the 1993 film starring Bill Murray (Ramis, 1993). The character played by Bill Murray, Phil Connors, P.C. is anything but politically correct and lives everyday repeatedly for perhaps 10,000 years, until he changes from a selfish to selfless person. The *Groundhog Day* film reference implies less boredom in terms of time doing things—there was always something to do. The meaning is derived from the quality of day-to-day accomplishments during the long days. In this sense, soldier experiences in Iraq became highly routinized and monotonous—a "creeping banality."

Cultural deprivation

Cultural deprivation in the Sinai in the 1980s connected to perceived restrictions rather than actual rules. The restrictions linked with the desert environment and a lack of people in communities. Other than a few service members, a few Bedouin tribesmen would emerge but spoke no English. Noted earlier, Wattendorf (1992) found very few complaints regarding cultural deprivation in Saudi Arabia in 1990 other than alcohol prohibition.

In Iraq, General Order #1 prohibited alcohol use for the U.S. Army. However, the Navy, Marines, Air Force, foreign workers, local nationals, American civilian contractors, and DOD personnel had differing rules regarding the consumption of alcohol. This relative deprivation caused considerable consternation among U.S. Army soldiers, especially on the FOB and in places that had diverse groups, and the different rules played out in practice. Near-beer and tobacco products were, however, readily available to the soldiers and were consumed conspicuously.

Additionally, for those leaving the FOB, there was a great deal of cross-cultural interaction between U.S. service members and Iraqis. The amount of interaction ranged among policing neighborhoods, working with translators, employing Iraqis, and befriending locals. In two cases, I was involved in getting to know Iraqis. One was a local merchant and his wife who had established a sewing shop and kiosk selling trinkets and other items on the FOB. We welcomed the new owner to the neighborhood as it were, intentionally patronizing his business and sending colleagues there to help stand up his business. We learned a great deal about Iraq from this merchant and his wife as we shared stories about our families and about their experiences living under the Baathist regime of Saddam Hussein. Tragically, the owner and young daughter were assassinated in December 2004—likely owing to his newly found success coupled with his direct affiliation with the Americans.

Another local Iraqi was a former military major with a Ph.D. in organization behavior. He, too, was married and had four children—the eldest two sons were physicians, the eldest daughter was oriented toward medicine, and the youngest daughter dreamt of a career in music. Despite his success and wealth, he opted to remain in Baghdad, and he established a business employing roughly 600 research assistants. My new friend and colleague spent a great deal of time on his cellular telephone as he and his family constantly tracked one another's movements and safety around Baghdad. After returning to Iraq following a training visit to the United States, he fled Iraq for his and his family's safety. He continues to move in and outside of Iraq and works through his business headquarters. I emphasize these relationships to show that culturally, it is fairly effortless for American soldiers to establish relationships with Iraqis—especially for the significant length of time they spend in Iraq—and many have.

I spoke with American soldiers who developed similar and even deeper relationships with Iraqis. They mentioned working with them on a daily basis for an entire year. For example, a 25-year old Army captain, with whom I spent 1 day, had become very friendly with Iraqis in his area of operation. The Iraqis he worked with were managing garbage collections in a large area of Baghdad and were directly supported by American forces. The Army provided funds to purchase garbage trucks, security, compounds, and salaries. We spent an entire workday visiting two locations. We went to the home of one of the Iraqi managers. The captain spent hours in the home sipping tea and passing the time while the manager's children and neighbors played and interacted with the American soldiers and myself outside as we cautiously socialized and guarded the patrol vehicles and the perimeter from an attack.

Lack of privacy

The lack of privacy in a military forward-deployed context refers to a form of boredom where there is an inability to find personal space. Military missions dating back to the American Revolution did not provide soldiers with personal space. In extreme contrast, for many, if not most U.S. Army soldiers in Iraq, there was an unprecedented amount of personal space—especially for the senior non-commissioned officers (NCOs) and most officers. Many FOBs used mobile home-type trailers to house soldiers. There were two types of trailers—"dry" and "wet" trailers. A dry trailer had three rooms with separate entrances, an air-conditioner-heater combination, and a window. The room was roughly 10′ by 10′ featuring double matching bed frame and mattress with sheet, pillow, pillow case, and comforter, night stand, metal closet, and a fire extinguisher. Community hot and cold showers, sinks, and toilets were within a short walk in another trailer.

Wet trailers were two 12′ by 12′ rooms furnished with a shower and WC shared in the middle. Senior NCOs and officers generally had a wet trailer. Many supported an underground economy paying a few extra dollars for personal maid service to the Filipino domestic workers on the FOB contracted by a private firm to clean laundry and community areas.

Lower-ranked soldiers doubled up in the 10′ by 10′ room described above. Not unlike college dormitory sophomores, they easily divided the room for increased privacy with closets, draped blankets, and other privacy walls. Some soldiers commented that they felt their lodging in Iraq exceeded the lodging at many posts in the United States. Wong and Gerras (2006:1) refer to the FOB as a "home away from home" with its rich amenities. In their ethnographic report on Iraq, they provide a telling example of FOB life:

> ...the conditions on FOBs generally allow soldiers to escape the harsh environment of Southwest Asia in order to rest. Air conditioning and comfortable beds are critical luxuries in providing rest for soldiers. One infantry team leader commented, "I've got a bed, nice actual mattress, not those little foam things. I have got my sheets, my covers, my pillows, and all my pictures. I just try to keep everything like I would at home"
>
> (2006:5–6)

Many soldiers in Iraq conducted shift-work—generally, 12 hour shifts. Theoretically, they could be off-cycle from their roommates—one on days and the other on night. Obviously, leaders had significant privacy in a single room. Soldiers at other places occupied palaces and similar "captured" buildings of the deposed Baathists or military of the former regime and managed to create livable and private dwellings. Indeed, the isolation was so prevalent that many officers I spoke with avoided their individual rooms because of isolation. They preferred to "work" a longer day—16 to 18 hours—and only sleep in their trailer or "hooch," a term that reemerged from the past and is derived from a tent-type shelter or dwelling used by American soldiers in the jungles of Vietnam.

The lack of common areas created the turn toward the private. When there were a handful of public events, very few soldiers turned out. For example, on July 4, a comedian and an all-female AC/DC cover-band named *Thund-Her-Struck* (2006) performed open-air on a wooden stage in front of the post exchange next to a Burger King housed in a trailer. The area is vast and can accommodate a few thousand people. However, the concert attracted a mere 150 to 250 people at the peak on a FOB with tens of thousands of people. Similarly, given the large numbers of soldiers on the FOB, other events around the FOB had limited patronage, including an outdoor swimming pool with tent cover and converted recreation center from Saddam Hussein's former bathhouse next to his private mosque. The latter housed a bank of computers with free Internet access, a TV and couches, both ping-pong and pool table, an extensive library of paperback books, kitchen snacks and, most notably, a large film-screening room with large and posh couches and comfortably air-conditioned. I systemically visited the location at least twice per week looking to interview soldiers and encountered few to none. Indeed, the proprietor, an American civilian, with a somewhat ambiguous status, was exceptionally helpful and engaging when he was not asleep—which was often.

To overcome the structural imposition of the private soldiers socially constructed public spaces. I observed soldiers creating social engagements by congregating in small groups of two to four on the stoops of their "hooch"—

usually at the end of a long day or in the early morning. With only two narrow steps to the door, book-ended by four-foot-high sandbags, stoops did not facilitate a conducive or comfortable gathering space, but it worked for standing, mingling, and smoking. Smoking cigars and cigarettes or dipping tobacco products (all selling well at the post exchange) seemed to be the one small group activity sanctioned by soldiers in these contexts—especially fortuitous for men—who are far less apt to plan a social event that does not involve alcohol. Cigars became the social lubricant favored by officers and other senior leaders. Cigars burn longer than cigarettes and facilitate longer conversations. Cigarettes and other tobacco products were the vice for junior enlisted soldiers, although, leaders also smoked cigarettes. Cigarettes burned quickly and offered more ephemeral and fleeting engagements. Further, soldier pressures to smoke existed on and off the FOB among American soldiers, Coalition Forces soldiers, and Iraqis who regularly greeted Americans with a cigarette or expecting one. Smoking became normative as it helped lubricate and facilitate social interaction and stave off another form of boredom—isolation—both on and off duty and on and off the FOB.

Isolation

Isolation refers to a form of boredom involving limited contact with others on the home or some other front of significance to the soldier. Years before, mail and telephones were not readily available in the Sinai or Saudi Arabia. In the Sinai, the early researchers noted that isolation was manifested in a temporal and spatial element—a sensory deprivation. Time of day, week, and even month, impact soldiers, commonly known as "Creeping Bedouin Syndrome." Over time, isolation could be somewhat overcome. However, it never matched the current level of access afforded many American soldiers in Iraq on FOBs (Wong and Gerras, 2006).

For American soldiers in Iraq, televisions and television on computers, especially CNN, was on in most places where soldiers congregated. Computer accessibility ranged for soldiers including venues such as "offices," Internet cafés, recreation centers, increasingly supplied via cafés owned and operated by Iraqis, and in individual "hootches" with high-speed Internet access. Telephone banks were similarly available in morale telephone trailers, and increasingly soldiers in Iraq had access to cellular telephone technology. Daily contact with family was prevalent.

In many of the FOBs in Iraq, soldiers had unprecedented communication access to the United States—in some cases, the communication ability was better in Iraq than at military posts in the United States. Computers were readily available in work spaces on the FOB. There were at least three Army-sponsored "Internet cafes" with a bank of 8 to 12 computers in air-conditioned trailers on Camp Victory—one of the large FOBs in Iraq. Each had a soldier serving as sentry to regulate use and check identification cards (note that virtually all soldiers carried weapons into these trailers as they did everywhere on and off the FOB). I visited the cafes at least twice day. They remained continually occupied day and night. Most use occurred before and after meals—6 am and pm and 12 am and pm. Soldiers appeared to be surfing the net as well as checking e-mails. Some used instant messaging; however, I am not sure with whom or where—on the FOB or with someone in the United States or somewhere else on the planet. Coalition Forces used the communication resources regularly, too. Most of the soldiers were younger, but civilian contractors and Coalition Force soldiers such as Poles and Estonians used them as well. I never noticed soldiers on a pornographic site, and such sites were officially off-limits to soldiers. An Iraqi father and son had established a for-profit Internet café during my last week in Iraq. It was somewhat more comfortable and consequently cleaner than the Army cafes, most of which had become overused, with broken chairs and wrecked peripherals and infested with the dust of the desert that got into everything on the FOB. However, other than myself and a few officers, I saw no customers patronizing the new Iraqi-owned and operated café that notably required a fee for use as well.

Soldiers had begun wiring their trailers with Internet access and personal laptop computers, cable television, and other electronic features including microwave ovens and small kitchen appliances. With live and cable TV access to computers and subsequently Internet chat rooms, blogs, discussion groups, and all major and minor on-line news sources, soldiers essentially had all the same media, perhaps more, than most undergraduates have in their dormitories on college campuses around the United States. Moreover, other mass media sources were readily available in post exchanges, including popular magazines such as MAXIM and other similar magazines (no "pornography" is sold) as well as the daily and traditional *Stars & Stripes* newspaper. Soldiers could receive materials from the United States and elsewhere via regular mail and packages. Letters and packages took roughly 2 weeks time from the United States. In the summer of 2004, DHL Global maintained deliveries of packages and envelopes all over Iraq, including Baghdad and on the FOBs.

The post exchange at Camp Victory—known affectionately as "Wal-Mart"—sold thousands of DVD titles, music CDs, a range of high-tech gadgetry and electronic entertainment devices, and popular books and magazines. Increasingly, Iraqis sold bootleg and pirated copies of American and foreign DVD films on the streets of Baghdad and on the FOB. For research purposes, I purchased two popular films at the time on one disk —*I, Robot* and *Fahrenheit 911*—for a nominal fee. Both recently had been released that summer in U.S. theatres. The quality was fair, but both had obviously been video-taped in a theatre screening or showing.

Thus, many soldiers in Iraq—especially Baghdad—were less than isolated from the home-front and aspects of the popular culture. They had a range of communication media available to them to connect with a host of others significant to them as well as mass media and popular culture materials. As Wong and Gerras similarly found, soldiers are "distant, but not disconnected" (2006:13).

Time and space

The loss of spatiotemporal reality characterizes boredom and highlights the relationship to time and space. Many soldiers, leaders, and others referred to their time and space situation in Iraq as akin to the popular American film *Groundhog Day*—the feeling of being lost in time and confined to place— living the same day over and over again in the same place. In Iraq, there were similar elements to previous U.S. experiences in the Sinai and Saudi Arabia with some new developments. Even MG David Petreaus referenced *Groundhog Day* and soldier accoutrements to describe the Iraq experience. He wrote:

> But we're all working to make life as livable as possible for our soldiers, to provide them an occasional break from what inevitably is a "groundhog day" existence and to ensure that there are opportunities to relax in reasonable surroundings during downtime.[3]

Groundhog Day fits the time-displacement film genre. Other popular American films in this genre include *It's a Wonderful Life, Peggy Sue Got Married,* and the *Back to the Future* series. Characters move to different times in either the past or future. Similarly, soldiers in Iraq quickly experience a displacement of time and space after a few days on the ground in Iraq. This time and space sensory deprivation is referred to as Creeping Bedouin Syndrome in previous U.S. deployments in deserts. It involves feelings of dislocation and disorientation. The open spaces, sometimes desert orientation, and lack of weekly rhythms in Iraq, was how soldiers equated their experience with the film *Groundhog Day.*

In terms of deployment length and uncertainty, soldiers in 2004 knew their tour to be roughly 1 year in Iraq. Further, it was typical to see a tour extended for 2 to 6 months beyond the twelfth month. Shorter deployments for other services fostered a sense of relative deprivation for U.S. Army soldiers. Similarly, many civilian contractors, Coalition Forces, and DOD civilians moved in and out of the community on differing schedules than Army soldiers—potentially exacerbating feelings of relative deprivation. Like Saudi Arabia, there were specific milestone events in Iraq that marked time such as the Coalition Forces returning sovereignty to the people of Iraq in June 2004 and, later that year, the national elections that occurred in January 2005. Such events brought both high and low points for soldiers. For example, the days leading up to the "transfer of power" created tension for possible increased attacks. U.S. commanders enforced that all U.S. soldiers in Iraq would uncharacteristically wear their "full-battle-rattle"—Kevlar vests with protective plates and helmet—regularly on the FOB during their day-to-day activities. Despite these milestone events, the situation for the rank-and-file soldier in Iraq was ongoing—"24/7" in soldier jargon—and consequently, soldiers collectively responded to events and created events at all hours of the day or night.[4] Thus, perceptions of time quickly move from clock to event time. Sleep patterns were disrupted. The Iraqi weekend was Thursday and Friday—with Friday the Muslim holy day. Soldiers easily lost track of the days of the weeks as many did not take time off from their duties. Thus, Groundhog Day became the label for one's days in Iraq—the same, continuous, and mundane things day in and day out.

An additional manifestation of loss of time and space reality was mass and communication media. The role of the communication media placed events around the world in different time zones directly into the soldiers' experiences. For example, soldiers in Iraq participated in the senior high school graduation ceremonies at Wiesbaden American High School, in Wiesbaden, Germany via video teleconferencing. Others oriented themselves on the families' schedules in order to link up via communication in real time. With time differences in Iraq ranging from 1 to 12 hours depending on the home base of soldiers' families (e.g., Turkey, Germany, United States), novel interpersonal communications evolved with loved ones and friends. Access to mass media such as CNN and other televised information, and real- and lag-time information, displaced the soldier as well.

Discussion

In the summer of 2004, Iraq for the American soldier resembled the wartime experiences of American soldiers in Vietnam and Europe during (not after) WWII more than recent peacekeeping missions in the Sinai and the prewar desert environment of Saudi Arabia.[5] Like Vietnam, soldiers spent at least 1 year in Iraq. Some spent longer, and others have been back on second and third "tours." Some moderate levels of underutilization existed for soldiers by location—such as those confined primarily to the FOB or in less-than-hostile regions and neighborhoods in and around Baghdad. Underutilization certainly did not exist for medics and other medical personnel on the FOB and anyone required to go off the FOB in a convoy. These soldiers experienced hyperutilization on and off the FOB. Missions off the FOB were highly intense, with the potential for danger constantly present. Most FOBs remain dangerous. An extreme example is a lone mortar rocket on December 21, 2004 that killed 24 people and wounded 64 at Forward Operating Base Marez in the northern city of Mosul, Iraq.[6] The FOB had received errant mortar fire about 30 times before, but this incident had the most tragic impact.

Cultural deprivation was evident in Iraq although perhaps not to the degree soldiers might appreciate. Interaction with Iraqis was all business, all the time, rather than in any leisure way, as American soldiers had found in other wars, in other places, and at other times.[7] Very little to no cross-cultural fraternization existed except perhaps with interpreters. Soldiers traveled to and visited historical and sacred sites such as Babylon and the Spiral of Samarra, but mosques and other sacred sites were generally off-limits for American forces. Likewise, visiting homes of Iraqis occurred. However, too much interaction could be dangerous for both Americans and Iraqis.

Privacy was available to American soldiers in Iraq. Certainly, they were more private than in early wars. Many soldiers in Iraq lived in private or semi-private rooms, including those living in captured buildings. This was especially true for officers and senior NCOs. However, privacy created a new and unique problem. The emphasis on providing relative individual privacy was at the expense of shared social spaces that structurally restricted informal soldier-soldier and soldier-leader interaction during leisure time on the FOB. Common areas facilitated soldiers finding a social space to talk, debrief, and share and discuss socioemotional issues. In many cases, informal social interaction relieves stress, serves as a coping buffer, and contributes to social cohesion directly and to task cohesion indirectly. In the extreme, informal interaction may stave off severe deviant acts resulting from a lack of integration and regulation such as suicides that, in Iraq among American soldiers, have remained, to date, conspicuously high.

Americans in Iraq qualify as the least isolated in U.S. history. In many ways, soldiers had more access to the broader world from their sparse accommodations in Iraq than back home in garrisons such as Killeen, Texas; Hinesville, Georgia; Tacoma, Washington; or Watertown, New York. They had unprecedented access to significant others and the larger American and global society through a host of communication media including cell phones, satellite television, snail mail, e-mail, and the Internet. There continues to be ongoing and increased use of communication media among deployed soldiers.[8] Likewise, soldiers in Iraq had a range of mass media available to them—similar in number but albeit different in quality, as Vietnam (Kroupa, 1970). More people knew the location of their soldier in Iraq and contacted them than they might otherwise have if she or he were stateside. Essentially, home-front was virtually on the war front and vice-versa. Finally, changes in spatiotemporal reality continue. Yet, the context has changed for American soldiers. The Creeping Bedouin Syndrome for those in the deserts of the late twentieth century (that continues today) morphed into an urban experience in Iraq known as *Groundhog Day*—using a 1993 film starring actor Bill Murray trapped in the parochial Punxsutawney, Pennsylvania as a metaphor for time displacement.

Boredom was evident in Iraq in 2004, but it easily vacillated toward and was camouflaged by its polar opposite—overload. Social saturation, distractions, responding to others, and lack of privacy characterize overload in Baghdad for the American soldier. In this sense, communication media and mass media socially saturated soldiers with information and requests for information—medium-communicated talk begets talk. Moreover, pervasive distractions about the war emanated from multiple sources. Insurgents kept soldiers preoccupied with security (this is what they are best at) from their overall efforts—indeed, the other elements of their mission in 2004—rebuilding the economy, recreating infrastructure, and stabilizing local and national politics. Additionally, soldiers responded to a host of others not traditionally in their chain of command. This included reservists and the National Guard, coalition soldiers, other service members, American and foreign national civilian service workers, civilian contractors, and Iraqis. Finally, while soldiers had privacy, they were concomitantly snared by their privacy with overflowing spectacle, escapism, and gadgetry, not the more genuine and wholesome things they might like or require in their private time and space. Overload initially masked boredom for soldiers in Iraq, but ultimately they became bored. In Klapp's words, they experienced a deficit in the quality of life. The noise of information overload dominated the experiences of the soldiers on the FOB—distracting and blurring and thus precluding meaning.

The social dimension of the war in the global war on terror continues to feature combat. Yet, it is unlike the "combat ..." of yore that Williams and Brewster characterize in WWII as "... actually experienced and consisted of periods of intense activity and excitement punctuating the periods of routine and boredom" (Williams and Smith, 1949:87–88). It is likewise dissimilar to the infantry life Roger Little observed in Korea in the 1950s where "the faces had changed but the story remained much the same" (1965:189)—with intense activity and excitement punctuated by large periods of boredom. Boredom in Iraq featured ongoing potential for activity and excitement punctuated by isolated moments of intense violence.

Military sociologists and psychologists have co-located boredom with other variables in the military. Studies of military populations have linked boredom to a number of outcomes including antisocial behavior (Glicksohn et al., 2004), cohesion at different points of a deployment (Bartone and Adler, 1999), heroin (Ingraham, 1974) and tobacco use (Cronan et al., 1991; Forgas, and Meyer, 1996), computer-mediated social network usage (Kurashina, 2000), soldier morale (Cresciani, 1989), stress (Bartone et al., 1998), and cognitive failure (Wallace et al., 2003). In Iraq, I observed no antisocial behavior, drug and alcohol use, or cognitive failure. However, increased computer usage and networking, fluctuations in morale, stress, and pervasive tobacco use existed and commingled with information overload and boredom in new ways.

Conclusion

This chapter provides a window to the most mundane feature of Iraq for American soldiers—boredom. It builds on previous research on boredom in a military context and helps us contextualize the soldier's experience in Iraq in five themes. The five elements of boredom are underutilization, cultural deprivation, isolation, lack of privacy, and loss of spatiotemporal reality. There was some select underutilization, some cultural deprivation, limited lack of privacy, and noticeable isolation. There was pervasive loss of spatiotemporal reality but perceived and labeled something different for Iraq veterans. In essence, the day-to-day experience of Iraq in 2004 contained elements of all previous wars and peacekeeping missions experienced by American soldiers. The typical American soldier and Iraq War veteran back in the United States will find much in common with his or her fellow veterans of foreign wars.

The previous and current chapters sought to construct for the reader a representation of the ephemeral cultural and historical life of American soldiers in Iraq. I will return to this interpretive and inductive approach in two of the later chapters. I hope these and later chapters will provide more depth of understanding of the experience of American soldiers. The next three chapters take a diversity turn. These chapters feature survey data from responses of soldiers across a range of topics on survey instruments. The chapters provide a more generalized experience of American soldiers in Iraq, Kuwait, and Haiti by identifying patterns and relationships across many subjects while concomitantly featuring the variety of views held by American soldiers in the post-9/11 era. Moreover, they provide comparisons between three groups to place the findings in a historical context. The chapters underscore similarities and differences representing the varied experiences of American soldiers.

3   Troop morale

The social psychology of American soldiers

> We have here a mine of data, perhaps unparalleled in magnitude in the history
> of any single research enterprise in social psychology or sociology.
>
> (Samuel A. Stouffer, *The American Soldier*, 1949)

Introduction

The previous chapter addressed the boredom factor in the experience of
American soldiers in Iraq. Here I continue to highlight the social psychological
experience of soldiers in Iraq. Like boredom, many of the topics addressed
in this and later chapters concern military sociologists of previous American
wars.[1] This chapter focuses on areas emphasized by researchers in the past
who illuminated the boots-on-the-ground experiences of soldiers, including
perceptions of preparation for deployment to war, satisfaction with their
duties, everyday experiences in the war zone, and morale at multiple levels.
The chapter closes with anchoring the findings of American soldiers with those
of previous American wars. Overall, American soldiers in Iraq reported being
prepared, satisfied, working long hours, and having satisfactory morale, with
officers reporting more in all categories compared to enlisted soldiers.

War in Iraq: preparation, satisfaction, the day-to-day life, and morale of American soldiers

Preparation for deployment

Military readiness is the bottom line for military leaders and their troops.
On surveys, I asked both Iraq deployed soldiers in 2004, American soldiers
returning from Kuwait in July 2003, and American soldiers who had returned
from Haiti in 1995 questions about their level of preparation for their deployment.
Questions went to two levels of preparation: personal and unit preparation.[2]

Research conducted in 2003 showed that American soldiers serving in Iraq,
Kuwait, and Qatar identified some noteworthy individual preparation for the

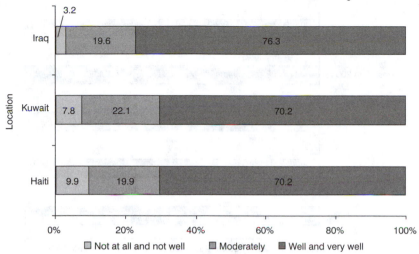

Chart 3.1 Percentage of American soldiers responding to their level of preparation for the current deployment by deployment location

Note: Bars may not equal 100 percent due to rounding error

deployment (Moskos and Miller, 2004). Forty-five percent of the active duty soldiers reported to be well or very well prepared compared to 30 percent of reserves and only 22 percent of the National Guard troops. In another study, focus group research of American Iraq and Afghanistan veterans pointed to significant soldier preparation for their missions and reporting that the training they had received was appropriate to the eventual mission (Hosek et al., 2006). Moreover, preparation remained important as it linked to stress and intentions to stay in the military.

The data in Chart 3.1 show the distribution of preparation for the three different groups. For the July 2004 Iraq troops, just more than 75 percent reported being "well" to "very well" prepared. The Haiti veterans come within 15 percent, but the Kuwait veterans distributed evenly across all three levels of preparation.

For unit-level preparation, two additional data points for the Iraq veterans are revealing. Chart 3.2 shows Iraq veteran data for September 2003 prior to their deployment and again in February 2004 and July 2004. The Kuwait veterans in July 2003 and Haiti veterans in February 1995 are included for their rating of their unit's level of preparation. Unit preparation went up noticeably once the soldiers were 6 months into the experience. For soldiers looking back, those deployed to Kuwait and Haiti, just more than one-half for both groups felt prepared. Comparing individual preparation (Chart 3.1) with unit preparation, Iraq veterans were more prepared, Kuwait veterans were much less prepared, and Haiti veterans reported more preparation then those in Kuwait.

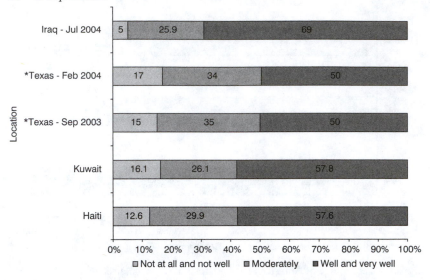

Chart 3.2 Percentages of American soldiers responding to their level of preparation within a division (Iraq soldiers at September 2003, February 2004, and July 2004) and other deployment locations and times

Source: *Adapted from 1st Cavalry Division, 2004
Note: Bars may not equal 100 percent due to rounding error

Comparisons of soldiers are available across U.S. Army rank groupings and their rankings of "well" and "very well" prepared. Chart 3.3 shows that rank and level of preparation were positively related—positive preparations go up with rank. Unit-level preparation is slightly lower than individual readiness, except for the lowest ranks. The lowest-ranked soldiers had the least confidence in their preparation compared to their units suggesting some personal anxiety but a more general confidence level in fellow soldiers and leaders. Officers and E1s to E3s were slightly more positive toward preparation than E4s and NCOs. All Iraq veteran perceptions of preparation are higher than Haiti veterans (not in the chart but, again, they reflected back on their deployment rather than during). Officers, more than 80 percent individual and 75 percent unit, were perhaps the best judges of actual preparation, and these leaders viewed themselves and their units as most prepared—perhaps showing more confidence in themselves and the potential of their units to always be better.

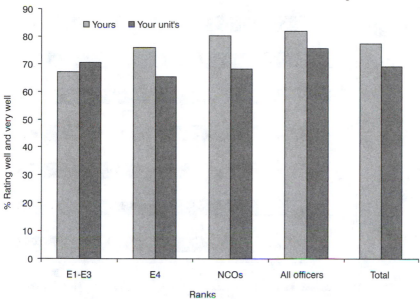

Chart 3.3 Percentage of Iraq veterans responding to their personal and their unit's level of preparation for the current deployment by rank

Note: Bars may not equal 100 percent due to rounding error

Job satisfaction in Iraq

American soldier job satisfaction is a major concern for military leaders. Satisfaction concerns date back to WWII. Personal satisfaction links to a number of outcomes, including overall well-being, fighting edge and motivation, reenlistment intentions, serving as a positive representative of the organization, and desire to remain in whatever specific military occupational specialty the soldier serves. Compared to the WWII satisfaction levels, American soldiers are markedly similar in some ways and different in others. The data in Chart 3.4 show that the higher the rank, the more the job satisfaction in Iraq. The two lowest-ranked groups were more satisfied (upper 30 percentiles) compared to WWII infantrymen but not higher than soldiers in the Pacific (55 percent) at the time (Stouffer and DeVinney, 1949). Indeed, the Haiti veterans reported the lowest satisfaction. Officer-reported levels serving in Iraq were equal in satisfaction (75.6)—just under (72 percent) combat aircrews in WWII (Stouffer and DeVinney, 1949).

The workday in Iraq

In-depth interviews with American soldiers in the earlier parts of Operation Iraqi Freedom (OIF) in 2003 found them to be living in austere conditions following

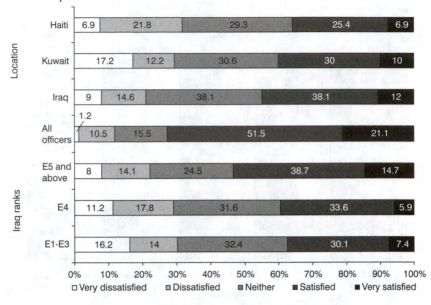

Chart 3.4 Percentage of American soldiers responding to how well satisfied they are with their current job by deployment location and Iraq veterans by rank

Note: Bars may not equal 100 percent due to rounding error

the initial invasion and the following 3 weeks of continuous combat engagement wherein even the embedded media reporters shared in the deprivation (Wong, et al., 2003). A RAND report on the day-to-day work of veterans of OIF correlated long duty days—including preparing for deployments and work on deployments, rather than the deployment itself—as a reason for likely not wanting to remain in the Army (Hosek, et al., 2006). Veterans reported long working hours and long work weeks as the norm rather than the exception. The findings are consistent with reports from soldiers reported here. Interestingly, non-deployed soldiers reported similar stress of long work hours and workload stress compared to those deployed. This included preparing soldiers to deploy and providing the rear detachment support. This suggests that military life during war in general—not necessarily deployments—is a major demand of the job.[3]

The day-to-day life of American soldiers has long been of interest to researchers. How soldiers spend their days in a combat zone clearly dates back many years. Historians have written about these experiences, but it was only in WWII when we began to understand fully how soldiers spend their day based on direct observation. U.S. Army soldiers in Iraq are generally on 12- to 15-month deployments in 2004 (deployments differ for specific Army branches and other service branches to include 60- and 90-day and 6-month tours). Most Army members received 2 weeks of rest and relaxation (R&R) break, and most returned to the United States. A holiday could, however, range from Qatar to Germany to Thailand to Ireland to back home and on to Disneyland. Many soldiers opted to forgo their 2-week R&R.

The soldiers I observed in Iraq encouraged soldiers to take 1 day a week as downtime to rest, relax, take care of personal matters, and run errands. I observed that many officers opted to forgo their off day—more often than not. I think most managed their affairs quickly and returned to their duties. Reasons for this commitment to duty included professionalism, the shear volume of work, and to stave off boredom—specifically isolation.

In the survey, specific questions were asked of soldiers of their day-to-hour workdays. The data in Chart 3.5 above provide the average workday on their current or most recent deployment for the three groups. Overall, three-fourths of American soldiers on all deployments put in long days. American soldiers in Haiti put in the longest workday: Just above 40 percent reported 15 or more hours per day. More than two-thirds of Iraq veterans reported working a 12- or more hour day. Looking closer at the data, more soldiers had longer days in Iraq than in Haiti and Kuwait.

A typical day in Iraq involved a 12-hour day with one day off sometime in the week. However, rank is somewhat correlated with hours worked. The more senior the soldier, the more hours put in beyond the typical 12 in the duty day. The data in Chart 3.6 show that officers represent the group with the highest percentage, working 15 or more hours per day—about 45 percent followed by

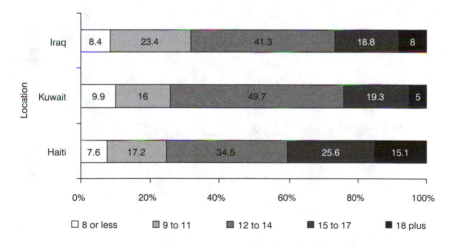

Chart 3.5 Percentage of American soldiers responding to the average number of hours worked per day on their most recent deployment by deployment location

Note: Bars may not equal 100 percent due to rounding error

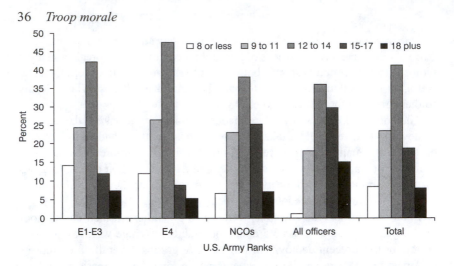

Chart 3.6 Percentage of American soldiers in Iraq responding to average hours per duty day by U.S. Army rank

Note: Bars may not equal 100 percent due to rounding error

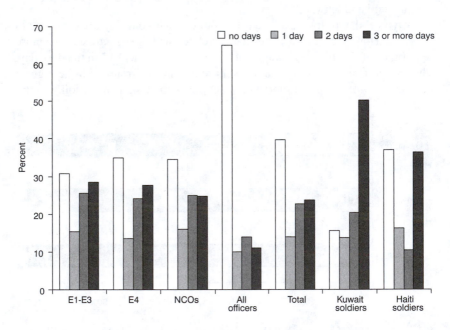

Chart 3.7 U.S. Army ranks of Iraq, Kuwait and Haiti veterans

NCOs with 30 percent. A handful of junior enlisted soldiers put in days beyond 12 hours.

Next featured is time off during the deployment. Again, the leaders of the Army units I worked around encouraged their soldiers to take a day off in the week to manage their affairs, rest, relax, and recharge physically and mentally. The data in Chart 3.7 show that similar to hours worked, officers were less likely to be able or choose to take time off. More than 60 percent of officers had no days off in the 30 days preceding mid-July 2004. Indeed, I witnessed officers bringing reports and other duties back to their sleeping quarters to busy themselves throughout the day and night. For many, keeping busy and focused helped pass the time in Iraq. The time spent is, however, consistent with soldiers from Fort Drum, New York who had been deployed to Haiti. Many worked long days.[4] The soldiers in Kuwait as a group had more downtime. However, they had been preparing to return to the United States in the 30 days prior to completing the survey.

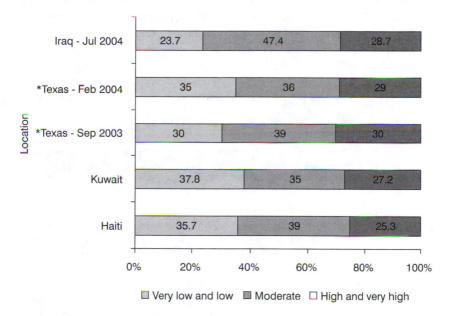

Chart 3.8 Percentages of American soldiers responding to their level of morale within a division (Iraq soldiers at September 2003, February 2004, and July 2004) and other deployment locations and times

Source: *Adapted from 1st Cavalry Division, 2004
Note: Bars may not equal 100 percent due to rounding error

Morale in Iraq

In the survey administered in Iraq, American soldiers had three direct questions about morale: individual, unit, and all troops deployed.[5] Fortunately, there had been some earlier morale questions for comparison data collected by the senior military leadership in 2003 and early 2004 from the same units. The percentages in Chart 3.8 show the ratings from American soldiers who participated in the OIF soldier survey at three points: September 2003 and February 2004 (both prior to deploying) and July 2004 in Iraq; Kuwait veterans in July 2003; and Haiti veterans in February 1995. All of the groups are rating their own level of morale. The top three bars of Chart 3.8 represent OIF soldiers at three different points in time asking them the same question. The other two are different soldiers at different times.

Overall, individual-level morale looks to be evenly distributed—almost a third had low, a third had moderate, and a third had high morale. The standout statistic is Iraq veterans with the lowest percentage reporting low morale. Keep in mind that only the July 2004 data are from soldier reporting *while* deployed. In other words, deployed soldiers, halfway through their deployment in Iraq, overall, show the highest level of individual morale over prior to deploying or having completed a deployment!

Next, soldiers rated their unit's level of morale. The percentages in Chart 3.9 show percentage ratings for three different periods: Iraq veterans (July 2004),

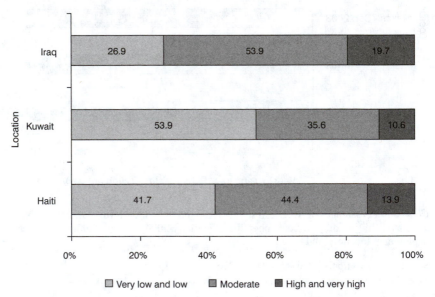

Chart 3.9 Percentages of American soldiers responding to their unit's level of morale by deployment location

Note: Bars may not equal 100 percent due to rounding error

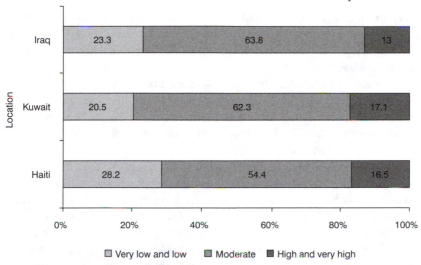

Chart 3.10 Percentages of American soldiers responding to all troops deployed level of morale by deployment location

Note: Bars may not equal 100 percent due to rounding error

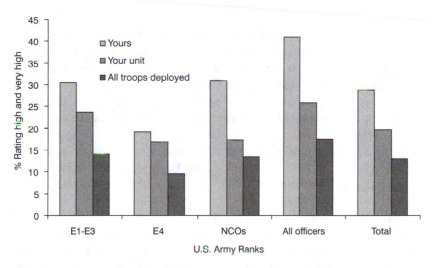

Chart 3.11 Percentages of American soldiers responding to your morale, your unit's morale, and all deployed troops' morale as high and very high by U.S. Army rank for Iraq veterans (July 2004)

Kuwait veterans (July 2003), and Haiti veterans (February 1995). Similar to the individual level morale, the outstanding percentage is the 26.9 percent of soldiers during OIF in July reporting low morale compared to the more than 40 percent for the other two groups.

Finally, soldiers are asked to rate the level of morale for all deployed troops. The data in Chart 3.10 show the rating distribution of all troops deployed and their level of morale for the three groups. Again we have some consistency—a general pattern of roughly three-fourths of soldiers repeating moderate to very high levels of morale overall.

Now, the analysis takes a slightly different approach. I provide comparisons across U.S. Army military rank groupings from junior enlisted soldiers (E1–E3 and E4), NCOs, and officers and comparing individuals reporting their own level of morale, their perception of their unit's level of morale, and their perception of morale levels for all troops deployed. The rank groups are comparable with the total. The percentages in Chart 3.11 are for soldiers ranking morale levels as high and very high. Across all the ranks, more soldiers reported their individual morale higher than that of their unit followed by all troops deployed. In other words, the closer to their own experience, the higher their morale. Officers had higher morale levels than enlisted soldiers.

Discussion

Social psychology owes a great deal to World War II. It was during WWII that social psychology exploded onto the field of scholarship with an applied, interdisciplinary focus on social issues in the military. Never before had such a human-oriented research enterprise been undertaken. That research left a legacy that was unparalleled in human history. Many years thereafter, the field of social psychology grew and splintered into three distinct faces— psychological social psychology, symbolic interactionism, and social structure and personality (House, 1977). More recently, the three theoretical perspectives have individually expanded and blended, and become less contentious. They are all increasingly diverse but at the same time complementary of one another in their orientations (Burke, 2006).

Clearly, social psychology has something to do with both the social world and individual psychology. The two domains are importantly different. When my students are on the fence about majoring in sociology or psychology, I like to tell them that psychology is under the skin and sociology is outside the skin. After letting this percolate a bit, I point out that psychology takes the individual as the unit of analysis. The focus is on internal processes and mental activities such as personality, drives, motivations, memory, and emotions. Sociology is outside the individual and focused on structured dimensions that include gender, age, religion, ethnicity, sexual orientation, social class, ability level, and other group memberships anchored in structures and contexts especially social institutions and culture. Social psychology is the intersection of these two levels of analysis—the macro or societal level and the micro or individual level. I like to romanticize the development of the field a bit by accentuating the expansion of social psychology in the aftermath of WWII and *The American Soldier* series (Hovland et al., 1949; Stouffer et al., 1949: vol. I; Stouffer et al., 1949: vol. II; Stouffer et al., 1950).

During and immediately following WWII, many studies oriented on the social experiences of war and focused on the relationship of individuals to social institutions such as in politics and the military but included medicine, economics, entertainment and leisure, and education. Many (male) scholars served in the military during the years of the draft. Some were draftees, and others volunteered, wanting to serve the mission in some capacity; many brought their scholarly expertise to bear on social issues in the military.

From their observations during WWII, sociologist Robin M. Williams, Jr. and social psychologist M. Brewster Smith (1949) provided the best characterization of combat as a social situation. They emphasized that combat definitions may vary by many features including location in the combat environment and length of deployment—especially between the Atlantic and Pacific theaters of war. The setting of combat in WWII for those with boots on the ground included risk of injury, physical discomfort including lack of sleep, no sex or intimate gratification, isolation, exposure to death, restrictions of personal movement, uncertainty, value conflicts, lack of individuality, lack of privacy, boredom mixed with anxiety, and poverty. They noted that in WWII, soldiers endured significant stresses, sustained exposure to combat, and remained overseas for years at a time, yet managed to tough out the experience with some satisfaction. More specifically, a mere 21 percent of infantrymen reported satisfaction with their current job compared to 55 percent of all enlisted service members in the Pacific Ocean areas and 72 percent of combat air crew members flying bombing missions (usually out of England).

In Korea, Roger Little spent time with rifle platoons and found the conditions comparable to WWII, "…harsh, primitive and 'close to the ground'…faces had changed but the story remained the same" (1965:198). Charles Moskos characterized the combat situation in Vietnam as "absolute deprivation" (1970:14) compared to relative deprivation. Relative deprivation suggests that an individual evaluates his or her situation by reference group comparisons. In the Vietnam case, the world of the combat soldier was narrowly defined by his individual rotation system—365 days in Vietnam with soldiers very aware of their return date: DEROS (Date Eligible for Return From Overseas). Their own day-to-day survival consisted of "…routine physical stresses of combat existence [and] include: the weight of the pack, tasteless food, diarrhea, lack of water, leeches, mosquitoes, rain, torrid heat, mud, and loss of sleep" (Moskos, 1970:141).

Post-Vietnam U.S. peacekeeping missions placed soldiers in a much different situation. Boredom dominated the day-to-day environment in the Sinai (Harris,

Rothberg, Segal, and Segal, 1993). From group debriefing interviews of soldiers after the U.S. invasion of Panama, we gleaned that the relatively quick mission had only a momentary resemblance to traditional war of previous generations (Ender, 1995). John Wattendorf (1992) found somewhat similar forms of boredom in the U.S. buildup to the first Gulf War 1 year after the invasion of Panama. In the 1990s, American soldiers again found themselves in destitute social environments in Somalia and Haiti (Miller and Moskos, 1995; Rosen et al., 1999).

Morale: What Is It and So What?

Morale is a catchall concept capturing a whole range of ideas including esprit de corps, cohesion, satisfaction, well-being, and interpersonal adjustment. Morale has to do with a capacity of people to maintain their belief system, usually connected to their institutional goal or mission. Applied more often in contexts requiring physical and mental courage, such as sports, it is especially relevant in the military. The famous nineteenth-century military strategist Carl von Clauswitz (1832/1968) emphasized the importance of morale as a major issue in soldier functioning. He connected it with moral and physical will. He also emphasized the importance of national morale—home-front will to sustain and support the war and the destruction of the enemy's morale; their will to fight is fundamental in war. Military psychologists most recently define it as "motivation and enthusiasm for accomplishing mission objectives" (Britt and Dickinson, 2006:160).

In Volume I of *The American Soldier* series, morale had a broader working definition where "[morale] might be thought of as an inference from group behavior, verbal or nonverbal, as to cooperative effort toward some common goal" (Stouffer et al., 1949:83). As noted earlier, one group of American soldiers did possess unusually high levels of morale during WWII—combat flying personnel in the Army Air Corps (Janis, 1949). Their duty had some of the highest risk of death for some units, even higher than for ground troops. The results contradicted perceptions of "common sense." Certainly, compared to other elements of the Army, the Air Corps soldiers volunteered for the Air Corp once in the Army. They tended overall to be more educated (for the period, they were more likely to possess a high school diploma), viewed their units and missions as elite, and were viewed as superior because of selection and skills training. They could also go home after completing a designated number of missions (infantry soldiers could not).

Today, these findings make similar sense when we think of American soldiers in Iraq and Afghanistan who are more educated than soldiers of previous wars, view themselves as somewhat select because of their volunteer status, receive elite treatment by senior leaders, and clearly have dangerous missions. Perhaps most important, they are highly trained—arguably the most trained and skilled soldiers in the history of the world. Most important, reported morale is higher than what one would expect—again subverting common sense—that dangerous missions connect with high soldier morale.

Today, the U.S. Army recognizes the importance of morale. In its most important publication for military leaders, the morale definition states:

> Morale is the human dimension's most important intangible element. It is a measure of how people feel about themselves, their team, and their leaders. High morale comes from good leadership, shared effort, and mutual respect ... High morale results in a cohesive team striving to achieve common goals. Competent leaders know that morale—the essential human element—holds the team together and keeps it going in the face of the terrifying and dispiriting things that occur in war.
>
> (Department of the Army, 2006:7–8)

Morale and Iraq

Much is made of American soldier morale in wartime, and much had been made about morale in Iraq. During the summer of 2004, news reports, especially televised news, were reporting low levels of American troop morale in Iraq.[6] Yet, only two systematic research studies had reported morale during the war and showed contradictory findings. Between the summers of 2003 and 2004, popular press stories in both print and televised features highlighted cases of low morale among American forces based on morale data. The 2003 study by a U.S. Army mental health advisory team assessed morale at two points in time and found it markedly low. With a sample of 756 soldiers, more than half (52 percent) reported low and very low personal morale, and almost three-fourths (72 percent) reported the same for unit morale (U.S. Army Surgeon General HQDA G-1, 2003). Yet, about the same time, Charles Moskos and Laura Miller (2004)—well-known and experienced military sociologists—surveyed 389 American soldiers in November and December 2003 in Kuwait, Qatar, and Iraq. One question served as a proxy for morale: their "spirits" most of the time. They compared active duty, reserve, and National Guard soldiers. Roughly, 15 percent of each group reported usually low spirits with the remainder reporting "sometimes good and low" and "usually good" spirits. Similarly, American soldiers responded to questions about their spirits during WWII. Enlisted and NCO spirits were similar but lower than officers, but about half of officers in Iraq reported "usually good" and three-fourths of WWII officers were about the same. It is notable that the spirits for enlisted and NCOs were much lower in WWII.

Conclusion

Again, the purpose of this book is to represent and highlight the experiences of American soldiers in Iraq from their perspective and for the perspective of others concerned about and interested in the troops. The data feature how experiences range for soldiers in Iraq. This chapter has met all three purposes. The chapter focuses on four long-established and critical areas of social psychological research related to soldiers: preparation, satisfaction, day-to-day life, and morale. These elements are crucially important to soldiers and leaders. In essence, American soldiers felt well prepared for their current mission. The higher rank showed greater perceived preparation for the current deployment. In some cases, even the lowest-ranked soldiers felt their education and experience had prepared them for their most recent deployment. Second, soldiers reported to be satisfied with their military experience and satisfaction correlated with rank—officers were the most satisfied. Day-to-day existence in a war zone has a long history of study. Reflecting on their day-to-day existence in Iraq, soldiers appeared to be putting in exceedingly long hours during the workday and week. Little downtime existed except to eat and sleep—and I noticed that "take-out" was a common occurrence at the dining facility. Officers work exceptionally long hours, more than enlisted soldiers. It is unclear what keeping busy might mean for enlisted soldiers: perhaps simply it is "busy work." Most notably regarding morale, data reported here are contrary to popular perceptions and at least one other study at the time. A large percentage of American soldiers in Iraq, halfway through a year and potentially longer deployment, reported their individual level morale to be high, with officers reporting the highest levels of morale. Similarly, they reported higher-than-expected morale for their units as well. While a minority of soldiers had low morale, overall the soldiers had higher morale than at other points in their military careers, including back home at garrison.

In the end, we see variety among the experiences of soldiers as well. Many soldiers felt less than prepared for the missions and thought their units and the military in Iraq were ill-prepared. Many soldiers felt very unsatisfied, worked fewer hours than others, and noted their own and their unit's morale and that of troops in Iraq to be low. Preparation, morale, time worked, and satisfaction positively correlated with the rank of soldiers, with officers being the most positive of all troops.

The results confirm results from earlier studies but offer new perspective on how American soldiers experience war today. In this chapter, a history of social psychological research on American soldiers is provided. The research traces back to *The American Soldier* studies of WWII. The next chapter continues the social psychology of soldiers. The focus is on attitudes toward social issues—particularly often-contested social issues in American society. There is a continued social comparative approach between American soldiers of Iraq, Kuwait, and Haiti, with some comparisons to past military and civilian leaders as well.

4 Fusion and fissure

American soldier attitudes toward social issues

I am not sure why the sections on domestic and social issues were included in this survey. I don't see how this relates to a deployment. It seems to me, not to make accusations, that this portion of the survey is designed to get a feel for deployed soldier attitudes and possible voting direction in the up coming presidential election. The questions included in those sections are some of the questions and issues that are major issues discussed in relation to the election campaign. I sincerely hope that they will not be used as a gauge to determine the potential vote of the deployed soldier. If a sense of distrust is detected, you are right. It is there.

(37-year-old white male Warrant Officer, married with one child)

Introduction

This chapter continues the thread of representing the social psychology of American soldiers in war with a particular focus on civilian and military similarities. The last chapter focused on the traditional areas researchers have studied of soldiers' experiences—preparation, satisfaction, day-to-day life, and morale. Here, the focus is on broader social issues less directly connected to the individual level of military readiness of the soldier but nonetheless important as it gets into the mind of the American soldier. This chapter looks expansively at American soldiers who step over the line between civilian life into the arms of Uncle of Sam and will someday return to civilian life. Specifically, this chapter focuses on attitudes toward salient American domestic and broader social issues on the public agenda at the turn of the twentieth century to include opinions about such matters as school bussing to traditional gender roles to handgun control. Additionally, soldiers share their perspective on attitudes on topics such as social morality, personal values, and the military.[1] The chapter concludes by discussing the relationship between American civil society and the military as a separate culture. I conclude that we have entered a new era of civil-military relations—one oriented more toward fusion rather than a fissure between the two spheres. Overall, the chapter inserts soldiers into social issues and gives the reader insight into their thinking. The major finding is that American soldiers look more like their diverse fellow Americans than not.

The civilian-military junction

Before presenting attitudes of the soldiers, it is important to differentiate between two approaches that people often consider when thinking about the military—in particular, how can the U.S. military serve to protect a society while simultaneously maintaining a separate set of norms and values from the host civilian culture it protects? If there is a divide between military and civilian cultures, military social scientists point to two competing perspectives. On the one hand, the American Army promulgates a different set of values than the American society it serves.[2] Early in army recruit training, or "boot camp," new military personnel are inculcated with a new language and ethos for survival in military life. Essentially, the military resocializes America's sons and daughters to the demands of the total institutional context with the expectation that they internalize and assimilate the new value system—a system oriented to fighting and winning the nation's wars. For example, by preparing young men and women to kill, we subvert the larger societal value of not killing.

The demands of military life include the risk of physical or mental injury or death, long working hours and shift-work, frequent relocations, short- and long-term separations from place of residence and others significant to them, residence in foreign countries, constraints on behavior, and working in a masculine-dominated culture (M.W. Segal, 1989). These demands exist individually in many other occupations. For example, police work is dangerous and male-dominated yet does not require residence in foreign countries or frequent relocations. Collectively, these demands characterize the major elements of U.S. Army life.

In terms of values, the Army espouses a unique set that, similar to the collective demands, are somewhat different than the values of the larger American society. The seven Army values include loyalty, duty, respect, selfless-service, honor, integrity, and personal courage. One civil-military view is that some of these values contravene American values—for example, selfless-service conflicts with individualism, and duty and loyalty conflict with freedom. An alternate civil-military view is that the armed services are also composed of different types of people who do not forsake their civilian culture. Service members are generally younger and overrepresented by males relative to the larger society. Hence, the divide between military and civilian cultures may less reflect a different value system or simply reflect the types of people who enter military service. Finally, others may view the demands and values as practical matters of the profession balanced against occupational prestige, service to the nation, and economic security. Essentially, old values are retained, new values integrated and the two values systems are rationalized to co-exist.

The bottom line of the findings presented in this chapter is that American soldiers are neither bipolar nor to one extreme or the other in their attitudes toward social issues. They are diverse in outlooks. They lean more toward being civilian-soldiers than soldier-civilians. They look more like than dislike Americans along sociopolitical lines. Thus, the promulgated gap that exists in American society is perhaps a political gap rather than a civil-military attitude gap. The goal of this chapter is to present the attitudes of American soldiers in Iraq across domestic and larger social issues from the perspective of the soldier and provide insights into who American soldiers are.

A useful measure of attitudes is to use a comparison group to help contextualize the findings. One constructive source of comparison is a comprehensive study that found military leaders, civilian leaders, and the general public responses to a broad spectrum of social, foreign policy, and domestic issues to have both similarities and differences (Holsti, 2001). Granted, these studies appeared prior to 9/11—considered perhaps the demarcation point for the entry into a new era in civil-military relations—yet they provide the only point upon which to compare and contrast American soldier attitudes. It is this study and others that I will use to represent and compare attitudes of U.S. enlisted soldiers, senior noncommissioned officers, and officers deployed to Kuwait in 2003 and Iraq in 2004.

Attitudes

American domestic and social issues are two major attitudinal topics at the turn of the twentieth century. The two scales operationalize the responses based on a five-point Likert scale.[3] First, the domestic social issues scale has 14 forced-response item statements (see Appendix 4.1). The statements query respondents about a range of what can be considered controversial domestic issues such as school bussing, traditional gender roles, and handgun control, among others. Seven items are politically "conservative," and seven are politically "liberal." This strategy allows for reversing coding of the items.

The second scale has six forced-response item statements reflecting broader moral issues and values statements (see Appendix 4.2). People in 1989 and 1999, including active and reserve military leaders, civilian veteran and non-veteran leaders, and the public, including both veteran and non-veteran samples, responded to these statements (Holsti, 2001). I used these same statements for two survey comparison samples of Kuwait veterans in 2003 and Iraq troops in 2004.

I begin with an examination of the domestic issues comparing the six groups from the late 1990s and two samples of American soldiers in Kuwait and Iraq. The data in Table 4.1 provide percentage results from the eight groups. Overall, across six groups, there was most agreement with using any budget surpluses to reduce the national debt rather than to reduce taxes, leaving abortion decisions to women and their doctors, placing stringent controls on the sale of handguns and, with eight groups, permitting prayer in public schools. There was least overall agreement with banning the death penalty, reducing the defense budget, and relaxing environmental regulations to stimulate economic growth. Military and active reserve leaders felt strongest about budget surplus both within the groups and across all issues. Civilian veteran and non-veteran leaders were similar in their attitudes toward abortion, how to use a budget surplus, and handgun control.

The Iraq soldiers surveyed in 2004 had the strongest positions on leaving abortion decisions to women and their doctors (73.3 percent), permitting prayer in public schools (75.8 percent), and encouraging mothers to stay at home with their children rather than working outside the home (30.3 percent). They collectively responded most strongly about the death penalty and nuclear power plants—a mere 13.2 percent feel positive toward banning the death penalty, and 22.4 agree with easing restrictions on nuclear power plant construction. They were fairly in line with their comrades who served in Kuwait—the largest differences surfacing among busing children in order to achieve school integration, permitting prayer in public schools, and barring homosexuals from serving in the military.

Comparing veterans of Iraq and Kuwait with civilian and military leaders, there was both similarity and difference. Noticeable divergences exist on issues such as bussing, the budget, the environment, tuition credit, school prayer, power plants, social inequality, and handguns. There was more consistency in attitudes with abortion, gender roles, education and the budget, homosexuality, and the death penalty. Notably, there are sizeable gaps in attitudes among military leaders and Iraq veterans on such issues as busing and national debt. Domestic issue findings showed a variety of positions and a diversity of attitudes.

Next is a turn to the moral issues and values statements held in American society (see Appendix 4.1). The data in Table 4.2 show the most attitude agreement overall with the first statement in the table: "The decline of traditional values is contributing to the breakdown of our society." The highest attitude-level agreement for all groups, except public non-veterans, felt collectively most strongly that "American society would have fewer problems if people took God's will more seriously" (79.5 percent). Not all felt this strongly. Responding directly to the question, a soldier wrote: "The 'God's will' question is tricky. Depends on which person's interpretation of God's will we use. Plus it would be hard for the country to adopt a God's will policy and keep freedom of religion" (21 year old, white male, E4, single and never married).

The least agreement was with the more liberal and cultural relativistic statement: "The world is changing and we should adjust our view of what is moral and immoral behavior to fit these changes." Exceptions were for civilian non-veteran leaders who agreed least with the statement: "Civilian society

Table 4.1 Percentages of selected American group attitudes toward specific domestic issues

| | Percent that "Agree somewhat" and "Agree strongly" | | | | | | | |
| | *Triangle Institute Security Studies 1998–1999 (Holsti, 2001)* | | | | | | | |
Domestic issue statements	*Military leaders*	*Active reserve leaders*	*Civilian veteran leaders*	*Civilian non-veteran leaders*	*General public veterans*	*General public non-veterans*	*2003 Kuwait veterans (n=185)*	*2004 Iraq veterans (n=968)*
Bussing children in order to achieve school integration	21.9	16.6	21.5	37.9	—	—	45.2	63.5
Using any budget surpluses to reduce the national debt rather than to reduce taxes	84.6	79.6	75.3	76.4	—	—	44.0	55.8
Relaxing environmental regulations to stimulate economic growth	19.2	29.5	30.5	20.8	—	—	34.3	41.0
Providing tuition tax credits to parents who send children to private or parochial schools	52.5	55.3	50.0	43.2	—	—	36.3	38.7
Leaving abortion decisions to women and their doctors	64.9	67.6	75.8	77.9	—	—	72.0	73.3
Encouraging mothers to stay at home with their children rather than working outside the home	51.1	46.8	57.7	41.0	—	—	27.2	30.3
Permitting prayer in public schools	73.8	73.3	53.6	46.6	80.0	74.6	62.4	75.8
Reducing the defense budget in order to increase the federal education budget	14.0	11.1	33.7	51.4	—	—	34.3	39.0
Barring homosexuals from teaching in public schools	44.4	41.6	29.0	18.1	—	—	33.5	40.8
Barring homosexuals from serving in the military	—	—	—	—	—	—	38.9	53.8
Easing restrictions on the construction of nuclear power plants	31.9	33.5	44.1	28.7	—	—	14.2	22.4
Redistributing income from the wealthy to the poor through taxation and subsidies	23.5	17.1	31.8	45.6	44.9	53.7	47.3	54.8
Banning the death penalty	10.4	7.8	24.3	37.3	—	—	7.1	13.2
Placing stringent controls on the sale of handguns	69.2	54.1	68.1	79.3	—	—	47.6	52.0

Source: Adapted from Holsti, 2001

Note: A dash ("—") implies question not asked or no data available

Table 4.2 Percentages of selected American group attitudes toward selected social, moral, and values issues

| | Percent that "Agree somewhat" or "Agree somewhat" | | | | | | |
| | Triangle Institute Security Studies 1998–1999 (Holsti, 2001) | | | | | | |
Social issue statements	Military leaders	Active reserve leaders	Civilian Veteran Leaders	Civilian non-Veteran Leaders	General Public Veterans	General Public non-Veterans	2004 Iraq Veterans (n=968)
The decline of traditional values is contributing to the breakdown of our society	88.6	88.6	78.3	67.0	83.4	81.5	81.8
Through leading by example, the military could help American society become more moral	70.3	72.1	56.6	37.4	—	—	63.1
The world is changing and we should adjust our view of what is moral and immoral behavior to fit these changes	10.1	19.3	24.5	33.6	—	—	48.0
Civilian society would be better off if it adopted more of the military's values and customs	77.0	72.9	44.5	25.0	47.8	33.5	52.9
American society would have fewer problems if people took God's will more seriously	60.6	62.3	54.6	48.0	79.5	81.7	67.2
All Americans should be willing to give up their lives to defend our country	80.2	84.0	77.2	60.0	72.7	67.9	66.2

Source: Adapted from Holsti, 2001

Note: A dash implies ("—") question not asked or no data available

would be better if it adopted more of the military's values and customs" (25 percent).

In terms of moral issues, Americans soldiers of Iraq agreed most that the decline of traditional values is what contributes to the breakdown of society (81.8 percent). Likewise, two-thirds of all soldiers in Iraq agreed, first, that the military could help American society become more moral. Second, American society would have fewer problems if people took God's will more seriously, and third, all Americans should be willing to give up their lives to defend the country. Soldiers were split on two items—the American society adoption to a changing world and adopting military values and customs.

Comparing the veterans of Iraq with the civilian and military leadership and the general public overall, there were a few surprises and some noticeable fission. First, overall civilian and military attitudes were in the directions many might expect to see them—more conservative. In terms of cultural relativism, however, almost half of Iraq veterans (48 percent) were more liberal than even the next highest group at one-third—civilian, non-veteran leaders. Similarly, Iraq veterans in 2004 were far less in agreement with military leaders and other veterans on two notable issues related to the military: "Civilian society would have fewer problems if people took God's will more seriously" and "All Americans should be willing to give up their lives to defend our country." In other words, soldiers in Iraq said they see somewhat separate military and civilian values and customs and the more military values are not necessarily the most desirable of those who are outside the military. Likewise, there was less agreement for a draft than military leaders.

Politics and attitudes

Last, veterans themselves compare for differences and similarities controlling for their political affiliation (table not shown). Table 1.1 in Chapter One (pp. 10–11)featured the distribution of political orientations from self-reports of soldiers. First presented are divergences. The democrats—traditionally more liberal on social issues—are in the directions we would expect them to be. In some cases, the gaps were wider and narrower, depending on the topical area.

Second, in the widest gap areas, 20 percentage points or more included the following. First, democrats agreed more with reducing the defense budget in order to increase the federal education budget (29.1 percent difference); placing stringent controls on the sale of handguns, (27.4 percent); leaving abortion decisions to women and their doctors (20.6 percent difference); and bussing children in order to achieve school integration (22.4 percent difference). Republicans agreed more with the statement regarding barring homosexuals from serving in the military (22 percent difference).[4] Worth noting, Iraq veterans reporting their political affiliation to be third-party independents (TPI), and the "other/none" fell in between various areas suggesting these political affiliations may represent elements of both.

Two other noteworthy percent differences of 20 percentage points or more between political ideologies included the following. First, there was a difference between democrats, republicans, TPIs, and other/nones regarding relaxing environmental regulations (27.5 percent is the widest). The TPIs agreed least with this statement. Second, the TPI were 21.4 percent more likely to agree that mothers maintain traditional gender roles. Democrats and those reporting other/nones were very close in agreement regarding redistributing income between the wealthy and poor.

Turning to social issues, there were four instances of 20 percent points or more differences between groups. First, republican soldiers were more likely than democrats to agree (25.9 percent difference) that all Americans should sacrifice in defense of the United States. Democrats were more likely then the republicans to agree (25 percent difference) that the world is changing and the U.S. should change its morality accordingly. Third, republicans more than democrats were likely to agree (20.3 percent difference) that civilian society would "be better off adopting military values and customs." Finally, republicans and democrats more than the TPI and other/nones agreed (24.7 percent at the widest) that American society would have fewer problems if people took God's will more seriously.

Discussion

The intersection of the armed forces and society is well covered. Many social scientists have acknowledged three significant waves of civil-military relations in American history—the post-WWII period until the end of conscription in 1973, the post-Vietnam era until the end of the Cold War, and the post-Cold War period (Bachman et al., 2000; Feaver and Kohn, 2001b; Feaver et al., 2001; Holsti, 2001; Segal et al., 2001). When thinking of civil-military relations, military social scientists hold that the gap between the military institution and the larger society may expand and contract at different moments in history. Examples of wide or narrow gaps include a military with a disproportionate number of republicans, a military that does not mirror the larger society in terms of race, class, and gender, greater reliance on contractors to fulfill military functions or, finally, a disproportionate number of current members of the U.S. Senate or Congress who are themselves veterans or have children who are veterans of Afghanistan or Iraq. As well, the civil-military culture gap is examinable in terms of general attitudes toward differing domestic and social issues.

Research suggests that political conservatives are generally more in support of going to war than liberals and moderates (Rohall et al., 2006). If people in the military service tend toward conservatism and republicanism, differences in support for going to war is somewhat explainable in part by political values.

In a comprehensive review of the empirical attitudinal literature during the Vietnam War in the 1960s and first half of the 1970s, Charles Moskos (1976) concluded that youth attitudes move to the left the farther one was from the military. ROTC cadets were noted to be less militaristic than cadets at service academies but more so than their non-ROTC undergraduate peers. More recently, Guiseppe Caforio (2003) developed an ideal type of the service academy cadet across a number of countries including the U.S. Three of the four characteristics of the typical cadet include (1) interest in the military, (2) desire for adventure, and (3) wish to serve one's country. An additional finding is that endo-recruitment exists among service academy cadets—cadets are from military families—suggesting there is a perpetuation of the military mind, self, and society in the U.S. military today and across other nations.

Many scholars in the 1990s forecast that the military and the larger society had headed into divergent directions in terms of social attitudes between the military and the larger society. Subsequent empirical research concluded the differences to be less than acute as originally speculated. Indeed, the modest gap that existed may have since narrowed even more. The aftermath of the so-called Global War on Terrorism following the September 11, 2001 terrorist attacks in the U.S, other terrorist attacks around the world, and new quasi-military groups under the umbrella of homeland security, have ushered in a fourth wave of understanding at the intersection of the armed forces and society.

Gaps can exist between the military and society. One major perspective in explaining the attitude differences between military and civilians is a self-selection effect: that people who enter the military share different values than their civilian counterparts. Another perspective is that the military inculcates values of conformity and hyper-masculinity. At no point is that masculinity tested more than in a forward-deployed context. No past research has studied soldiers in a forward-deployed context and their attitudes toward social issues.

Research shows that socialization *and* self-selection account for what little divide exists between military and civilian attitudes, depending on the issue (Bachman, et al., 2000). The authors use survey data from the *Monitoring the Future* project, comparing male responses to surveys given just prior to high-school graduation and again 1 or 2 years later. As a result, differences between time one and two would certainly be attributable to socialization. While all students showed strong support for the military, students entering the military reported more support for greater military spending and greater military influence in the U.S, among other topics. These differences largely reflected selection effects wherein socialization effects are simply enhancing the selection effects. The authors conclude, however, that there is limited evidence that military personnel are increasingly alienated from the larger society. Perhaps those who self-select are simply aligning their attitudes with their new found, future role—wherein attitudes are attempting to be jived with perceived expectations.

Other studies published in the last few years confirm the narrow gap hypothesis. For example, Snider and colleagues compare the attitudes of three groups of students: West Point and ROTC cadets and civilian college students at Duke University (Snider et al., 2001). They conclude that the three groups are relatively similar in what they know about the military but their collective knowledge is limited overall. Using a similar sample, political conservatives and males are generally supportive of going to war compared to liberals, moderates, and women (Rohall et al., 2006).

Based on recent research we have labeled the narrowing gap the "civil-military fusion" and label it as a fourth wave in civil-military relations in the United States (Rohall et al., 2006). This is not so much a civil-military gap closure, or even a garrison state; rather it is a coming together of sorts, through a mutual militarization of civilian life and civilianization of military life.[5] Evidence of a fusion would be increased knowledge on the part of the public regarding military issues and affairs, a diversity of attitudes among soldiers, and consistent patterns of attitudes toward a number of issues between the larger society and soldiers—essentially a blurring of the military culture and the American society where each reflects the other. The attitudinal findings presented here—especially the latter two—support the fusion thesis.

Conclusion

In this chapter, American soldiers shared their attitudes on social domestic and moral issues. The representations of soldiers anchor in the military social science literature on the 1990s that focused on a civil-military gap. While some scholars in Europe continue this line of inquiry, few in the United States have followed up the earlier barrage of U.S. studies. The current military environment in the post-9/11 era offers a new and important context in which to assess attitudes. A new era of civil-military relations in the U.S. has emerged—a modest civil-military fusion. Support for this position exists through (1) the U.S. military continuing to be involved in wars in Iraq and Afghanistan, (2) U.S. troops and the military in general viewed favorably in the response to disasters around the world in Pakistan and Indonesia and at home following hurricanes Katrina and Rita, and (3) reporters constructing positive portraits of soldiers and providing in-depth coverage of the human dimensions of their experience. Finally, the results reported here and elsewhere point to a diversity among American soldiers and their attitudes aligning more with the political views across the nation. In other words, there is no particular military attitude or mind-set.

The purpose of this chapter was to compare and contrast the attitudes of military and civilian leaders with American soldiers of Iraq and Kuwait. The chapter focuses on two groups—veterans of Kuwait near Iraq at the end of a six month deployment and veterans in Iraq midway through a military tour of Iraq in the summer of 2004—both with Operation Iraqi Freedom. It employs an objectivist approach to viewing social and domestic issues, giving the respondents a list of issues and having them check their level of agreement. Most research has focused on officer pre-commissioning, officer, and senior leader samples. The present study offered two unique contributions to the civil-military attitude gap literature by comparisons with deployed American soldiers in a combat environment, including enlisted soldiers—the bulk of the armed forces, their self-reported political affiliations, and a replication of previous studies in a new sociopolitical environment—the post-9/11 context.

Overall, political affiliations and their associations seem diverse in the Army among deployed soldiers. Soldiers are fairly equally split along republican, democrat, and third-party lines. However, a great number of soldiers reported their political affiliations as "other" or "none." It is unclear why the larger percentage exists. One explanation might be soldiers' unwillingness to report their political affiliation during a forward deployment, months prior to a major presidential election and with a divisive war around the world, among the American public, and split down political lines. The opening quotation in the chapter highlights the point in the words of an American soldier in Iraq in 2004. Another argument is that traditional remnants of political neutrality among soldiers—especially during and in a military deployment—are prevalent. Accountable research will shine a brighter light on any relationships of particular groups to these questions. None of the findings regarding extreme views of domestic or social issues account for this divergence. Moreover, the data here suggest political engagement on the part of soldiers along a number of social, political, and domestic issues.

Responses to both domestic and social issues were consistent in the direction expected for conservative or liberal views. Half of the items on the domestic issues scale were reverse-coded to account for reliability and validity. All 14 statements were in the expected direction for both democrats and republicans. This finding shows that identifying with either major political party in the military follows their American peers in the larger society.

Consistently and collectively, soldiers feel the most strongly about the life-and-death issues Americans experience, such as abortion and the death penalty. However, they also feel strongly about prayer in public schools. An interesting finding is their level of disagreement regarding the role of mothers in society: Soldiers appear less traditional than what many might expect from within the organization of a masculine dominated culture.[6] Equitable agreement exists for the items remaining and disagreement for the less than life-or-death issues. Again, this is likely more consistent with civilian attitudes to include the less than traditional attitudes toward the roles of women.

In terms of social issues, God and Caesar (religion and the military) dominate the perspective of soldiers: This finding should not be a surprise to readers. Soldiers split along other issues suggesting a somewhat modest civilian orientation when it comes to change, values, and customs.

Again, the divergences among issues along political lines are consistent. Only 5 of 14 items are dramatically divergent—with modest differences along political lines. There is more similarity than dissimilarity. Again, this might suggest some modest consistency with civilian attitudes. In contrast, there is more dissimilarity along political party lines and values—pointing to a modest political gap regarding social values. This divergence along party lines is consistent with previous work at the pre-officer commissioning levels where politics mattered more than institutional affiliation (Rohall et al., 2006). The results are consistent with previous work on enlisted soldiers, and it points to the possibility of a very narrow gap held by others (Snider et al., 2001). Moreover, it shows that even during war, political engagement of soldiers is not foreign, and they are not extreme in their orientations. Indeed, mainstream is the norm when it comes to politics, a finding found among first-term enlistees as well (Segal et al., 2001).

In essence, there is no profile of the typical American soldier. She or he resembles others on the outside or in senior leadership positions. They have a varied point of view on most pressing social and domestic issues that concern Americans. All in all, American soldiers—veterans of Operation Iraqi Freedom—hold varied attitudes toward sociopolitical issues. There is no one American soldier attitude. The findings are along political party lines regarding traditional domestic and social issues; American soldiers are not of a single mind-set, yet, neither is there a complete mosaic of diversity perspectives either. This latter finding likely relates to some self-selection along political party lines into the all-volunteer military force. Future research remains with a need of continued systematic and multivariate analysis controlling for additional variables such as gender, race/ethnicity, religion, socioeconomic status, rank, and increasingly likely degrees of physical abilities or sexual orientation. In the next chapter, I go beyond the U.S. borders and provide the point of view of soldier attitudes toward foreign issues.

5   Over there

American soldier attitudes toward foreign issues

If men define situations as real, they are real in their consequences.

Thomas Theorem[1]

Introduction

The famous German military strategist Carl von Clausewitz stated that war is a "mere continuation of policy [politics] by other means" (1832/1968:119). However, along the continuum between positive peace and all-out war, there is a range of means that involve how American soldiers deploy in the politico-military world. The previous chapter featured attitudes of American soldiers toward domestic social and moral issues on the American agenda. The varied attitudes of the soldiers point to a relative disappearance of a civil-military gap in the post-9/11 world. This chapter continues the line on attitudes and focuses on global topics and foreign policy issues, all of which the U.S. military might play in following national and international decisions. Clearly, foreign affairs and their accompanying wars are a concern of all soldiers.

The role of the United States in conflicts abroad has greatly expanded in the past 100 years. In addition to traditional war fighting, the U.S. and other militaries are increasingly called upon for peacekeeping duty around the globe (Gravino et al., 1993a). One of the first peacekeeping missions began in earnest in September 1920 when Poland petitioned the League of Nations to assist with a conflict with Lithuania. Today there are military peacekeeping missions around the world including the ongoing Multinational Force and Observers (MFO) in the Sinai (Gravino et al., 1993b). In recent years, the U.S. military greatly expanded its role beyond fighting and winning the nation's wars and into Military Operations Other than War, with national building in Haiti; humanitarian relief in Somalia; disaster relief in Florida, Louisiana, Pakistan, and Indonesia; and more recently a global war on terror in Afghanistan and Iraq and stability operations in both places. The question is: How do soldiers, especially those who experience the war in Iraq, feel about these and other types of missions and the roles they may find themselves involved with in the future? Do they differ in attitudes on foreign issues? The overall conclusion is that

American soldiers today remain primarily Americentric but have a worldview and an expanded appreciation and definition of the nation's defense.

Attitudes toward foreign issues

Four different scales access American soldier attitudes toward foreign policy and trans-cultural orientations (see Appendices 5.1 to 5.4). The four scales used were (1) attitudes toward foreign issues,[2] (2) attitudes toward likely future roles and missions of the military,[3] (3) attitudes toward types of uses of the armed forces,[4] and (4) attitudes toward peacekeeping.[5]

The percentages in Chart 5.1 present the findings for American soldiers' attitudes toward foreign others and personal trans-cultural experiences. Overall, the three groups—Iraq, Kuwait, and Haiti American soldiers—show similarity on the issues. The one item with the most divergence was difficulty working with foreign nationals: an 18 percent difference between American veterans of Kuwait and those of Iraq. It is noteworthy that the Kuwaitis have long been an ally and the Iraqis, relatively, only recently. Otherwise, there is no more than eight percentage points between the three groups. Soldiers felt most strongly (near 90 percent) about not trusting foreign nationals as much as people from

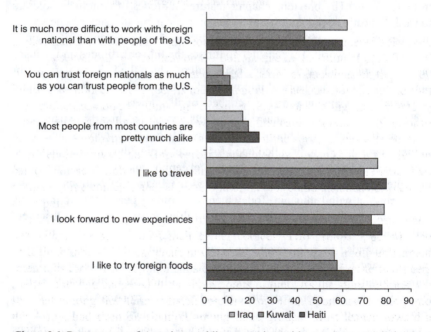

Chart 5.1 Percentages of American soldiers agreeing with statements toward foreign issues by deployment location

the United States, and three-fourths liked to travel and looked forward to new experiences.

Soldiers split somewhat on liking to try foreign foods and having difficulty working with foreign nationals compared with people from the United States. The table can be split into two categories: orientations toward others, the first three items; personal orientations, the latter three. Overall, the groups felt more strongly about their negative orientations toward peoples of other nations than positive about their experiences outside of their own cultural context. American soldiers with Iraq experiences felt the most strongly about others compared to the other two groups.

There is a consistency across generations of American soldiers in the Sinai in 1994 and today (Gravino et al., 1993a). Similar to the Sinai soldiers, there was no trans-cultural orientation toward others, but there was a personal trans-cultural orientation. Most remained untrustworthy of foreign nationals and disagreed that people are "pretty much alike" across national boundaries, and a majority reported it more difficult to work with foreign nationals than with Americans. Unlike liking to travel, trying foreign food, and looking forward to new experiences, all positive attitudes declined over the course of the deployment in the Sinai; the three groups here have the majority appreciating variety despite deployments in less-than-favorable cross-cultural contexts. Essentially, today's American soldiers oppose being more global than previous generations. As a soldier responded on what the United States is doing in Iraq:

> Betray its heritage and tradition by accepting a role for which it is not designed, not prepared for, and not fully committed to accomplishing. The UN-doctrine, nation-builder crap is better suited for the Salvation Army than the U.S. Army. History mocks nations that use its militaries for anything except the conquest and extermination of those who offend it.
>
> (20-year-old, white male E4 married with no children)

The percentages in Chart 5.2 present the findings for the second scale— American soldier attitudes toward likely future roles and missions of the military. Overall, similar responses stand out. One major difference exists between Iraq and Haiti veterans and Kuwait veterans regarding the use of both chemical and biological weapons—approximately 20 percent difference between the latter and former two groups. Note the time at which Kuwait veterans were completing the surveys—in 2003, when in Iraq there remained a strong belief that Saddam Hussein possessed weapons of mass destruction including biological and chemical weapons, and the military prepared for the likelihood that he would use them as he had on the Kurds some 10 years prior. Indeed, the U.S. government had made a case against Iraq and justified an invasion based on what turned out to be faulty intelligence that such weapons were available. American veterans of Kuwait were likely answering the survey in this social context. However, despite the "intelligence," only one-third of

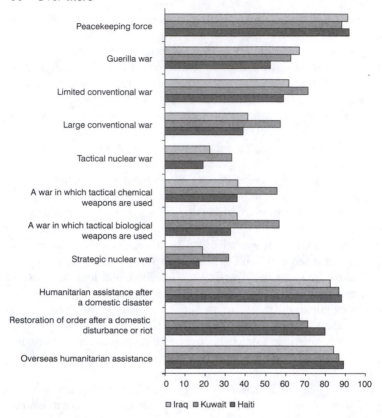

Chart 5.2 Percentages of American soldiers responding to "Likely" U.S. involvement in kinds of deployments in the next 10 years by deployment location

the American soldiers returning from Kuwait thought a war using chemical or biological weapons was likely.

In general, in terms of the types of roles and missions the United States is likely to encounter, all three groups reported operations other than war to be considerably more likely than more high-intensity conflicts. More specifically, all three groups of soldiers believe the least likely scenario of war deployment in the next 10 years would be the highest intensity of nuclear wars, tactical or strategic: in other words, a tactical nuclear war involving specified smaller-scale nuclear attacks versus more strategic types—generally launching a full-scale nuclear war. Plus, for all three, limited conventional war was roughly 20 percent more likely than a large-scale conventional war. The top three types of missions they do foresee would be very-low-intensity operations other than war including peacekeeping, overseas humanitarian assistance and humanitarian assistance after a domestic disaster. For example, a soldier noted the importance

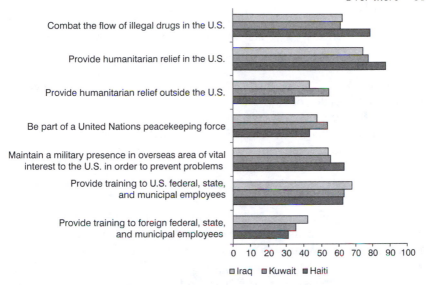

Combat the flow of illegal drugs in the U.S.

Provide humanitarian relief in the U.S.

Provide humanitarian relief outside the U.S.

Be part of a United Nations peacekeeping force

Maintain a military presence in overseas area of vital interest to the U.S. in order to prevent problems

Provide training to U.S. federal, state, and municipal employees

Provide training to foreign federal, state, and municipal employees

0 10 20 30 40 50 60 70 80 90 100

□ Iraq   ▨ Kuwait   ▪ Haiti

Chart 5.3 Percentages of American soldiers supporting types of operations other than war use of the armed forces by deployment location

of humanitarian assistance and wrote, "I believe that doing more humanitarian efforts, perhaps improving more roads and residential areas would please the general local national public and may quell some anti-coalition sentiment" (21-year-old white male E4 never married).

For the Haiti veterans, humanitarian missions occurred in the early 1990s. They include Operation Restore Hope in Somalia; peacekeeping in Kosovo, Bosnia, and the Sinai; and disaster relief in Florida following Hurricane Andrew. Such missions likely influenced Kuwait and Iraq veterans as well. These findings are consistent with studies of American reservists from 10 years earlier except they were less likely to believe the U.S. would actually be involved in any high-intensity missions (Gravino et al., 1993a).

The percentages in Chart 5.3 show the percentages for American soldiers' attitudes toward support for the uses of the armed forces in nontraditional situations. These sets of statements move somewhat beyond hypothetical future scenarios to actual areas that the soldiers may experience. Again, overall, similarity dictates. No more than 10 percent differences exist between the groups except for drug interdiction and humanitarianism. Haiti veterans felt stronger about these two issues than the two more recent groups of soldiers. Least support was for providing training to foreign federal, state, and municipal employees—ironically, a job that occupies a significant number of U.S. Army forces in Iraq beginning in 2004 and continued thereafter for some time.

Overall, American soldiers are diverse in their attitudes, yet, they are Americentric warriors—they are oriented toward American interests. As a soldier penned to me:

> Anybody should be willing to defend their country. But if we protected our borders better, other terrorists couldn't get in and families wouldn't be torn apart because we suspect someone might think about attacking us in the future. Helping other countries is good and all, but 900 soldiers dead and countless wounded on false pretenses and no end in sight. Let us help ourselves.
>
> (22-year-old white male E4 married with no children)

Soldiers split on the uses of soldiers for operations other than war, with more favoring using them for Americans. The further away from home and the more traditional the military conventions—meaning warrior skills exclusive of others—the less supportive soldiers appear to be for using American soldiers.

Finally, the last chart in the chapter (Chart 5.4) shows the percentages for American soldiers' attitudes toward peacekeeping. Peacekeeping has been the most prevalent area of research among military sociologists in the last 30 years. Overall, group responses continued to show fair uniformity except for Kuwait veterans. They interestingly agreed less that peacekeeping is boring, but that peacekeeping operations are appropriate missions for their unit—keeping in mind that these are primarily combat support soldiers reporting. Essentially, they are not bored by peacekeeping; rather, they should be doing something else.

The top two overall areas of most agreement were that a soldier considered well trained in basic military skills requires additional training for peacekeeping and that reservists can perform peacekeeping missions as well as regular military personnel. Unarmed peacekeeping duty had the least agreement—soldiers just "ain't wantin'" to go nowhere without a weapon. Next, the other three least agreement areas were that peacekeeping missions are appropriate missions for the unit and that peacekeeping assignments help a soldier's career, and should be performed by military civilians rather than by soldiers. This latter finding continues the adage often attributed to the late military sociologist Charles Moskos, put forth by former United Nations Secretary-General in a 1962 speech Dag Hjalmar Agne Carl Hammarskjöld, and commonly the unofficial motto of UN peacekeepers: "peacekeeping is not a job for soldiers, but only a soldier can do it."

Similar to the mid-level officers of all military branches studied previously (Avant and Lebovic, 2000), it appears American soldiers today are fairly in touch with a changing world and changing missions. There was not a prevalence of negative attitudes toward peacekeeping missions. Indeed, they appear in line with their brothers and sisters of a previous generation (Segal et al., 1998; Segal and Tiggle, 1997). One soldier described his unit's mission in Iraq as "The

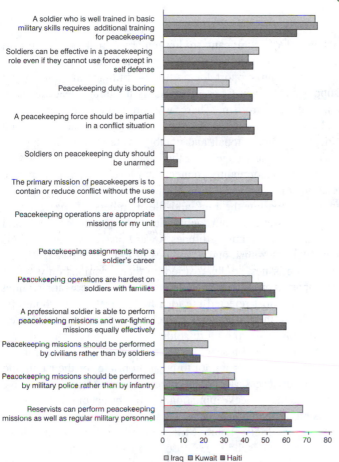

Chart 5.4 Percentages of American soldiers agreeing with statements toward peacekeeping by deployment location

Peace Corp." Similar to earlier cohorts, most rejected the idea that peacekeepers should be unarmed or that civilians should accomplish peacekeeping duties. A soldier in Iraq described his mission as twofold: "provide peace and security to the people in our area of operation." And, like most soldiers from both the reservist units and the active units from previous studies, the soldiers here felt peacekeeping was not appropriate for their unit and that peacekeeping was not necessarily good for their careers. Confirming the attitudes of soldiers from a previous generation (Miller, 1997), there is no "dominant view" among today's American soldiers when it comes to foreign policy issues other than possessing a weapon while doing it.

Discussion

In the 1990s, a handful of significant studies emerged that helped inform us about peacekeeping and soldiering. First, Avant and Lebovic (2000) found officers to have strong support for traditional military missions while concomitantly supportive of new types of missions including peacekeeping, drug interdiction, and antiterrorism. There was an important finding that officers connected greater support for any type of mission if they perceived there to be presidential, congressional, and notably, American public support for the mission. The researchers concluded the officers to be in touch with a changing world. Yet they concomitantly connect their level of support to public support of expectations for them and their soldiers.

In another study, comparing the rank-and-file members of the reserves, researchers found consistency—both active-duty American soldiers and reservists alike did not have negative attitudes toward peacekeeping missions and might embrace both traditional and new types of military missions (Segal et al., 1998). On specific issues, soldiers varied on their positions on whether soldiers should be impartial and that they could be effective in reducing conflict without the use of force. Most rejected the idea that peacekeepers should be unarmed or that civilians should conduct peacekeeping missions. However, the more missions deployed on, the more soldiers felt civilians could do the mission (Reed and Segal, 2000). Most soldiers, from both the reservist unit and the active unit, reported peacekeeping not to be appropriate for their unit and that peacekeeping was not necessarily good for their careers. Many of the active Army units had attitudes that peacekeeping might better be accomplished using military police units rather than the infantry.

In 1994, military sociologist Laura Miller found no "dominant view" among American soldiers in Macedonia. Those who had completed their tour reported less enthusiasm about the mission than those only a few weeks into the mission. Overall, soldiers had mixed views about this particular mission, with most noting the benefits of at least a temporary real-world deployment over the suppression and degradation of their combat skills sitting at home.

Another important study about attitudes of American service members and most closely aligned with the present study was carried out by military sociologist David Segal and military psychologist Ronald Tiggle (1997). I replicated three of their scales here. They surveyed a reserve component of the 505th Parachute Infantry Regiment out of Fort Bragg, North Carolina. This unit was headed for a 6-month rotation with the MFO in the Sinai and were surveyed at three 4-month points—1 month into being activated and in preparation for the deployment, 4 months later (1 month into the deployment), and 4 months later (4 month before the unit returned to the United States).

First, in terms of the types of roles and missions that the United States is likely to encounter, most reservists found operations other than war to be considerably more likely than more high-intensity types of conflicts. However, this pattern declined the longer they were in the deployment. Contrary to previous studies, they were more likely to believe the United States would actually be involved in high-intensity missions. Second, the researchers noted no emergence of a "trans-cultural orientation." Most remained untrustworthy of foreign nationals, disagreed that people are "pretty much alike" across national boundaries and, by the end of the deployment, a majority reported it more difficult to work with foreign nationals than with fellow Americans. Liking to travel, trying foreign food, and looking forward to new experiences all declined during the course of the deployment. Finally, regarding peacekeeping, many agreed with supporting the minimal use of force, peacekeeping would require special training, impartiality, and reduction of conflict, but this reduced somewhat with time in the deployment. Agreements with peacekeeping assignments being good for their unit and good for careers declined over time. Many disagreed with the statement that "this mission could be performed by unarmed personnel." Declines on other items exist as well, and the researchers concluded that the reserve soldiers, like active-duty soldiers before them, increasingly become disenchanted with the mission over the course of the deployment. In sum, disenchantment with the mission coupled with the more they moved from evaluating perception to evaluating their actual experience.

Conclusion

In this chapter, I featured attitudes toward foreign policy issues and the varied roles the U.S. military might play following national and international decisions. The following four areas received attention: (1) attitudes toward foreign issues, (2) attitudes toward likely future roles and missions of the military, (3) attitudes toward support for the uses of the armed forces, and (4) attitudes toward peacekeeping. Soldiers definitely have attitudes toward foreign issues and the new missions they may encounter, and they define for themselves what their attitudes are, often based on their actual experiences with deployment.

The traditional view of the purpose of the U.S. military is to fight and win the nation's wars. Clearly, this role has been expanded in the past quarter-century into real-world, non-combat missions including peacekeeping, nation building, disaster relief, and more recently fighting global terrorism. Nevertheless, how have soldiers responded to this—especially those having recently been involved in missions? Previous research has pointed to variability among American soldiers and their being positive toward peacekeeping and other foreign policy issues. They believed missions in the future were likely to be nontraditional and of low intensity. They were more oriented toward U.S. interests and less toward trans-cultural orientations. American soldiers serving in Iraq and Kuwait are not unlike soldiers from other wars, other missions, other places, and other times— at least in recent times. Embedded into their social reality are peacekeeping and missions other than war. They have an expanded definition of defense beyond fighting and winning the nation's wars, a finding close to what we find among American college students as well (Rohall et al., 2006). They certainly are as Americentric as their peers from a generation before—supporting that they are nationalistic and not "global citizens"; however, they are more trans-cultural. If their attitude is an indication of future behavior, we can expect they will continue to define the situations as real and valid and to continue to do what the nation has expected of them. In particular, they appear to appreciate working in varied capacities beyond the U.S. borders.

This chapter concludes the representation of American soldier attitudes on larger domestic and foreign issues. The next chapter presents results from experiences of American soldiers in Iraq based on their perceptions of social control mechanisms. The questions provided American soldiers opportunities to assess whether they view themselves as innovative professionals or as human tools. Specifically, soldiers responded to six queries including opportunities to be creative in their day-to-day activities in Iraq and whether characteristics of the McDonaldization thesis—efficiency, calculability, predictability, control, and the irrationality of rationality—shapes their experience more or less.

6 McSoldiers

Human tools or innovative professionals?

Make sandwiches for Geraldo Rivera (seriously!).
(28-year-old white female junior officer, married)

Nothing is quick, nothing is efficient. In fact, all operations are overly planned and analyzed ... so much to the point that things are dangerously inefficient.
(21-year-old, white male E4, never married)

Introduction

The previous chapter highlighted attitudes of American soldiers toward foreign policy–related issues that may or may not one day engulf their life as soldiers or civilians. This chapter turns to the day-to-day work of American soldiers in Iraq, specifically using the McDonaldization thesis as a framework, and provides them a forum for sharing their experiences in their own words. George Ritzer defines McDonaldization as "the process by which the principles of the fast-food restaurant are coming to dominate more and more sectors of American society as well as of the rest of the world" (Ritzer, 2004:1).

McDonaldization builds upon the sociological work of Max Weber (1921/1968) wherein the prototypical McDonalized organization would be extremely efficient, decidedly calculating, vastly predictable, highly controlling, and with irrationality overcoming the rational (Hajjar and Ender, 2005). Weber is a classical sociological theorist, and one of his main theories concerns bureaucracy and rationality in modern society. Ritzer has adopted Weber's theoretical conceptions for more contemporary time, specifically outlining five dimensions usable as heuristics to understand organizations: efficiency, calculability, predictability, control, and the irrationality of rationality. Most readers are probably familiar with the five dimensions. However, a brief refresher for the uninformed is appropriate. Later parts of the chapter cover discussions of applications of the McDonaldization thesis in other areas of social life.

Efficiency in the McDonaldization process refers to "the optimum method of getting from one point to another" (Ritzer, 2004:12). Superficially, efficiency is a good thing. It is pragmatic. After all, it is more attractive and hip to "read" a book on tape or see a movie over the book versus turning through the pages or getting your food on the fly through the ubiquitous drive-through window versus eating in the restaurant or cooking at home. The far deeper question begs, what are the social costs of being too efficient? Next, calculability in the McDonaldization process refers to "emphasis on the quantitative aspects of products (portion size, cost) and services offered (the time it takes to get the product)" (Ritzer, 2004:12). Can billions of consumed burgers be wrong? Does not counting and assessing consumables make us a better society? Should not our SAT (Standard Academic Test) scores and a college GPA (grade point average) determine our destiny? The deeper question begs, what are the social costs of being fixated on numbers? Next, predictability refers to the "assurance that products and services will be the same over time and in all locales" (Ritzer, 2004:13). In the world of McDonalds, a Quarter-Pounder in New York City is the same in Hockenheim, Germany; Ho Chi Min City, Vietnam; Yokohama, Japan; and Liverpool, England. The virtually identical product from block to block and continent to continent is on the surface comforting to many. Predictability is consistency. However, a cliché begs the question, is not variety the spice of life? Control references the tendency in McDonaldized systems to exert *control* over people, usually through uses of nonhuman technologies (Ritzer, 2002:3). McDonalds has come to control individual choices (based on their own in house calculated research studies). Individual products such as a burger, fries, and drinks are now clustered products with individual numbers, and employees regularly encourage customers to order the numbers rather than specific combinations of items. Finally, the irrationally of rationality, according to Ritzer, "is that rational systems serve to deny human reason; rational systems are often unreasonable" (Ritzer, 2002:20). This fifth dimension highlights some of the potential dangers of this process and it gives this theory a critical angle. Despite the advantages of McDonaldization as a purely rational system (e.g. significant profits, customer choices, speedy service at times), it produces some irrational consequences. To expand on the notion that McDonaldization limits people from fulfilling their human potential, Ritzer presents a hopeful picture of the future that encapsulates his concern: "Unfettered by the constraints of McDonaldized systems, but using the technologies available made possible by them, people would have the potential to be far more thoughtful, skillful, creative, and well-rounded" (Ritzer, 2002:22).

Can the McDonaldization thesis be applied to the military profession and soldiering in Iraq? Overall, the findings below are consistent with the overall theme of diversity. Many soldiers describe examples of all five elements of the McDonaldized thesis, and many do not. Among the notable elements of McDonaldization, the irrationality of rationality occurred most often. The contexts included both on and off the Forward Operation Base (FOB)—both in the work world and on their downtime on the FOB. Officers were more likely to have identified irrationality than enlisted soldiers. At the same instance, a host of soldiers reported much creativity in Iraq. The bottom-line finding up front is that American soldiers report situations of being McDonaldized—not enough to be labeled McSoldiers—as just as many report opportunities to be innovative, creative, and adaptive—essentially some level of autonomous professionalism.

The American McSoldier?

One might expect the prototypical bureaucracy—the U.S. military—to be ripe for McDonaldization (Segal and Segal, 1983). Recent studies support the thesis (Gehler, 2005; Wong, 2002). First, Wong (2002)—while not referring to McDonaldization directly—has identified two elements of McDonaldization: control and predictability. Each intervenes in U.S. Army company commanders' ability to be innovative in their mid-level organizational leadership. This finding emerges despite the rhetoric of leadership at the time calling for transformation and empowering junior leaders to be more innovative and adaptive to a changing external environment. Wong (2002) says:

> Put bluntly, the Army is relying on a leader development system that encourages reactive instead of proactive thought, compliance instead of creativity, and adherence instead of audacity. Junior officers, especially company commanders, are seldom given opportunities to be innovative; to make decisions; or to fail, learn, and try again...this move to over-centralized control results ...(p. 3).[1]

Wong examines the training cycle of units from the perspective of the company commander. He argues that training prescribed from higher headquarters and virtually every component involves responding to directions wherein even occasional disruptions and conflicts are outside the control of the commander. Current and emerging leaders receive assurance that the next year will be same not only over time but also from one place in the Army to another—what Ritzer would call *predictability*. Wong never refers to McDonaldization, but I would argue he clearly locates two elements of the process in the training regiment of U.S. Army junior officers.

In a separate study, we identified some elements of McDonaldization process more directly (Hajjar and Ender, 2005). Using data from a large-scale study of U.S. Army officers, we uncovered some evidence of McDonaldization in the U.S. Army.[2] We identified practices and illustrative deleterious effects of McDonaldization, including stifled creativity, reduced leadership effectiveness, and hindering of the profession. Examples of all four dimensions of McDonaldization—efficiency, calculability, predictability and control, and ultimately the irrationality of rationality—were evident. Both studies, however, are more conceptual than empirical, more retrospective than immediate, and focused on training rather than real-world, practiced contexts of McDonaldization.

Finally, Wong (2004) did conduct some real-world analysis through 50 structured interviews of lieutenants and captains in Iraq in the spring of 2004. His major finding was that junior officers in Iraq were adapting well to an environment characterized as complex, ambiguous, and dynamic. For example, they were not specifically trained for duties requiring simultaneous war fighting, conflict resolution, and nation building. He concluded that an entire cohort of junior leaders was coming of age as "...adaptable, creative, innovative, and confident in their abilities to handle just about any task..." (Wong, 2004:15). Such skills transcend what one would expect of a McDonaldized organization. This provides a real-world, military context for the application of the creativity and adaptation and the McDonaldization thesis—soldiering in Iraq. Soldiers are not particularly McDonaldized and are fairly creative.

American soldiers serving in Iraq received a series of open-ended questions on a survey designed to tap into each dimension of the McDonaldization thesis and creativity (see Appendix 6.1). The responses of soldiers below will shed auxiliary light on the process and assess whether soldiers in Iraq were becoming or resisting the McDonaldization moniker.

Elements of McDonaldization in Iraq

Efficiency in Iraq

Soldiers were asked whether the tasks seemed to be completed quickly and efficiently in their unit and by them specifically, but not necessarily to the best possible quality. Just more than one-half the soldiers (53.8 percent) provided a response to this open-ended question. Of those, more than one-half (57.8 percent) said "yes," and 13.9 percent provided a "no" response. Less than 10 percent (9 percent) wrote "no comment," "don't know," or "not sure." Just above 7 percent (7.3 percent) made some other type of comment.

Most of the no responses simply read "no." Some qualified their "no" with a tone of pride and matter of factness. A typical response quipped, "The guys I work with make it personal and are on point to do the very best they can with what they have or don't have to work with" (36-year-old, white male E6, married for the first time). Another wrote, "All tasks are accomplished with a fair amount of accuracy" (34-year-old African-American male, NCO, no children). Another quipped, "Tasks are completed to standard. That's our job" (34-year-old African-American male NCO with two children). Finally, another insists, "What my unit does is done efficiently at all times and with the best of quality" (28-year-old, white female private, remarried with one child at home). Some soldiers seemed a bit hesitant in their responses. A 26-year-old, white male private, married and with two children at home, said, "I can't think of any."

The "yes" responders provided more details because the question had directed them to. The soldiers provided a range of examples reflecting on the detriments of efficiency. The more salient shortfall areas according to soldiers included tasks in general, time, quality of life areas, security, reports, equipment, patrols and searchers, and "everything." However, the top area that received the shortest attention according to soldiers was maintenance. "Maintenance" manifested in efficiency in a number of areas. One soldier extolled,

> The biggest task in the ASB is maintenance. We hold our own and do quality work. However, we are not as efficient and cannot work as quickly as we need to. Parts are our major hurdle, both for ground maintenance and aviator maintenance. The problem is there is a bottleneck on parts flow at the division SSA, MGB. Repair parts are received in theater from the states faster than parts can be received from the Division SSA to units.
>
> (37-year-old white male warrant officer, married)

Other soldiers lamented the primacy of security over maintenance: "Maintenance of control and parts and equipment. We are stretched too thin to accomplish the mission to the best ability" (22-year-old Hispanic male private, married for the first time, no children) or,

> Mission related tasks (i.e., maintenance) take a back seat to tower and gate duties. Some shops all but close just to man our positions. Gates and towers seem to be protecting guards for the next shift rather than a FOB with operating motor pools and maintenance shops.
>
> (35-year-old white, male E6 married with four children)

Soldiers also provided examples of other areas such as tasks. "Tasks" are essentially professional "to-do" duties for soldiers. Some tasks fell short of accomplishment. One 26-year-old junior officer wrote, "There is always room for improvement on execution of tasks."

"Time" was similarly identified as something not provided. Another 24-year-old junior officer, engaged with no children, shared: "When someone from our company is called to do a mission in someone else's zone it is usually a 'hey-you' mission that has always worked out but could have gone smoother if we had more time."

"Quality of life" issues lacked the quality they deserve, according to soldiers. Examples from soldiers included "sleep," "physical training" and "returning to work after only eight hours down time."

Additionally, soldiers identified "Reports" as not being the quality they deserve. A junior officer bemoaned, "Routine reports to higher HQ [headquarters]." Soldiers identified the managing of equipment as lacking quality. A 25-year-old African-American E4 wrote, "Breakdown in issuing our equipment."

"Patrols and searchers" lacked the quality they deserved, according to a number of soldiers. An example was what a soldier called "presence patrols"—where units simply have visibility in a neighborhood.

Last, some soldiers simply said that "Everything in Iraq" lacked quality. Along these lines and reflective of the statement, soldiers wrote about a number of areas in their area of operation including training, especially weapons training, dealing with anti-mortar fire, guard duty, planning, dealing with Iraqis, and manpower shortages as efficiency culprits.

In terms of rank, only officers differentiated from the enlisted ranks. Officers were more likely to report a lack of quality in their performances. In many ways, this reflects their leadership roles and their "big picture" perspective on the mission. In the end, they are responsible for the success of the tasks, missions, and war in general. They were more likely to see shortcomings in the quality of accomplishments. However, what stands out was the high number of soldiers that identified some lack of quality in a range of different areas under their jurisdiction.

Predictability in Iraq

Roughly 71 percent of soldiers surveyed responded to the question about predictability in Iraq. Responses factored into four categories. Among those who responded with something, just above one-third (37.9 percent) said predictability was not a problem for their unit and/or the Coalition Forces in Iraq. Of those, almost half (45.3 percent) said "yes," and another 8 percent said "sometimes." Another small proportion (8.8 percent) provided some other comments or said "no comment" or that they "don't know."

For the "no" responses, soldiers usually simply wrote a definitive "no" or "NO!" in capital letters with an exclamation point. Others qualified their responses. First, some noted how their unit was conscientious regarding predictability and projecting patterns of movement. Responding to the predictability question, a male E4 wrote: "Overall, no. We are aware of these predictability situations, so therefore everyday would be different as far as mission wise." A senior-level NCO, married with two children, attributed the success of being unpredictable to leadership:

> No, I believe through our BN's centralized planning process (e.g., our Go-No-Go process for tactical convoys), key leadership CDRs, 1SGs, CSM, and staff pull brain cells together in order to plan, prep, and execute—employing the units with the utmost of its capabilities.

A male company-grade senior officer with one child and married placed the reason for the lack of predictability on soldiers:

> No. We are unpredictable in the conduct of our operations … hence no casualties during the deployment. The challenge is to maintain the vigilance and battle focus in that regard in order to avoid the plague of the C word. Complacency!

Those who said "yes" provided examples. Most of the examples fell into two categories, predictability outside the FOB—mostly travel patterns on routes in and around Baghdad and behavior in general on the FOB. Regarding "Travel Routes," soldiers left the FOBs in convoys of usually three or more vehicles. Entering and exiting a FOB was fairly well guarded but certainly fixed. Because of the roads in and around Baghdad, travel was noted as predictable by many soldiers. A 22-year-old female junior officer, single with no children, wrote: "We run convoys to and from the same point. If that is where the supplies are, that is where they [the insurgents] go." A 27-year-old white male sergeant, married with one child, scribed:

> Yes, during convoy missions, we do not leave everyday, but we do leave on the same exact time. The route we take is very predictable. During convoy ambushes, the enemy knows aircraft will come to provide cover which makes it an easier target.

Similar to vehicle convoy routes, helicopter pilots noted similar route problems. A 30-year-old Asian-American female junior officer, married with no children, and a pilot lamented:

> I would say so because I know the schedule we fly soldiers to and from other camps at roughly the same time each day. We also always sat on meals at the same time, each time, which would be a great opportunity for the enemy to conduct a rocket/mortar attack.

Indeed, this latter incident occurred at a Coalition Forces FOB dining facility in Mosul, Iraq just before Christmas in 2004. 24 were killed including 15 Americans and 64 wounded (Redmon, 2004).

On the routes, soldiers noted problems not with routes but with times. A 30-year-old white male staff sergeant with one child and married for the third time, shared: "Yes, we have IED sweeps from 2100–0900. Every 3 hours a different unit goes out. We have to stay out there for 3 hours to do something that takes an hour. There are a lot more things." A 25-year-old white male private and single observed,

I work inside the FOB. But I know when we do our little patrols we always [emphasis in original] go the same route. I think its a flaw with people in the military who do things the exact same way every time or else how would you be squared away?

Noted above is the incompatibility between a traditional bureaucracy such as the military where being "squared away" means you are successful at your job, yet the new environment of the war in Iraq required more of a different way of thinking to be successful.

Another soldier noted how the process linked with IEDs and targeting seems a bit more complicated and haphazard, asserting,

As far as IED's go, they don't really need to study our schedule. Just some need to see us then blow it as we go by. As far as ambushing us, they just need a plan for them to escape. Our patrols are predictable, not necessarily times, but when we patrol we cover our sector. It's easy to attack us when we were driving down the same streets day after day. There's no way around it for us on the streets we chose. All we can do is change it up. The enemy just picks the spot where they want to hit us and then escapes.

(25-year-old African-American male, sergeant married with one child)

A 27-year-old white male, single junior officer, however concludes with the inevitability of the process:

Yes … While individual patrols take measures to avoid being predictable; it would be easy for the enemy to pattern the frequency of patrols through a given sector at given times. While higher maintains situational awareness and disseminates, there are no measures to avoid repetition.

In addition to routes and times outside the FOB, there was predictable behavior in terms of more "General Day-to-Day Behavior" on the FOB. There were common predictable practices on the FOB. A 22-year-old white female private pointed out, "Yes [we're predictable], my unit has PT formation six days a week, same place and time every single day."

Others underscored how predictability on the FOB envisaged behavior off the FOB as well. A 26-year-old Hispanic male, single junior officer scribbled,

Yes [we're predictable]. Every Tuesday convoys from all over Baghdad head to Victory North [a large FOB] to draw funds to spend on the units. You can only go on Tuesday because that's the only time the contracting place is open (Tuesdays from 0700–1200). This makes no sense at all.

Soldiers responded to sources of predictability as an issue larger than the control of the individual soldiers and small units and inherent in the organization of the U.S. Army. A 33-year-old African-American female, sergeant with two children and divorced recognized, "… the Army follows all its teachings and seems to have trouble adjusting to doing it differently … because they [the insurgents] know our training strategies." A 24-year-old white male junior officer, single with one child, pointed out, "The enemy knows our ROE, but since that is somewhat non-negotiable …" implying that the overall rules of war predict behavior for Coalition Forces. Finally, a 27-year-old Native American male junior officer, engaged with no children, noted his personal struggle with the larger structure of the organization:

> Yes [the Army is predictable in Iraq]. The Army's standards are its own enemy in this unconventional war. You have to go against your usual way of planning to be able to stay one step ahead of the enemy and so far this company as a whole has done this well.

Since most of the research on innovation and adaptability has been undertaken with officer samples, I examined the responses on predictability by military ranks. I compared junior enlisted soldiers, NCOs, and all officers. There were no outstanding differences in responses. The lowest ranked soldiers (E1 to E3) did have a somewhat higher percentage of "Yes" responses—20 percent more than NCOs.

Quantification in Iraq

Calculability in the McDonaldization process refers to "an emphasis on the quantitative aspects of products (portion size, cost) and services offered (the time it takes to get the product)" (Ritzer, 2004:12). The question asked: "Are there any statistics or numbers that you feel get too much attention in Iraq?" Almost two-thirds (61.3 percent) of the soldiers responded to this open-ended question with some written responses. Of those, half (50 percent) said "yes." The next largest group was "no" (35.6 percent) and again two groups of less than 10 percent, each responding either "don't know," "no comment," or some other response.

The "no" responses are of interest as many go beyond the singular response with a qualification. For example, one soldier said, "No. I think the American people should know what is really going on in Iraq" (27-year-old white E4, married with three children). Another goes even farther and stressed, "No, Americans and all countries involved have a right to see the harsh reality of war" (33-year-old African-American E6, married with two children). Another viewed quantification as a form of social control writing: "Nope, not at all. What is the value of a human life, combatant or noncombatant? The world needs to know; otherwise "very highers" would move us around like chess pieces" (24-year-old African-American male, single junior officer). Another saw the body count as important, writing: "No, I think it is important for all Americans to know how many brave soldiers have paid the ultimate sacrifice for the freedom of others." (24-year-old Pacific Islander male, engaged to be married with two children).

Most of the respondents elaborated on their "yes" responses. Virtually every response encompassed "Media Attention." Soldiers had a strong position on mass media, how it portrays their individual and collective experiences, and it came out in the representations of casualties. The responses of quantification fell into four major categories: "Death," "Media," "Prison," and an "Other" category.

Most of the soldiers felt there was too much mention of "Death" in the media. Responses generally involved casualties in general and American, insurgent, and Iraqi civilian casualties. For example, one soldier wrote, "Yes, casualties happen in war. The risks are substantially less than in any previous conflict we've been in. The media blows it out of proportion" (28-year-old white male junior officer, never married). Others shared: "The numbers of casualties I feel are exploited in the media, without showing comparison of actual battles and total personnel in country" (30-year-old white male private, divorced) and

> KIA IED Incidents—there is way too much attention. Our media is diabolically focused on the sensational and the morbid. Too much goodness is ignored and the picture painted back home is wholly skewed to the negative. A real travesty lending truth to the saying…"the first casualty of war is the TRUTH" [original in caps].
>
> (34-year-old male field-grade officer, married with one child)

Soldiers also wrote about "Civilians being Killed." Two soldiers put pen to paper: "The news always talks about how many "civilians" were killed, but it doesn't mention that some of these civilians are really insurgents carrying RPGs and AK-47s" (32-year-old white female E5, never married). Another wrote:

> Casualty figures in general. Also it can be a very quiet day in the AOR and there may be one event but that's what is on the news. Also, the news media is not getting the whole story. My favorite—a car bomb kills 3. They fail to mention the three were the bad guys and the bomb blew up early and killed them.
>
> (34-year-old white male field-grade officer, married with two children)

Another major topic was whether stories showed the "Brighter or Darker Side of Events and Day-to-Day Life in Iraq." Below are a number of examples in the words of soldiers:

No particular statistics that I'm aware of, however; the notion that Iraq in general, Baghdad in particular, is in flames and chaotic as depicted by the media. I think this is misleading the world populous. But, as they say about the media, "Where's the glory in reporting on the positive stuff?"

(43-year-old African-American male field-grade officer, married with one child)

I feel the only news you ever hear is when something bad happens. They should push the number of schools we have rebuilt, lives saved, hands shaken, etc. Not the number of people that hate us. Because I know in my zone there are a lot more that like us than hate us.

(24-year-old white male junior officer, engaged)

Too much attention is given to what politicians and generals (to me there's no difference between the two) have to say about the great things going on in Iraq. They are not the ones out here on the ground. They stay in their MR conditioned offices and attend meetings and listen all day to people who tell them what they want to hear.

(26-year-old bi-ethnic male junior officer, single)

One last significant area of media commented on by soldiers involved the "Prison Humiliations." Two soldiers composed: "Yes, also the prison abuse, they have been abusing their own people for years, I am not condoning the actions of American soldiers but I am saying it is getting too much publicity (21-year-old male E4, legally separated) and "The fucking prison scandal gets way too much attention. The Iraqis don't care. They know Saddam did a whole lot worse" (27-year-old white male E4, remarried with no children)

Other responses related to quantification features included leadership issues, the countdown to troop withdrawal, Saddam Hussein in the news, and the amount of mortar fire in the Green Zone. A soldier noted, "Saddam is in the news way too much" (25-year-old white female junior officer, engaged). In another example, a soldier suggested, "Safety statistics are being overdone at the individual level considering we get hit when we are driving. Original flak vest works great. Improve vehicles" (24-year-old white male junior officer, married with one child).

Finally, a cross-tabulation comparing how the counting of things was overemphasized via responses by rank shows no significant differences. Officers were, however, somewhat more likely to respond "yes" and "no" and more likely to say "yes" than enlisted soldiers.

Control in Iraq

In the McDonaldization process, control refers to the tendency of systems to exert *control* over people, usually through the utilization of nonhuman technologies. This question had the largest number of respondents. Just more than three-fourths (75.9 percent) of the soldiers responded to the question dealing with control. Of those who responded, fewer than half (45.6 percent) wrote "yes." Half (50.6 percent) wrote "no." The remaining 5 percent had some other response.

Most of the "no" responses did not add any additional comments to their responses. A handful of soldiers wrote something like the following: "We are free to conduct our missions with limited restrictions, no major issues" (43-year-old Hispanic male warrant officer, married with three children).

It is the "yes" responses where there was more writing. The elaborations on the "Yes" responses fell into three categories: "General Control," "Controls on the FOB," and "Controls from Rules of Engagement" (ROE).

The fewest responses, about 15 percent, were types of "General Control" where the soldiers did not identify any specific forms of control—only that they felt controlled. Two typical responses in this category included "Rules imposed make me feel as though I'm being treated like a child" (32-year-old white male sergeant, married, no children) and "There are too many little rules that make everyday living harder" (38-year-old white male E4, married, no children). Some of the general rules included rules about gear. One typical example: "Side shields and riot face shields being worn by gunners ... being issued gear that I can't use, for example, Wiley X's eye wear glasses...I must sign for and carry Wiley X [protective sunglasses]?" (20-year-old white male private, never married).

A third of the "yes" responses had to do with "Rules and Regulations" on the FOB. Most of the responses had to do with alcohol, sex, clothing, and buddies. A soldier succinctly noted, "I can't consume alcohol or fuck. You go figure" (no demographic information available). Another wrote more suitably, "No alcohol or opposite sex interactions make it difficult, at least for me, to unwind" (29-year-old white male E4, single). Another soldier was more practical: "I feel soldiers should be allowed two beers a week" (22-year-old Native American E4, single). A mission-focused example included:

> We should be permitted to drink. The Iraqis drink and I am often invited to have a drink with other professional Iraqis. I am unable to explain why we cannot drink because I do not understand it. Everybody else (such as the British, Poles, CPA, Iraqis, NGOs, etc.) is permitted to do so. Intoxication is prohibited by UCMJ when on duty—that should be the standard, but some regulated social drinking should be permitted.
>
> (36-year-old white male field-grade officer, married no children)

Another order on the FOB involved no "Sexual Relations among Soldiers." A soldier responded to this policy:

> Yes, one rule is too restrictive: No talking to females. We are treated as if we are children and not grown American soldiers. What comes next, tell us how to breathe? And yet they expect us to go out and get shot or blown up.
>
> (26-year-old Hispanic male E4, married)

Another major control mechanism felt by soldiers on the FOB had to do with "uniforms." A few examples represented their concerns:

> Leadership is getting stupid. Yes they are. We are not allowed to wear our PT uniform (shorts and T-shirt) unless we are doing PT even in your time off. You are only allowed to wear one brand of sunglasses and must wear them; even in the base camp we must carry our weapon at the ready. You are not allowed to flip up the cuff of your shirt in the hot conditions.
>
> (20-year-old white male E4, engaged)

> No alcohol. People need a drink every now and then (although I don't drink). Also, no Do-Rags. This is not a problem in living quarters; should be able to have them. No civilian attire—should be able to feel comfortable. No PT's in recreation area—it's a recreation area. We should feel comfortable having fun.
>
> (24-year-old African-American male private, legally separated with two children)

> No PT's [shorts and t-shirt] in the DFAC. DCU's are actually dirtier than PT's. When working outside and not under attack, you can't have soldiers take off DCU tops. It is bad for morale when orders are dictated by personnel not dealing with same issues. Good discipline is important, but, so is reality. When a leader dictates that a rule is in place (such as can't take off top), while they are in A/C, SUV's, and work in A/C buildings?
>
> (33-year-old Hispanic/Latina female senior NCO, married with one child)

American soldiers were expected to always walk around the FOB with a "Battle Buddy." Many soldiers objected to this ruling. One soldier entered,

> They must have a BATTLE BUDDY [original in caps] rule (Can't go anywhere alone). Sometimes you may want to use the phone, or go get something to eat, or use the computers. If no one else is around or wants to go then you can't go.
>
> (23-year-old African-American male E4, single)

However, soldiers appear to have felt the most strongly and wrote the most about the "Rules and Regulations that Restricted off the FOB"—specifically, half of the responses had to do with the rules of engagement (ROE). They identified a host of areas they felt controlled them. In the only instance I read or heard of a soldier using a derogatory statement against the Iraqis, a soldier wrote: "You can't win a fist fight with your hands tied (Hajji huggers)"[3] (27-year-old white male E6, married for the first time).

More typically, the responses were "Other Oriented and Culturally Relative." A soldier wrote,

> Yes. I understand that force protection is a big issue, but I would like to interact with the locals more. It would help me and my buddies understand the Iraqi people and their culture, and I think that it would show the Iraqis that Americans aren't all that bad.
>
> (32-year-old white female sergeant, single)

Another soldier provided a more sober response:

> There are sometimes when you wonder is it even worth pulling the trigger. I mean, in our training we were more or less taught that if a kid comes running up with a box, towards the vehicles, to shoot. But now we're scared we will spend the rest of our lives in prison. I know we shouldn't just shoot and we wouldn't but there are times we could have probably been taken out (killed) by hesitation because we are scared of consequences. The squad leaders should have more control without being scared of the suffering consequences. They are our immediate supervisors. They are our leaders. The higher ups put them there, not us. If you don't trust them then don't put them there.
>
> (26-year-old white male E4, never married)

Some of the ROE had to do with "Driving in and around Baghdad." A 29-year-old ethnically Other male junior officer, married with no children, put pen to paper:

> With transfer of sovereignty [ToS], leaders stated units would follow traffic laws (such as speed limits, not forcing cars out of lane, turning only where legally supposed to, etc) unless tactical situation dictates otherwise. Although this guidance appears to be sensible on the surface and can be followed if situation allows, unit TTPs are based on enemy TTPs—not because units have larger vehicles with weapons and can do it. The ToS did not change the enemy TTPs.

When studying perceptions of control across ranks, there was minimal variation. Senior NCOs were slightly less likely to say "yes"—this is somewhat understandable as they are the social control agents on the FOB. E1s to E4s were the most likely to say "yes" as they are the benefactors of the rules and regulations imposed by the social control agents. The finding goes similarly in the opposite direction with the "no" respondents.

Irrationality in Iraq

Again, irrationality refers to reasoned systems that have become unreasonable. Ritzer refers to this aspect as the irrationality of rationality. Soldiers responded to an open-ended question with a follow-on qualifier: "What are the most unreasonable things that the chain-of-command has asked you or your unit to do? How did you (or your unit) respond to those requests?"

Almost two-thirds (62.4 percent) of the soldiers responded to this question. Of these, 56.6 percent noted some unreasonable taskings. However, almost every soldier complied with the tasking or order—they met the mission—despite their perception of the unreasonableness of it. A third (32 percent) replied that no unreasonable requests were asked of them, and 11.4 percent either did not know or had some other response.

Unreasonableness manifests generally and in two specific areas: on and off the FOB. A typical "General" comment on unreasonableness was: "Nothing has been asked of me that I feel was unreasonable, except to come to Iraq in the first place, under false pretenses" (35-year-old white male junior officer, never married). Another confessed, "Come to Iraq. I got on the plane instead of going to jail" (21-year-old white male E4, married with one child).

Again, the one FOB unreasonableness had to do with work and leisure, most with a few cases of leadership issues: "OS Transgressions" and "Quality of Life Issues." One example was a mechanic going outside of his area of expertise, who wrote, "Send a Bradley mechanic to an air conditioning class for HMMWVs. I went to the class" (29-year-old white male junior officer, married with one child). One inside the FOB quality-of-life issue was:

> The biggest complaints have not come from what happens out in the zone but from what happens in the FOB. During training we were talked and talked to about the "switch." [This refers to] being able to go from ready to kill to relax mode once in the FOB. The soldiers are never able to fully relax. For example, they have to get fully in DCU just to run and grab a coke (PT's are not acceptable). [This is] just one example that is going to take a toll on the individual soldier that could lead to problems.
>
> (24-year-old white male junior officer, engaged)

An example of "Unreasonable Leaders" wrote, "Lend a vehicle and an E4 from my detachment to go get wood for the BN XO so he could build a deck in front of his trailer. We executed the mission" (26-year-old white male junior officer, married with no children).

Outside FOB activities involved mission issues linked with "Gear" and "Mission Behavior." A gear example was "wear seat belts on combat convoy in the city…wore it" (19-year-old white male private, engaged). One other soldier provided a bit more detail about gear and relation to mission effectiveness:

> Well, I think the most unreasonable thing is that we were asked to wear those shoulder and side body armor panels when it clearly says on them "warning with no ballistic inserts—no penetration protection." And how we responded? We're still wearing those things.
>
> (24-year-old Hispanic male E4, never married)

"Reckless Missions" were also distinguished. A 23-year-old white male E4, single, quipped, "Run missions into hostile neighborhoods with ghetto-rigged, broke-ass trucks. Even in danger of being stuck there. We were told to make it happen so we did. A good soldier just does his/her job."

An example of "Limited Personnel" was "To do more mission than we have people to task for those missions. Suck it up and drive on, you can't argue with someone who won't listen" (23-year-old white female junior officer, never married). Another wrote, "They ask us to do more than we are capable of—as if we have more soldiers than we really do. We fight and sometimes we win or we lose and soldiers pull double/triple duty" (25-year-old white female junior officer, married).

Officers as a group identify more unreasonableness than enlisted soldiers. Officers were 15 percent more likely than E1 to E3s to report some type of unreasonableness that they nevertheless complied with.

American soldier creativity in Iraq

The McDonaldization thesis does not account for creativity. McDonaldization does allow for niche markets. In this case, smaller and more specialized productions emerge in contemporary life while larger, traditional mass markets spread across the social landscape but miss these special areas (Ritzer and Stillman, 2001a). In a military context, especially in Iraq, there is research suggesting officers are becoming adaptive leaders in Iraq while the larger organization is more traditional and bureaucratic. In the survey, soldiers wrote in their own words if they were experiencing creativity in Iraq (see Appendix 6.1).

Again, almost two-thirds responded (63.3 percent). Of those, again, more than one-half (56.4 percent) said that their units used creativity. Just less than a third (30 percent) said "no." Another 14 percent provided either "don't know," "no comment," or some other response. The majority of "no" responses were simply no. Some soldiers qualified their "no." A typical example came from a 35-year-old white male captain: "No. Our unit is now in the battle rhythm. It's the same thing day after day, not much change going on."

Among the "Yes, we are creative …" responses were four categories—"General Creativity," "Up-armoring Vehicles," "Improving the Work and Living Spaces on the FOB," and "Specific People that are Generally Creative" such as leaders or rank and file soldiers who were adaptive and resourceful in creating success or situations for success.

A number of soldiers wrote statements suggesting there was for them a "General Environment of Creativity" in Iraq. Some typical examples included "Yes, by doing whatever is necessary to complete the mission" (22-year old white male private) and "My unit is under-strengthened so everything is creative" (30-year-old racially "Other" male E6, engaged with four children). A 25-year-old white male junior officer, married, wrote:

> Yes, we are an Air Defense unit operating as an Infantry unit. We have none of the same equipment or even the required number of personnel. Currently we use mechanics as dismounted Infantry soldiers. Our soldiers do what they have to do to accomplish the mission of the day and survive.

Highly creative situations had to do with up-armoring vehicles. A topic that received a great deal of press is when then-E4 Thomas Wilson asked then-Secretary of Defense Donald Rumsfeld on an international and live broadcast on December 8, 2004, "Why do we soldiers have to dig through local landfills for pieces of scrap metal and compromised ballistic glass to up-armor our vehicles?" (Associated Press, 2004).

Two examples of "Up-armoring vehicles" earlier that year included, "After one of my buddies was killed by an IED we put armor on the sides of our trucks and ballistic windshields" (22-year-old white male E4, single), and "Our unit did not receive any up-armored Humvees while deployed. Our maintenance team was able to make our Humvee into a somewhat, hard-shelled Humvee using steel and a blow torch" (24-year-old Hispanic male junior officer, single). Finally, another shared: "My soldiers successfully adjust to all changes. They're creativity is limitless—from armoring vehicles to washing clothes. As long as they are given freedom to maneuver, they will find a way to do the job" (30-year-old white male junior officer, married for the first time). Two examples of "Improving the FOB":

> Our level II medical treatment facility (tent) has been constantly improved upon [since] our arrival (e.g., floors, lighting, air conditioning, layout, organization, etc). Also, the defense of our FOB (e.g., Aerostat early

warning detection and intelligence gathering, patrols, mini-medcaps, maximizing use of terrain and weapons system obstacles, etc.).

(38-year-old bi-ethnic male senior NCO, married with two children)

Always. We conduct postal services for over 16,000 soldiers. We've had to adjust two times. First for the 1st Armor Division's extension [in Iraq] almost tripling the amount we service, but doing an awesome job of accomplishing the job with less manpower than we were supposed to have.

(26-year-old white male E5, married with two children)

Examples of "Creative Living" included "We bar-b-qued on the 4th of July ... nice stress break" (32-year-old African-American male junior officer, single with one child). A 26-year-old white male E5, married with two children, put pen to paper: "My Unit has given us a lot of things to help us with down time— weight room, TV Room, Ping-Pong, and volleyball. To me, help people by giving them stuff to do and not feeling bored and lonely."

Two soldiers provide representative examples of obtaining resources on the FOB. A 25-year-old Hispanic female E5, married, jotted down, "Yes. Our commander practically acts as the S4. She has gotten POC's to add air conditioning in the trucks, bullet-proof windshields, and doors. So many examples, but yes, we do adjust fire when we need to" and

The unit is excellent at creative adjustment. Almost every improvement we have made on our checkpoint has been done with a M88 recovery vehicle and most of the suggestions have come from soldiers. We have dramatically changed the layout of the checkpoint and our patrol TTPs with little help from higher.

(26-year-old white male junior officer, never married)

There were also soldiers who wrote about creativity through the "Improving the Missions" responses. A soldier wrote, "We have created our own flyers to explain to the locals why we are doing what we are doing. Also, we do water missions—taking fresh clear water to villages that were originally hotbeds of ... activity" (37-year-old field-grade officer, married with no children), and another shared: "Yes, while conducting a TCP we noticed the ING was not inspecting vehicles correctly. We stepped in, asked if we could search a vehicle, and did it properly. The ING soldiers immediately copied us and got the job done" (25-year-old white male junior officer, single). Last, "We are tankers without tanks. We had to learn infantry and MP operations" (26-year-old white male junior officer, single).

Finally, officers in Iraq reported more creativity than enlisted soldiers and NCOs—three-fourths compared to roughly half. This certainly is understandable as officers have a more operational view of military matters than enlisted soldiers that have more tactical, micro-level perspective. Despite this, it is noteworthy that half of enlisted soldiers and NCOs identified creative aspects in their deployments in Iraq.

Discussion and conclusion

The McDonaldization thesis first emerged in a 1983 publication in the *Journal of American Culture* (Ritzer, 1983). Later expanded into a book (Ritzer, 2004), the thesis has proliferated as evidenced from more than 156,000 Google Web-based hits. Web sites have emerged highlighting the ills of McDonaldization (McDonaldization.com, 2006), and Google Scholar yields over 2,370 references to McDonaldization.

New books have applied McDonaldization to various social institutions in American society including education (Hayes and Wynyard, 2002) and religion (Drane, 2002). A McDonaldization reader features the framework to explain a diversity of areas of social life including theme parks (McRides), chain stores (McChains), the criminal justice system (McCourts), the family (McMom), sex trade industries (McSex), the university (McUniversity), work (McJobs), and rib joints (McJoint), among others (Ritzer, 2004).

Scholars have used the McDonalization framework for other areas of social life far removed from the fast-food industry (Hajjar and Ender, 2005). Examples include an analysis of Korean mega-churches (Hong, 2003), Disneyland (Bryman, 2003), baseball parks (Ritzer and Stillman, 2001b), libraries (Quinn, 2000), pharmacology (Taylor and Harding, 2002) and physicians (Ritzer and Walczak, 1988). McDonaldization is not exclusive to the United States, and the thesis has applicability in cross-cultural contexts including global consumer culture in Hong Kong (Mok, 1999), Germany (Kemmesies, 2002), Scotland (Hartley, 1995), Israel (Illouz and Nicholas. 2003), India (Datta, 2005), and Europe in general (Ritzer, 2002).

This chapter examined the experiences of American soldiers from the perspective of the McDonaldization thesis but included the polar opposite as well—creativity. Overall, the findings are consistent with the overall theme of diversity. Soldiers show instances of adaptation, innovation, and creativity and McDonaldization in Iraq. Among the elements of McDonaldization, the irrationality of rationality occurred most often. Notably, most of the McDonaldization described was accounted for both on and off the FOB—both in the work world and on their downtime on the FOB. Officers were more likely to have identified irrationality than enlisted soldiers. As noted in Chapter 2, citing Wong and Gerras (2006), American soldiers refer to the FOB as a "home away from home" (pp. 21–22) rich in amenities. Thus, American soldiers desired some element of sensibility on the FOB where life on the FOB would compliment and provide an "away" from the conflict outside the gate. Accoutrements and activities such as uniforms, alcohol, gear, and sex alter the quality of life on the FOB, and soldiers expressed wanting more freedoms in and around these areas. Finally, many of the on-FOB complaints crossed all five McDonaldization elements.

On the other hand, American soldiers reported problems with irrationality in terms of a shortage of personnel to accomplish their missions off the FOB—a problem of much larger proportion reported at the sociopolitical levels and the Pentagon. Additionally, outside-FOB salient factors included the media, the rules of engagement, and avoiding predictable behavior at the tactical level.

Half of the soldiers said McDonaldization was not an issue. Quantification was not problematic per se—rather, it provided an outlet for soldiers to air their complaints about the media. They referenced portrayals of what they termed "negative press" such as too much emphasis on casualties. Such reporting contrasted with a desire for more positive press such as featuring small-scale success stories of American soldiers in Iraq. Outside the FOB, only a minority of soldiers reported predictability as problematic, whereas others said it was not—essentially, conscientiousness proved pervasive outside the FOB in terms of calculated unpredictability to undermine the enemy. Finally, efficiency provided the broadest range of examples given by the American soldiers in Iraq from tasks off the FOB to quality of life on the FOB. The most salient form of efficiency was negative maintenance. Essentially, equipment lacked the proper maintenance necessary to do the mission effectively. Social control as a McDonaldization element was reported the least often.

While McDonaldization characterized some experiences of American soldiers, creativity flourished in Iraq in the summer of 2004. More than half reported it, and the contexts of creativity and adaptation varied. Similar to McDonaldization, creativity occurred both on and off the FOB. Again, a notable area of creativity involved up-armoring vehicles, overcoming problems with maintenance, and a lack of personnel. Essentially, American soldiers innovated at the individual and small unit levels resulting from shortcomings at the broader levels—the levels where they lacked control such as deploying large numbers of personnel into the theatre of operations and supplying resources and equipment. Officers appeared especially aware of the ingenuity of their peers and subordinates and reported it more than the enlisted soldiers. Future research should continue to assess whether McDonaldization elements and creativity, innovation, and adaptation are on the rise or declining among soldiers.

The next chapter provides a relatively unique window into a specific group of soldiers—women. The chapter focuses specifically on female service members and their similarities and differences from their male peers who they served along-side in Iraq, Kuwait, and Haiti.

7   Real G. I. Janes

American female soldiers in war

> We have snipers, medics, and females. Our commander has thought of everything and every situation to get us ready.
>
> (21-year-old white male E4, remarried with no children)

Introduction

Sociologists have long written about American women in the military. Much of the research on women in the military deals with women's roles, primarily historical accounts (Campbell, 1984). There are but a handful of sociological studies addressing how uniformed women experience deployments and war. It is yet curious that female soldiers in general, and especially those in Iraq, continue to permeate the printed press and hold public interest.[1] From the controversy surrounding Private Jessica Lynch as a POW to the criminal Lynndie England and Abu Ghraib to the heroic 23-year old Sergeant Leigh Ann Hester, the first women to receive the Silver Star for Valor for close quarters offensive combat, to the undeniable inspirations of the late LTs Emily Perez and Laura Walker, female military service and the roles women occupy are unquestionably deserving of reevaluation in the aftermath of Iraq and Afghanistan.

American women soldiers are at the heart of the research findings in this chapter. The focus is specifically on how female service members compare and contrast with their male peers who served with them in Iraq, Kuwait, and Haiti. I re-present some of the topics from previous chapters with a comparison here of men and women. I conclude the chapter with some fresh perspective on comparative attitudes toward the varied roles women perform in the military. Overall, only minor differences distinguish American soldiers by gender on attitudes about military-related experiences. The one exception, ironically, is the role of women in the military.

American military women and wars

Women have participated and served in all American wars since the inception of the Republic (see Holm, 1992; U.S. Department of Veterans Affairs, 2006;

Wilson, 2006; Women in Military Service for America Memorial, 2006). The view of the expansion of women's roles in the U.S. military emerges best during and immediately following American wars. The role of women in and around the U.S. military institutionalized during and immediately following times of wars. Research on American women in the military has followed research on women in general with the exception of a number of publications during WWII (Friedl, 1996). While many served as camp followers on the American frontier as laundresses, cooks, and servants, others disguised themselves as men and served and led in combat. Female military historical figures include Margaret Corbin, Deborah Sampson, Lucy Brewer, and Loreta Velasquez.

Margaret Cochran Corbin, who lived from 1751 to 1800, fought in the American Revolutionary War alongside her husband, took his cannon position and fired following his death, and later was a casualty herself. She was the first woman to receive a lifetime pension from the U.S. government as a disabled soldier. Buried in the West Point cemetery at the United States Military Academy, New York, a monument honors her military service there.

During the American Revolution in the 1770s, women were generally restricted from formal and active involvement in the war. A few did, however, play military roles along with and following the death of their husbands or brothers. Some actually posed as men in order to serve. The most famous is Deborah Sampson, disguised as Robert Shirtliffe. She fought and served for more than 3 years during the early 1780s. She managed to go undetected until discovered by a military surgeon who was treating her for fever. More women probably served than is currently documented.

Through the 1800s, the role of women remained formally restricted to non-official, civilian roles in the health and nursing areas. However, women continued to disguise themselves as men—Lucy Brewer camouflaged herself as George Baker and served as a Marine on the ship *USS Constitution* during the War of 1812. A famous Civil War disguiser was Loreta Velasquez. Her husband served as a Confederate officer. She masked herself as LT Harry T. Buford. She glued on facial hair, bought a uniform, recruited her own soldiers, and commanded them in battle. Although soon discovered, she again rejoined as an infantryman, again received a promotion to cavalry officer, and was discovered a second time only after being wounded.

Women's roles unofficially expanded during the Civil War to include military roles in espionage, sabotage, and scouting. The famous ex-slave Harriet Tubman served as a scout for the Union Army, taking soldiers into the woods of the American south and surprising the Confederate forces. Military sociologist Mady Wechsler Segal (1989) refers to the social history of women and the U.S. military as women who serve "unconventional" roles despite exclusion from the "conventional" military (see D.R. Segal, 1989:113).

Women served heroically as nurses and physicians during the U.S. Civil War, and many received commissions, honors, and awards for their service.

Dr. Mary Walker received the Medal of Honor—the highest decoration in the United States military—for her service as a surgeon with the Union Army. Such service paved the way for women to serve officially as members of the United States armed forces in the twentieth century.

Approximately 1,500 female nurses served as contracted civilians during the Spanish-American War from 1898 to 1902. The vital utility of the nurses and no doubt their leadership under Dr. Anita Newcomb McGee ushered in greater formal recognition (D.R. Segal, 1989:115). In 1901, the U.S. Congress officially established the Army Nurse Corps as an auxiliary military unit. Later, the Navy Nurse Corps was established in 1908.

During later wars, the roles of women in the military expanded only to contract after the hostilities had ended. During World War I, about 33,000 women served in uniform, with the majority in the Army and Navy Nurse Corps, and many were highly decorated. General John J. Pershing requested that American women fluent in French deploy to France to serve as telephone exchange operators. Hundreds of American women aided the Army. The U.S. Navy and U.S. Marine Corps sent women to Europe as service members. Approximately 13,000 women enlisted as Marines and yeomen in the Navy. They served as clerical workers, typists, stenographers, telephone operators, recruiters, and translators, among others. They were the first group of women in U.S. history admitted to the status of full military rank. Because women could not technically serve aboard ship but needed to be aboard a ship to serve in the naval reserve, the Navy buried a tugboat in the mud in the Potomac River near Washington, DC. After the war, much of the integration that had occurred would backslide as women were no longer needed for service.

A major turning point for women's roles in the military occurred in 1920. Women fought for—and encouraged the U.S. Congress to increase—citizenship rights of American women, including the right to vote (the Nineteenth Amendment to the U.S. Constitution). Military integration of women continued to progress incrementally forward—in 1939, as the war in Europe raged, and the United States slowly drew down into WWII. Many anticipated shortages of male military personnel, and plans called for an auxiliary Corps for women. Some exposure to the role of women in the military in other countries may have influenced changing attitudes and perspectives in the United States.

In 1940, military conscription, suspended in 1919 following WWI, was reestablished. Seeking full citizenships rights, women's political groups lobbied for a more direct and legitimized role in the forthcoming war (D.R. Segal, 1989:116). Congress established the Women's Auxiliary Army Corp (WAAC) in May 1942, 6 months after the Japanese attack on Pearl Harbor. Thereafter, in July 1942, the Navy's Women Accepted for Volunteer Emergency Service (WAVES) followed and, in February 1943, the Marine Corps Women's Reserve both were established. In July 1943, the WAAC achieved increased military status and became an integral part of the Army, dropping the word auxiliary from its name and becoming the Women's Army Corps or WAC. It gave women greater military benefits. When the WAAC converted to the WAC, the Army Air Forces (AAF) had the highest retention rate of female service members of any command employing WACs. The Women's Air Service Pilots (WASPs) transported military aircraft to overseas military locations; they attached to the Army because the U.S. Air Force did not exist in WWII. The Army Signal Corps integrated women successfully as well.

In WWII Europe, the WAAC (and later the WAC) served in forward areas. Then General Clark ensured the acceptance and relative legitimacy of WACs by presenting them with awards for their success and allowing them to wear the green scarf of the Fifth Army. The women experienced equal treatment and enjoyed no special privilege. They moved and ate with the men and wore the same uniforms. There two notable social histories by the same author. The first is about an 855 all-African-American female but segregated unit—the 6888th Central Postal Directory Battalion—stationed in Europe during WWII (Moore, 1996). A mere 18 African-American women had served prior to WWII. The other is about the 500 Japanese-American women who joined the U.S. military during WWII (Moore, 2003).

By the end of WWII, roughly 350,000 women had served in the armed forces. Locations included stateside and overseas locations including Europe and the Pacific. Positions were in traditionally female fields—deemed appropriate for women at the time and freeing men for other jobs—such as administration, clerical positions, health care, and communications, with some later moving into parachute rigging, aircraft maintenance, and gunnery instruction (D.R. Segal, 1989:118). Forty-two had been POWs.

In 1948, the Women's Armed Services Integration Act gave women a regular status in the military. Only 2 percent of the total enlisted population could be female, and no more than 10 percent of the enlisted total could be officers. Requirements for enlistment included being 18 years of age and submitting written parental consent for women up to the age of 21. Other restrictions existed in the ranks for female officers: no command positions and no rank above lieutenant colonel. There were restrictions on their dependents, such as number of children. By the time of U.S. involvement in Korea in the early 1950s, approximately 120,000 women served on active duty. In addition to the nurses actually in Korea, many women served at support units nearby in Japan and other Far Eastern countries.

The decade of the 1960s witnessed less pressure for change from war but rather an increased pressure of all minority groups for greater citizenship rights. This included access to full military statuses. Military sociologist David Segal described the creation in 1966 of a Department of Defense task force created to study the role of women in service (D.R. Segal, 1989:119). After a year, a number of implemented changes added expanded opportunities for women including, for the first time, promotions to the rank of colonel and a lifting of the 2 percent cap on the percentage of female-to-male enlisted service members. Soon after, the number of women in the Army increased; however, they were never subjected to conscription—they were all volunteers. During the Vietnam War, 15,000 women served overseas in the combat theater, mostly as nurses. By the late 1960s, women continued to serve in segregated WAC units and continued to be excluded from the American service academies at West Point and Annapolis and at the U.S. Coast Guard and U.S. Air Force academies.

In 1973, the United States moved to an all-volunteer force that resulted in an unanticipated but immediate rise in the number of women willing to serve. By 1975, 95,000 enlisted women served on active duty (including my mother) and, by December 1980, 151,000 women comprised 8.8 percent of the enlisted force (D.R. Segal, 1989:121). In terms of officers, the U.S. Air Force had already opened Reserved Officers Training Corps (ROTC) through American colleges and universities in 1970, and the U.S. Army and Navy followed in 1972. In 1976, the U.S. service academies began admitting women. Non-combat assignments to ships occurred in 1978. In 1980, 22,000 female commissioned officers served in the U.S. armed forces.

The WAC as a segregated branch ended in 1980, and Army women were integrated into the regular armed services. A year later, the four branches of the armed services took different approaches to the number of women in uniform and the utilization of such women. The U.S. Air Force utilized women in almost all officer career fields, with women making up 12.6 percent of the total Air Force personnel; the Marines rely on women the least, with 4.8 percent of the force.

War again led to change. In December 1989, the U.S. invasion of Panama saw increased expansion of women's roles. About 800 of the 18,400 soldiers involved in the invasion were women. Their roles varied in the air and on the ground, from piloting troop helicopters while taking enemy fire through to CPT Linda Bray leading a military police platoon during a ground assault to capture a Panamanian Defense Forces compound.

One year later, more than 40,000 women deployed to the Persian Gulf, making up roughly 7 percent of all military personnel deployed for Operation Desert Shield. Thirteen women of the 375 American service members died, and two were taken as POWs in the Persian Gulf War—Operation Desert Storm (ODS). After ODS, American women could serve on combat aircraft and naval combat ships.

Since the first Persian Gulf War, military women participated directly in all major deployments around the world, including Honduras, Haiti, Somalia, Bosnia, Kosovo, and peacekeeping missions in the Sinai. The data in Table 7.1 shows the number of American women who officially deployed and served in select military conflicts from the U.S. Civil War to Iraq.

In general, the numbers of women and their representations in each branch of the service are directly proportional to occupational specialties available to

Table 7.1 Number of American women who officially served in select military deployments and conflicts from the Civil War to Iraq

Military conflict	Number of women who served
Civil War	Unknown
Spanish-American War	1,500
World War I	33,000
World War II	400,000
Korea	120,000
Vietnam	7,000
Panama	800
Persian Gulf (Desert Storm)	40,000
Somalia	1,000
Haiti	1,200
Bosnia	5,000
Afghanistan	on-going
Iraq	on-going
Total	609,500 plus

Sources: Department of Veterans Affairs, 2006; Wilson, 2006; and Women in Military
Service for America Memorial, 2006
Note: Numbers are approximations based on in theater estimates

them. The percentages in Table 7.2 show military positions and occupations open to women for selected years between 1981 and 2003. For example, in 2003, 99 percent of all the positions in the Air Force were open to women; 91 percent of the positions in the Navy; 70 percent in the Army; and 62 percent in the Marines. All positions in the U.S. Coast Guard are open to women. Overall, American women have made steady gains since 1776 in their ability to serve in the military, especially during times of war, with even more dramatic progress since 1971. However, women in the military do have a glass ceiling, as they are limited in the highest military ranks because of continued limits in specific branches of service (Hosek, et al., 2001).

Research on Women in the Military

By the 1990s, exclusion of women from direct combat roles continued. Combat exclusion varied from time to time and from service to service. There remained a number of concerns regarding gender-integrated military units and combat. The major issues debated about women in combat included mission readiness, cohesion, morale, pregnancy, physical ability, and attitudes toward gender roles. Mady Segal (1995) has theoretically outlined a model for military women's

Table 7.2 Percentage of military positions and occupations open to U.S. women, selected years, 1971–2003

	Positions				Occupations**			
Year	Army	Navy	Marine Corp	Air Force	Army	Navy	Marine Corp	Air Force
2003	70	91	62	99	91	94	92	99
1994	65	62	34	100	—	—	—	—
1983	52	40	21	90	90	86	96	98
1980*	—	—	—	—	95	86	96	98
1971*	—	—	—	—	39	24	57	51

Source: Segal and Segal, 2004 (reprinted with permission)
Notes–is less than .05 percent
2: *Enlisted only
3: **Occupations refer to specific military job categories (for example infantry rifleman or tank driver), while positions refer to the people actually employed in these occupations

participation in Western democratic nations such as the United States and Britain. The model provides testable hypotheses for specific variables under the rubrics of social structure, culture, and the military institution. Darlene Iskra and her colleagues (2002) expanded the Segal model to include non-Western nations such as Zimbabwe, Australia, and Mexico.

The earliest studies conducted by the Department of Defense showed that the presence of women did not decrease unit performance (Rosen et al., 1999). Recent studies report compatible performance between men and women in military training (Harrell et al., 2002). Another concern regarding the full integration of women involves perceived interference with male bonding and, as a consequence, unit cohesion. The research conducted in these areas are mixed at best suggesting there are some negative outcomes connected with mixed-gender units compared to single gender, but the findings were not consistently strong (Rosen et al., 1999:382). More research needs to be undertaken. Sexual and gender harassment continue as important areas of concern for women in the military in general and women at the military academies preparing for service (Bowling, et al., 2005; Carroll and Clark, 2006; Firestone and Harris, 1994; 1999; Matthews et al., forthcoming; Nelson, 2002; Rosen and Martin, 1997; Scott and Stanley, 1994).

Military deployments to war and operations other than war have consequences for military women. Air Force women have had persistent health-related problems, and many left the service because of family commitments, financial strains, and negative attitudes toward war following the first Persian Gulf War (Pierce, 1998; 2005; Weinstein and White, 1997). However, female American soldiers in Somalia adopted and internalized the humanitarian strategies more than their male peers and sought cultural explanations for Somali behavior rather than victim blaming—a strategy oft used by men (Miller and Moskos, 1995). Research leading up to the Global War on Terror showed perceptions of gender integration to have only a marginal impact on readiness, cohesion, and morale (Harrell and Miller, 1997). All in all, the social science research appears to support full integration of women.

Finally, the current Department of Defense assignment policy for women in the military states "… women shall be excluded from assignment to units below the brigade level whose primary mission is to engage in direct combat on the ground" (Aspin, 1994). The U.S. Army has a slightly more restrictive definition of women's role. A recent assessment of the policy to include interviews with key leaders and soldiers returning from Iraq finds compliance with the DOD policy but violation of the Army policy (Harrell et al., 2007). The study finds that commanders on the ground find the policies ambiguous at best and a hindrance if complied with to the letter. No research has assessed women's direct experiences during a sustained conflict. The research reported here fills some of the gap in knowledge. The present chapter provides active-duty female American soldiers a collective say about a number of dimensions related to their service experience from Forward Operating Bases in an intense and sustained real-world deployment that is Iraq.

American military women socio-demographics

In terms of gender representation in the U.S. military, the force has been traditionally male, and the number of women serving has expanded and contracted based on war mobilizations; yet, the roles they occupy have been expanding across history (Holm, 1992; Segal and Segal, 2004). As of September 2004, about the time the major survey reported here was administered in Iraq, women comprised approximately 17 percent of the total active duty military services (Office of the Under Secretary of Defense, 2007). The U.S. Air Force had the highest representation at 19.6 percent and the Marines the lowest at 6.1 percent. Women comprised approximately 15 percent of the active-duty Army in 2004, and enlisted women made up 83 percent of the female forces.

In the topics that I present here, women have fair representation in two of the studies and less in one compared to the populations in September 2004. For the Haiti study, women have an underrepresentation, with 31 women (6.1 percent).[2] For the Kuwait study sample of 185 veterans, there were 23 veterans reporting their gender as female (13.2 percent).[3] Finally, in the larger sample of Iraq veterans, 118 veterans reported their gender as female (12.4 percent).[4] While the numbers were low, the experiences of these deployed women were real-world.

In most instances, American women and men looked moderately similar in Iraq, Kuwait, and Haiti along a number of socio-demographic characteristics (table not shown). Women serving in Haiti and Kuwait generally were lower in rank. Iraq veteran women had slightly more education compared to the men. A larger percentage of African-American women were in Iraq and Kuwait than African-American men. To be sure, the largest percentages of women from the Kuwait unit were African-American women. While religion was fairly equally distributed, a slightly larger percentage of Kuwait women report their religious affiliation as "Other." Slightly more women veterans of Iraq and Kuwait reported a political affiliation as men. Obviously, among the officers who report their branch, virtually all the women were non-combat arms (although two report other combat arms and one in field artillery), and the men showed unequal distributions across all the branches including combat arms. Finally, while women in the present analysis tended to be lower in rank, they, like the men, shared deployment experience to a combat zone. What's more, fewer have a second tour overseas, and a fair number had one. In some cases, Army women had two or more deployments in addition to the current one in Iraq.

Family demographics

Female veterans of Iraq, Kuwait, and Haiti were noticeably less likely to be married and slightly more likely to be single, and this finding is consistent with the larger U.S. Army in 2004 (Segal and Segal, 2004). Iraq and Kuwait female veterans were more likely to be divorced. Male veterans were also slightly more involved than females in a significant relationship with an intimate other. Women veterans of Haiti were almost 25 percent less likely to have children than males. If they had children, they had fewer. The distribution of children is closer to equality with Kuwait and Iraq veterans, but women were more likely to be childless than their male counterparts.

U.S. women veterans and other issues

The social psychology of American soldiers in Iraq

What follows is a comparison of male and female American soldiers. Where appropriate, responses compare to the topics covered in previous chapters. I highlight both similarities and differences. The main finding is how similar women are to men on most topics, yet, they maintain some unique qualities specific to women as a group.

Chapter Three featured the overall results of morale. Again, soldiers responded to three different levels of morale. Overall, men and women showed markedly similar morale levels. Individual male and female soldier morale was similar for soldiers in Iraq and Haiti. For American soldiers returning from Kuwait, fewer women reported their individual morale to be high. Perceptions of unit level morale were unequal. Women veterans of both Iraq and Kuwait had lower perceptions of unit level morale than men. Haiti morale among the genders was equal. Perceptions of all deployed troops were moderately similar with the exception of Kuwait women, whose reported morale for all troops deployed was lower than men but not very low.

Chapter Three featured the overall results of preparation for soldiers' current military deployment. In terms of preparation for deployment, there were no differences between the men and women at the three levels—individuals, units, and all deployed troops.

In Chapter Three, the results showed how soldiers spent their work day. There were some slight differences in day-to-day work activities of veterans in the three regions. Male soldiers in Haiti and Kuwait report somewhat longer workday hours than women. Note that these two missions were less dangerous than Iraq. For those in Iraq, no differences materialized, with just as many men working 18-plus-hour days as women and just as many men as women working 8-hour or fewer days.

In terms of days off, the largest percentage of male soldiers who served in Haiti report no days off in the last month, and the largest percentage of women report 5 or more days off. A similar trend exists for Iraq, but the days off were 3 or more for women rather than 5. Kuwait veteran days were less divergent; women were more likely to report having taken days off than their male peers, suggesting perhaps less structured opportunities for women to soldier in Iraq than their male peers.

Chapter Three highlighted the overall findings of soldier satisfaction. While men and women having served in Iraq and Haiti claimed equal satisfaction with their jobs, males having served in Kuwait reported twice as much dissatisfaction compared to females, with more neutral responses to their levels of satisfaction. In terms of satisfaction with support of single soldiers and Army families, female veterans of all three deployments appear to know least about officers in high post positions and NCOs—almost half of women; twice as many as males. Further, for Haiti veteran women, more know less about chaplains. Women veterans of Iraq appeared to be more unaware of the level of support provided by their unit Family Readiness Group. This is understandable, as fewer women reported being married than men. In the Haiti veteran group, men equaled women, and the women veterans of Kuwait responded more favorably than did males.

Female soldier attitudes toward foreign policy issues

In Chapter Five, "Over there: American soldier attitudes toward foreign issues," the global topics focused on attitudes toward foreign policy issues and the varied roles the U.S. military might play following national and international decisions. Here is a comparison made between how men and women responded to these issues.

Males and females surfaced as moderately similar regarding foreign issues. They equally liked to travel, looked forward to new experiences, and to try foreign foods with women veterans of Haiti slightly more of the first two. There were no differences between males and females serving in Kuwait. While the majority of Iraq veterans agree that it is much more difficult to work with foreign nationals than with the people of the United States, more males agree than females. Similarly, there was disagreement with the statement that you can trust foreign nationals as much as you can trust people from the United States, and more male veterans of both Iraq and Haiti disagreed. Male Haiti veterans came out more neutral and female veterans more in agreement with the statement that most people from most countries were reasonably alike. These collective findings suggest women have a greater foreign empathy compared to male peers, regardless of mission type.

Female soldier attitudes toward uses of the armed forces, social issues, and values

Men and women differed on four social issues: "using the armed forces to combat the flow of drugs," "for humanitarian relief outside the US," "for training others," and "for maintaining a military presence overseas." Overall, female soldiers reported less support for these types of military missions than their male peers. Thus, female soldiers may have a narrower view about the role of the U.S. military than their male peers.

I asked Kuwait and Iraq–but not Haiti–veterans statements about social and domestic issues. Specifically, I asked them about levels of agreement regarding contemporary social and domestic issues and values. Women veterans of Kuwait differed from men on more than half of the items: bussing children, economics, the environment, homosexuality in the military, construction of nuclear power plants, the death penalty, and handgun control. On all these issues, women leaned more toward liberal agreement than the men. For Iraq veterans, women differed with men on different items: abortion, traditional roles for women, prayer in public schools, the defense budget, homosexuality in schools and the military, and handgun control. Essentially, women lean more toward a politically liberal perspective on these items with the exception of permitting prayer in public schools—they lean more in favor than male veterans.

Interestingly, men and women shared similar agreements and disagreements on the values issues. Twenty percent more males than females at least agree that all Americans should be willing to give up their lives to defend their country.

Again, 13 questions tapped attitudes toward peacekeeping. Men and women differed somewhat on their attitudes. Slightly more women veterans of Kuwait felt soldiers needed additional training for peacekeeping missions beyond basic military skills. In the same group, women agreed less that soldiers are effective in peacekeeping even if they cannot use force except in self-defense. More male veterans having served in Iraq and Haiti agreed that peacekeeping duty is boring. All three groups differed some on whether peacekeeping assignments helped a soldier's career. Women were more likely to be neutral as men were more likely to split evenly on their agreement and disagreement with the statement. Curiously, half of male veterans of both Haiti and Kuwait agreed that a professional soldier should be able to perform peacekeeping missions and war-fighting missions equally effectively. Eighty percent of Haiti female veterans agreed with this, but only one-third of Kuwait female veterans agreed. No gender differences surfaced among veterans of Iraq. The last item of peacekeeping statements states "peacekeeping missions should be performed by military rather than by infantry." Kuwait, Iraq, and Haiti female veterans were more neutral, but Kuwait males were more likely to agree or disagree with the statement, and Iraq and Haiti male veterans were more likely to agree. Essentially, women had less opinions on peacekeeping than men, which may be attributable to their limited deployment experience compared to men.

Of eleven kinds of military situations the U.S. might be involved in, parallel views existed for men and women for peacekeeping forces, guerilla war, humanitarian assistance for a domestic disaster, and overseas humanitarian assistance. Twice as many male veterans of Kuwait thought both limited and large-scale conventional wars might occur. More male than female veterans of Iraq and Kuwait thought tactical nuclear war to be at least unlikely. More female than male veterans of Iraq and Kuwait thought tactical, biological, and chemical weapons and a strategic nuclear war at least somewhat likely. Finally, and most notably, large portions of both men and women thought the U.S. might likely be involved in the restoration of order after a domestic disturbance (many of these soldiers had assisted in Florida following Hurricane Andrew) but women (93.5 percent) even more than men (78.6 percent).

Attitudes toward women in the military and combat

Is there a gender gap in the attitudes of women and men in the military and toward the role of women's service and combat? Research suggests women to be less supportive of military spending than men.[5] Gender and politics of undergraduates are predictors of attitudes toward the wars in Iraq and Afghanistan—at least in the early parts of the wars—and women overall showed less support for the wars irrespective of military affiliation (Rohall et al., 2006). Despite a desire of many women to prove their democratic loyalty to the nation through the right to bear arms and fight against all enemies foreign and domestic, early research by sociologists found little support for giving women the "right to fight" in the military (Segal et al., 1977). Recent research finds differences among attitudes of ROTC cadets around the country, with female ROTC cadets showing more support than their male peers for increased roles and positions for women in the military (Zeigler and Gunderson, 2005).

Two groups of veterans from Kuwait and Iraq received survey questions about their attitudes toward women in combat (I did not ask the question of

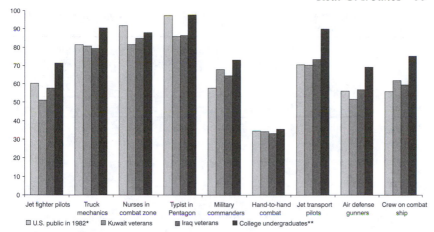

Chart 7.1 Percentage distributions for four American groups responding that women should perform specific roles in the military

Source: *Wilcox, 1992, **Matthews, Ender, and Rohall, 2004

Haiti veterans). The nine different positions were based on the question: What jobs women should or should not perform in the military. Response categories included "should," "should not," and "don't know/can't say." The percentage distributions in Chart 7.1 show the respondents who reported women "should" perform these jobs. The original question came from a 1982 random sample of adults in the United States on the General Social Survey not asked since 1982 (General Social Survey, 2007). The U.S. public data from 1982 are included along with Kuwait and Iraq veterans. For an additional comparison group, I included the findings from a separate but recent study of American college and university students (Matthews et al., 2004; Matthews et al., forthcoming).

Overall, the most support is for women as typists in the Pentagon, followed by nurses, truck mechanics, and jet transport pilots. There is least support for jet fighter pilots, air defense gunners, and crew on a combat ship. Hand-to-hand combatants received the least favorable responses by all four groups. Between groups, college undergraduates have the most "shoulds" for all categories except nurses, where the American public reported a higher percentage of "shoulds." College undergraduates differ most on combat domains except for hand-to-hand combat. Essentially, veterans today mirror the U.S. public of a quarter century ago!

The data in Table 7.3 show the distribution by gender for three of the four groups: (the U.S. public in 1982). The highest percentage of "shoulds" from all groups except Kuwait female veterans was for "women as typists in the Pentagon." The lowest percentage of "shoulds" for all groups was for "women as hand-to-hand combat soldiers." The percentages for these track

Table 7.3 Percentages for four groups (three by gender) responding that women should perform specific roles in the military

Roles of women in the military	U.S. public in 1982* All	Kuwait veterans, 2003 (n=185)		Iraq veterans, 2004 (n=968)		U.S. college undergraduates, 2003–2005 (n=1,977)**	
		Males	Females	Males	Females	Males	Females
Women as jet fighter pilots	60.4	48.6	73.9	55.5	73.5	60.5	89.9
Women as truck mechanics	81.5	79.2	91.3	77.8	88.9	89.4	94.0
Women as nurses in a combat zone	92.0	79.9	91.3	83.9	89.7	83.3	97.0
Women as typists in the Pentagon	97.3	85.2	87	85.3	93.2	98.2	98.2
Women as military commanders of military base	57.8	63.8	91.3	60.6	90.6	65.6	87.6
Women hand-to-hand combat Soldiers	34.4	33.1	39.1	30.0	54.7	23.9	55.5
Women as jet transport pilots	70.6	69.9	78.3	72.4	79.3	88.6	94.0
Women as air defense gunners in the U.S.	56.2	50.0	65.2	55.1	68.4	63.3	81.0
Women as crew members on a combat ship	55.9	59.9	73.9	57.7	70.9	69.0	86.9

Source: *Wilcox, 1992: **Matthews et al., 2004

in the thirtieth percentile range except for Iraq female veterans and female undergraduates from around the U.S. at 54.7 and 55.5 percents, respectively, and male undergraduates at 23.9 percent.

Overall, military males surface as the most conservative regarding the role of women in combat. These twenty-first-century male soldiers and now veterans are more conservative in recent years than the U.S. population 25 years earlier. In three areas are veterans males more open—women as commanders of military bases, as jet transport pilots, and crew members aboard combat ships—three areas where women actually currently serve in distinct numbers. Male college students follow the attitudes of their uniformed brothers except as truck mechanics, jet transport pilots, air defense gunners, and combat ship crew members. U.S. college women come forward as far more progressive—keeping in mind that some of these women might be future Army officers—with the only exception being women military commanders of a military base. Ironically, this position is more typical for military women! It is worth noting that the women veterans of Iraq showed progressiveness regarding the role of women in hand-to-hand combat, as this implies the infantry. Many American women in Iraq have performed these types of duties alongside men.

Discussion and conclusion

Women have a long history of serving as soldiers dating back to the American Revolution. Historically, we see that American minority roles in the military increase during wars, and the needs for service members increase. Roles seem to expand during war and then contract somewhat during peacetime but rarely to the prewar level. Women's numbers follow this trend over the past 230 years. We know that women want and do move into these new roles with some zeal. However, we know somewhat less about women's attitudes overall, relative to men during wars and their attitudes toward different kinds of military missions. This chapter has filled some of this knowledge gap. The chapter has focused on social psychological subject matters such as morale, performance, satisfaction, day-to-day activities, values, and attitudes toward foreign, social, and domestic issues.

Overall, men and women had the same levels of morale, with women perceiving morale slightly lower among contexts. Perception levels of preparation for the deployments mirrored morale. Women worked shorter days in Haiti and Kuwait but not in Iraq. In Iraq, they did take more time off than males. Both appeared equally satisfied; however, women report that they and higher-ranked leaders are out of touch with one another. They are similar on values.

On attitudes, they are equal in their attitudes toward foreign issues, except men trust others less and would work less with foreign nationals. Such an orientation places women more in line with the needs stressed in the U.S. Army Marine Corps (2007) *Counterinsurgency Field Manual*—affectionately called "COIN." Quizzically, women show less support for using the armed forces for some missions outside the United States yet, they are traditionally more liberal about social issues than their male peers. Women appear to think peacekeeping can be done in addition to other missions but are more likely to say additional training is necessary for such duty. Women appeared more neutral on many of the peacekeeping issues, with men more likely to have a range of opinions— explained perhaps through experience. On the likelihood of future missions, the two groups differed some. A slight pattern exists for women regarding nontraditional missions, and men thought traditional wars would be the likely scenarios of the future.

Finally, women are noticeably more progressive than men regarding the roles of women in combat including female veterans and female college undergraduates—yet all continue to be conservative regarding positions that involve direct contact with enemy—confirming the current Army policy but not the realities of Afghanistan and Iraq. This gender gap on the roles of women is highly pronounced. More important, women's equality role in the military is no longer simply theoretical, as women in college and notably outside the labor force assert their attitudes. Women veterans appear more progressive than their male peers, a difference that has historically been less pronounced during peacetime. This finding is noteworthy as experience may have increased confidence in many of these roles. Women in the military are closer to these roles than at any time in recent U.S. history. If history is an indicator, these attitude changes coupled with real-world exposure may push women's military roles closer to those of men once the dusts of Afghanistan and Iraq have cleared and the military and policy makers reflect and reevaluate what men and women have accomplished together on these two long and intense military engagements.

Again, this book is about diversity in the all-volunteer force, representing American soldiers through their positions and words in a real-world context and providing readers with a vista into the world of soldiering and Iraq. Notably we tend to think and perceive of women as different from men in a range of areas in social life and perhaps nowhere more different then when on the battlefield. The results provided here show women and men to be more similar than dissimilar in a host of areas. Given the history of American women in warfare, the contemporary war in Iraq may mark a milestone and turning point for the role of women in the military.

In the next chapter, I turn to soldiers and communication. The U.S. wars in Iraq and Afghanistan are the most communicated wars in U.S. history. Some have argued that many American soldiers in Baghdad communicate more and better than when they are home in the United States. The chapter focuses on types of communication media used and the satisfaction with the use of those media and provides a brief social history of media for interpersonal communication during military forward deployments.

8 Baghdad calling

Soldier communications with other fronts

My wife, she's writing the war's on CNN "It looks pretty bad from here…" You should see it from my end.

Ellis Paul, *Kiss the Sun (A Song for Pat Tillman)*, 2005

Introduction

In the last chapter, I focused on the available research findings around American women soldiers in war. The focus is on how female service members compared and contrasted with their male peers whom they served with in Iraq, Kuwait, and Haiti. I examined and presented some of the topics from previous chapters but with a comparison of men and women. The chapter concluded with a topic only specific to that chapter, in particular comparison of attitudes toward women in roles in the military.

In this chapter, I turn to American soldiers and their communication behavior during war. This chapter focuses on types of communication media used by soldiers in Iraq, Kuwait, and Haiti and satisfaction with the use of those media, followed by a brief social history of media for interpersonal communication. For American soldiers and their circles of significant others around the world, the wars in Afghanistan and Iraq are the most communicated in history. At this writing, American soldiers in Iraq communicate more and better to the world from their Forward Operating Bases (FOBs) in Iraq and Afghanistan than many from their home bases in places such as Fort Campbell, Kentucky; Fort Hood, Texas; Fort Drum, New York; or Fort Carson, Colorado. Leonard Wong and Stephen Gerras (2006) refer to the FOB as "…the home away from home for the American soldier" (pp. 21–22)—essentially, a communication technology rich home. Indeed, it would not have been extraordinary for two 19-year-old American soldiers in Baghdad, Iraq to be sharing a 10-foot by 12-foot room in a trailer. They might have a satellite dish with high-speed Internet access, two laptops, Skype cameras, an Xbox, cell-phone technology, a Blackberry, a Bluetooth, and a webcam; run a blog; and utilize a music sound system board to produce their own hip-hop mixes.

U.S. newspapers began reporting on the new modes of communication dating back to Operation Joint Endeavor—the U.S. involvement in Bosnia.[1] One of the first recent major newspaper stories about e-mail use by American soldiers and families appeared soon after the ground war in Iraq on the front page of the *Christian Science Monitor* (McLaughlin, 2003). Numerous stories appeared in international, national, and regional newspapers sources by 2005. Headline stories included soldier blogs (Knickerbocker, 2005), concerns about the home-front (Shanker, 2005), lifelines to being connected (Nguyen, 2005), and an in-depth piece on the front-page of the *New York Times* Science Section—usually reserved for medical, biological, and physical sciences but in this case a social science story by a freelance reporter stressing the ubiquity of soldier communication from Iraq.[2]

Communication media in the United States today

Twenty-first-century technologies have made American homes digital cocoons and individuals walking techno-graffiti as their hands-free/hands-on and ergonomically correct devices allow multi-task opportunities at the expense perhaps of their situational environments. Passing adults on the street talking into thin (thick) air or text-messaging is not atypical today, a habit only a few years ago that would have garnered quizzical looks and thoughts of homeless, paranoid schizophrenics conversing with the voices in their heads. In the new techno-rich environment, Bluetooths and other technologies make the once unacceptable acceptable. Teenagers can instant-message one another as they sit side by side in church, walk to class, or sit in the dentist's chair. All link in more efficient and instantaneous ways to the outside world than previous generations.

The electronic rich environment bears on the U.S. military and their families as well (Ender, 2005). Future soldiers born into these technologically rich communication contexts will no doubt expect to use such devices on their leisure time, while on duty, and certainly while deployed. The key to understanding soldier and Army family uses of personal communication media is the accumulation of communication media devices do not supplant. In others words, new personal communication media do not displace older media; soldiers and families add them to their repertoire of communication and information sources.[3]

Soldier, unit, family, and larger society communication today

American soldiers in Iraq and Afghanistan and anyone around the world significant to them participated in the most communicated wars in U.S. history. The short-lived, 13-week *F/X* cable television program featured a 2005 series called *Over There.*[4] Drama aside, it did a realistic depiction of both the home

Table 8.1 Soldier effectiveness ranking of seven communication media

Mode of communication: Most to least effective	
Telephone	Most effective
Face-to-face	↑
Mail	
Audio tapes	
Video tapes	
Email	
Facsimile (fax)	Least effective

and war front communication media sources used with soldiers linked by telephones and e-mail in real-time communications.

American soldiers in Iraq and Kuwait and those who had served in Haiti in 1996 received similar questions regarding their communications with the home-front. Questions addressed communication media and effectiveness, uses, satisfaction, and needs assessment of the deployed soldier.

Effectiveness of communication media

It is necessary to move beyond uses and gratifications to understand contexts associated with communication media. The idea is to discover the different types of communication media and different communication media activities (Schumm et al., 2004). Overall, both spouses and soldiers ranked the telephone and face-to-face communication as the most effective modes of communication for them (Ender, 2005). The results in Table 8.1 notably show real-time communication—face-to-face and telephone—as the most effective for soldiers in the mid-1990s. Notably, e-mail ranked far below where we would expect to see it ranked today. Indeed, I find American soldiers in Iraq and Kuwait ranked it higher compared to soldiers in Haiti just more than 10 years ago.

Types of communication media used

American soldiers in Iraq and Kuwait and those who served in Haiti reported on a range of sources of communication media usage. Table 8.2 lists 11 modes. Free telephones and mail refer to free morale calls available for soldiers to call home and postage paid letters delivered from a war zone without charge. For-fee or "paid" telephones and mail incur traditional charges for overseas calling; however, letter and package mail cost only traditional, domestic charges—in other words, it is similar to mailing costs within the continental United States. The data in Table 8.2 show that just more than one-third of American soldiers

Table 8.2 Percentages of American soldiers reporting using 11 different communication media almost daily while deployed by deployment location

Modes of communication	Iraq	Kuwait	Haiti
Paid telephone	10.3	7.1	2.7
Free telephone	4.6	19.9	3.5
Radio transmission (MARS)	0.4	0	0
Email	36.8	31.4	1
Facsimile (fax)	0.2	0	0
TV satellite hook-up	0.2	0	0
Audio-tape	0.1	0	0
Video-tape	0.1	0	0
Regular mail (free)	3.9	6.4	23.8
Regular mail (paid)	—	1.8	5.5
Package mail	1.7	—	—

Note: A dash ("—") implies question not asked of sample

used e-mail almost daily from Iraq. Further, using e-mail and for-pay telephones, such as calling cards and cell phones, rose dramatically for American soldiers in Iraq and Kuwait compared to their Haiti peers more than 10 years before. The use of regular mail (snail mail) declined, and most other media use remained about the same. While most sources of media continue to be available today for American soldiers, the computer appears to be consolidating those sources as well. For example, webcams, voice-transmission, scanning, and sending attachments via the internet have all but made Fax and audio and video tapes obsolete.

Farther, less than 10 percent reported hardly ever using e-mail, and less than 15 percent reported hardly ever using the telephone for pay (data not shown). E-mail use was reported by two-thirds of soldiers from two to three times per week to almost every day. In contrast, more than 90 percent reported having hardly ever used a video teleconference satellite hook-up. We can only assume that while e-mail was viewed in past wars as less effective, it has emerged in providing soldiers, their families, and other loved ones and acquaintances today as the conduit for communication activities such as keeping in touch, sharing timely and personal information, and showing support.

Satisfaction with communication media

I asked soldiers about their level of satisfaction with resources to communicate home during their deployment. The data in Chart 8.1 show the percentages of American soldiers having served in Haiti, Kuwait, and Iraq and their satisfaction across five levels from highly dissatisfied to highly satisfied. Further, Iraq

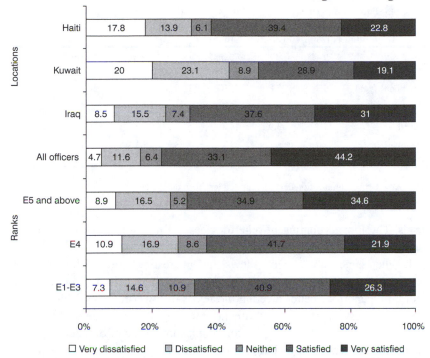

Chart 8.1 Percentages of American soldiers responding to "how well satisfied are you with resources to communicate home?" by deployment location and ranks for Iraq veterans

Note: Bars may not equal 100 percent due to rounding error

veterans are categorized into four rank groups—officers, E5 and above (literally all sergeants), E4, and E1 to E3, with the latter the least experienced and lowest-ranking soldiers. Overall, Iraq soldiers reported more satisfaction comparatively than their Kuwait- and Haiti-experienced peers. Further, among the ranks, rank positively correlated with satisfaction—the higher the rank the greater the satisfaction. Roughly, two-thirds of all soldiers reported being satisfied with the communication resources, although almost one-fourth were dissatisfied.

Finally, I asked soldiers about 10 specific communication media devices that best or least met their communication needs. The data distributions in Table 8.3 provide percentages. Again, I can compare the totals for three deployment groups and again categorize groups serving in Iraq according to military rank. Almost half (47.5 percent) of Iraq veterans reported e-mail as the best mode. For Kuwait soldiers, it was just above one-third (38 percent). For Haiti, e-mail was a lowly 2 percent. For Haiti soldiers, paid telephone and regular mail comparatively better met their communications needs. Telephones followed as best. Only 3 percent reported regular mail as best meeting their communication

Table 8.3 Percentages of American soldiers responding to "during this deployment, which of the following best meet your communication needs?" by Iraq veteran ranks, Iraq veteran total, Kuwait, and Haiti veterans

Modes of communication	E1-E3	E4	E5 and Above	All Officers	Total	Kuwait	Haiti
Telephone (paid)	30.2	27.8	26.0	18.9	25.8	24.0	45.0
Telephone (free)	23.3	19.6	21.7	13.2	19.6	26.6	24.8
Email	41.4	43.9	44.8	62.3	47.5	38.3	2.0
Regular letter mail	1.7	5.1	2.8	2.5	3.3	7.1	22.8

Note: All other communication devices reported less than one percent

needs. The low accounting of other devices did not warrant inclusion in the table.

In the same table, rank shows an interesting pattern for best-met communication media. Paid telephones, although reported the best for everyone, showed a pattern of better meeting the needs of lower-ranking soldiers (they have the lowest income). E-mail, the not-too-long-ago privilege of the middle class, continues to better meet the communication needs of officers compared to enlisted soldiers—a whopping two-thirds majority.

Next, I looked at communication media that least met the needs of American soldiers from the three different deployments. The distribution in Table 8.4 shows a great deal more variation in responses. The facsimile machine (Fax) met the least communications needs overall and with four percent of Iraq veterans reporting e-mail as not meeting their needs. Mostly, they reported fairly equally, but in low percentages, that all the communication media did not meet their needs.

Soldier gender and communication

In the previous chapter, I reported on differences between male and female soldiers and the social features of their deployment. I also looked at gender and communication patterns during the deployment. Few nuances surfaced in terms of communication media use and satisfaction. Haiti female veterans were slightly less likely to have ever used a free telephone. A larger majority of Iraq women veterans report using e-mail two to three times a week or more than men. Kuwait women veterans were twice as dissatisfied with communication resources as males. E-mail was reported as the means for best meeting the communication needs of men, and personal pay telephones were reported by women as the medium best meeting their communication needs. More Kuwaiti female veterans than any other used free telephone almost daily; more Kuwaiti

Table 8.4 Percentages of American soldiers responding to "during this deployment, which of the following least meet your communication needs?" by Iraq veteran ranks, Iraq veteran total, Kuwait, and Haiti veterans

Modes of communication	E1-E3	E4	E5 and above	All officers	Iraq total	Kuwait	Haiti
Telephone (paid)	13.8	15.2	12.0	8.8	12.6	3.8	15.4
Telephone (free)	11.4	16.8	13.0	12.6	13.8	18.5	18.8
MARS	13.8	10.0	13.4	18.9	13.5	8.3	11.6
Email	5.7	4.0	3.1	4.4	4.0	1.9	10.1
Facsimile (fax)	18.7	22.4	21.9	22.0	21.6	14.0	14.8
TV satellite hook-up	12.2	14.4	15.1	11.3	13.7	9.6	2.3
Audio tape	3.3	4.8	9.6	11.9	7.6	10.8	1.8
Video tape	4.1	4.0	2.7	3.8	3.5	2.5	5.1
Regular letter mail	13.0	6.0	4.8	5.0	6.4	17.8	10.1
Regular package mail	3.3	2.0	3.1	1.3	2.4	10.2	—
Other	0.8	0.4	1.4	—	0.7	2.5	—
Total	100.0	100.0	100.0	100.0	100.0	100.0	100.0
% of total	14.9	30.3	35.4	19.3	100.0	100.0	100.0

Note 1: "Other" included all of the above
Note 2: Columns and last row may not equal 100 percent due to rounding error

male veterans used free telephones hardly ever. Most males hardly ever used the regular mail, most women a few times a month.

Thus, there appears a modest gender gap in interpersonal communication media use in a forward-deployed context. Women communicated more. Female soldiers may require greater available and compensated sources of communication such as e-mail and paid telephones to cover their communication needs.

A social history of communication media in military forward deployments

American soldiers have consistently sought ways to communicate home when deployed. Civil War, War of 1812, WWI, and WWII American soldiers spent much of their downtime writing letters home. WWII letter writing and listening to the radio to overcome isolation and boredom were quite normal (Stouffer et al., 1949: vol. 1). WWII saw other sources of communication including a recording of soldiers' voices on wax (vinyl) albums and sent to the U.S. home-front (Avellar, 1942; Heggie, 1942). Home-front America mailed approximately 6 billion letters to American service members overseas during WWII (Litoff and Smith, 1990). By the time of the Korean War in the early 1950s, American soldiers used telegraph, radio, and telephone—in particular the Military Affiliate Radio System (MARS) (Westover, 1955). By Vietnam, mail continued to flow in voluminous numbers between the home and war front. Photographs and audiotapes provided additional modes of communicating and American soldiers continued to consume the popular press en mass (Kroupa, 1973). A decade passed before U.S. service members in the Western hemisphere used international calling cards to telephone home from their deployments in Grenada, Honduras, and Panama (Ender and Segal, 1996). The autonomy of the individual, lower-ranked soldier communicating with people in the United States was dramatized in the 1986 film *Heartbreak Ridge* starring Clint Eastwood and Mario Van Peebles—the only popular film about the 1983 U.S. invasion of Grenada.[5] Loosely based on an actual incident, Van Peebles plays a Marine lance corporal surrounded and trapped in a building without a radio man and taking small arms fire from Cuban nationals. He innovates and locates a telephone in the building, pulls out an AT&T credit calling card, popular at the time, and calls in an air-to-surface strike and other support to save his platoon.[6]

Increased telephone use during peacekeeping missions provided both positive and negative outcomes for soldiers, families, and leaders (Applewhite and Segal, 1990). E-mail, faxes from the desert, and voice mail first appeared during Operation Desert Shield and Desert Storm (the first Persian Gulf War). Much of the world connected to Southwest Asia through a host of communication media. Soldiers also went to war with appendages— Walkmans (Wattendorf, 1992)—the precursor to the iPod.[7] Voice mail made a debut during Operation Desert Shield (Jowers, 1991). Snail mail in the millions went to the desert (Mathews et al., 1990). Prisoners of war in the Gulf used eye-blinking and other body language to communicate messages about their conditions via videotaped broadcasts on television similar to how POWs used photographs and radio from previous wars (Fleming and Scott, 1991). This revolution in soldier communication use was not limited to the United States. Russian soldiers in Afghanistan following the Soviet invasion in 1979 (a war that lasted 9 years) communicated home with their families as well (Frolova, 1992).

Similar to the Grenada telephone call in *Heartbreak Ridge,* actor Mark Walberg plays an American soldier temporarily a POW during the 1990–1991 Persian Gulf War in the film *Three Kings* (1999). He finds himself locked in a dungeon-like room with boxes of contraband that includes caches of jeans, polo shirts, and cell phones. Trying many unsuccessfully, he eventually dials his wife in Arizona while essentially imprisoned in the Iraqi-Kuwaiti desert— an unlikely event. However, a more recent, and the only other popular, film about the first Persian Gulf War to date, titled *Jarhead* (2005) and based on the book of the same name by Anthony Swofford, depicts a more realistic use of telephone by soldiers. It features a bank of "morale" telephones in a tent with a sand floor and soldiers standing in line waiting to call home with poor and intermittent connections.

Prior to the end of the Cold War, research on soldier-family communications found excessive telephone credit card bills from soldiers making long distance calls from the Middle East during Operations Desert Shield and Desert Storm (ODS/S) (Booth et al., 2007; Segal and Harris, 1993). Further, one quarter of spouses reported difficulties communicating with their spouse in the Persian Gulf. Results from wives of soldiers deployed to Grenada showed they very much wanted to communicate during the mission. By ODS/S, many spouses reported a desire to learn information directly from their soldier. Reports and perceptions of distorted news media contributed to a contentious climate and mistrust of information. Additionally, a lack of perceived reliable information and rumors affected the fragility and stability of marriages both during and after the deployment.

Following the Persian Gulf War, a scattering of studies examined the role of communications media in the lives of the spouses of forward-deployed soldiers. Results from survey data provided evidence that communication media (including one- and two-way media) added new dimensions to the spouses' experiences of their soldiers' forward deployment and made devices for communicating to and from the home-front more widespread (Bell and Teitelbaum, 1993). Eighty-two percent of the spouses interviewed had made at least two telephone calls per month; 38 percent mailed one or more video tapes per month.

Almost a year later, the Los Angeles riots in May 1992 involved 2,500 active-duty U.S. Army soldiers from the 7th Infantry Division (Light), Fort Ord, California, following the acquittal of Los Angeles county police officers involved in the Rodney King beating. Owing to the interference of high-rise buildings with radio communiqués in the city of Los Angeles, soldiers turned to the relatively new technology of cellular telephones and pagers for operational communications—making it the first U.S. mission relying on cell phone technology; soldiers also used them to call their friends and loved ones (Wenger, 1994).

In Somalia in 1993, U.S. Army soldiers desired communication media, but they were not readily available (Gifford et al., 1993). Limited telephone use overcame the lack of telephony in and around Somalia and alleviated the stressful implications for soldiers and families. Problems with communication between front and home precipitated an innovative e-mail program that pleased many spouses by ultimately providing the speed, relative privacy, decentralization, and personal communication they desired (Ender, 1997). Soldiers and family members eventually sent approximately 10,000 email messages across the Atlantic from continent to continent.

Types of communication media available and used by spouses with their soldiers in Somalia included paid mail (87 percent), free mail (49 percent), telephones (36 percent), e-mail provided by the Army Community Service (27 percent), Army unit-provided email (34 percent), MARS (15 percent), fax (28 percent), and TV teleconferencing (4 percent) (Ender, 1996). Looking back, Somalia spouse communication appeared more connected to units than individuals (Bell et al., 1999). Three-fourths had problems communicating, and communication problems correlated with feelings of stress during the deployment. The most important communication activity appears to be the first contact: early first contacts and diverse communication devices mediate the initial sources of stress.

A year later in 1994, the United States sent troops into Haiti for Operation Uphold Democracy. For the American soldiers in Haiti, there was a continued range of personal communication media available to use as referenced in the findings earlier in this chapter.

A year or so later in December 1995, the U.S. mission in Bosnia, dubbed Operation Joint Endeavor, involved the United States and allied nations, such as Russia, deployed as peacekeeping forces. Some 20,000 American soldiers comprised Task Force Eagle whose responsibility involved putting into action the military elements of the Dayton Peace Accords. In Bosnia, American soldiers fully engaged their mission but also generated the use of a host of communication media from snail mail to e-mail. The U.S. Army arranged free mail for American soldiers to send small package and letter mail from Bosnia. In addition, an "Any Service Member Mail" program, similar to the one established during the Persian Gulf War, was established. The mail volume to service members averaged 40,000 pounds of mail per day. The First Lady at the time—Hillary Rodham Clinton—inaugurated a complimentary "Any Family Member" program for military family members in Germany to receive free, support-oriented mail from the American public. This initiated a trend toward increased public access to military family members that today creates new expectations for access, use, and satisfaction and new types of communication stresses for both soldiers and families.

Discussion and conclusion

This chapter focused on soldiers and communication during war. For American soldiers and their circles of significant others around the world, the war in Iraq is the most communicated in history. The chapter focused on types of communication media used and satisfaction with the use of those media and provided a brief social history of media for interpersonal communication during military deployments. Others have reported that American soldiers linked better to the world from their FOB in Iraq or Afghanistan than many were from their home bases. Again, the key to understanding soldier and military family uses—personal communication media does not displace older media; rather, soldiers and families add them to their repertoire of communication and information sources. There is a long and dramatically changing social history of communication media use during military-related forward deployments. The increase in access to a plethora of communication media has created new kinds of communication stresses on both soldiers and families. American soldiers in Iraq and anyone around the world significant to them participated in the most communicated wars in U.S. history.

The goal of the present analysis is to discover the different types of communication media and different communication media activities. Both spouses and soldiers ranked the telephone and face-to-face communication as the most effective modes of communication for them. Iraq and Kuwait veterans and those who served in Haiti gave a range of sources of communication media to report on their use—11 modes. American soldiers in Iraq and Kuwait used e-mail regularly and almost daily, thus rising dramatically over 10 years ago while regular mail (snail mail) has declined and most other media use has remained about the same.

Iraq soldiers were more satisfied than earlier soldiers, and rank is positively correlated with satisfaction—the higher the rank, the greater the satisfaction. Telephones and e-mail better meets the communication needs of soldiers. Finally, a modest gender gap in interpersonal communication media use exists.

The next two chapters turn to American soldiers and the long-term affects of serving during times of war. Moving away from how America soldiers perceived and experienced their time in Iraq, soldiers responded to questions about the long-term impact of deployments to Iraq. Essentially, is the Iraq deployment for them indeed an agent of personal change? First, is the war a turning point in their personal life and, if so, how? Also, more specific questions are included about reenlistment intentions and options, representing the military to others, and any civilian options they may have. Chapter Ten examines the ultimate sacrifice in Iraq—death in the ranks.

9 Turning point

Iraq as a change agent for American soldiers

Nothing endures but change.

Heraclitas

Seeing and knowing about friends dying really sucks. I see myself becoming bitter and growing up at the same time.

(24-year-old, white female junior officer, single no children)

It is not the strongest of the species that survives, nor the most intelligent, but the one most responsive to change.

Charles Darwin

Introduction

In our *Deviance & Social Control* course at West Point, we usually invite both a professional tattoo artist and a body modification expert to class. The tattoo artist recently shared an interesting phenomenon. In his late fifties with middle-of-the-back-length hair, a rugged outlaw-biker style, and patently patriotic, he shared that his most recent clients were Vietnam veterans. They are coming to commemorate their Vietnam service with tattoos. He said they had developed a newfound appreciation of their wartime experience and wanted to commemorate it with a permanent tattoo. Of course, these mostly drafted veterans participated in a war that became increasingly unpopular—even more so after the war ended. Back then, they wanted to ignore or put the experience behind them. However, the new wave of public esteem showered on soldiers returning from Iraq and Afghanistan appears to have concomitantly recast their Vietnam service experience in a more positive light. War and the aftermath of war constitute an increasingly public turning point in lives of soldiers (Hampson, 2008).

The idea of a war, or indeed one's veteran status, having implications for your life trajectory has been an important, necessary, and long-established area of study.[1] To begin, one might ask, is the military simply a job or more than a job or is it a calling? This question occupied military sociologists for a number of years during the late 1970s and 1980s (Moskos and Wood, 1988; Musheno and Ross, 2008). Originally proposed in 1977 by the late Charles

Moskos and gaining the attention of scholars as the institutional/occupational (I/O) thesis, the research emerged in the context of the all-volunteer military. It held that military (wo)manpower motivations on the part of volunteers could be placed on a continuum from an institutional "calling" to an occupational "job." Characteristics of the institutional volunteer are intrinsic, such as a calling to and for valuing of service, a life-style orientation that is comprehensive, all-encompassing, holistic, transcendence of self-interest, and the so-called "work" is oriented toward the higher good. Words such as *duty*, *honor*, and *country* fostered self-sacrifice for the institution. Further, positive public esteem showers down on those who serve. In everyday terms—one lives to work.

In contrast, people may work to live. The occupational model views military work as a job. Compartmentalized work in the gestalt of one's social life is the norm. Compensation is based on extrinsic reward such as money and financial incentives with motivations captured through salaries and bonuses. People specialize and segment their work-life. The marketplace drives recruitment.

Much of the research on the I/O has slowed in recent years as some scholars came to conclude that soldiers probably rationalized elements of both—that they could be both institutional and occupational: a pragmatic professionalism, one who is motivated by both intrinsic and extrinsic rewards (Woodruff et al., 2006).

The sociology of veterans shows the significance that individual or group military experience or even a war has for veterans versus non-veterans. For example, research shows that WWII veterans fared economically better than civilians (Smith, 2007; Teachman and Tedrow, 2004), that officers fared better than their civilian peers, but enlisted men fared less well than theirs (Dechter and Elder, 2004), and Vietnam veterans fared similarly in economic earnings compared to their civilian peers (Teachmen, 2004). Others found military service to interact with college education in ways most would not expect for both Vietnam era veterans (Teachman, 2005) and Cold War veterans (MacLean, 2005a; 2005b). Research also shows that drug use and criminal activity increased among disadvantaged youth who served in Vietnam (Wright et al., 2005).

In this chapter, both qualitative and quantitative results highlight future orientations of soldiers regarding the legacy on their lives of military deployment and military service in general. The research questions ask whether military service and deployment are perceived as a turning point in the lives of soldiers and, if so, how? Soldiers received questions about reenlistment intentions and options as well as their position on representing the military to others. Similar to other dimensions of deployments, veterans are akin across the years but, within the most recent experiences, Iraq and Kuwait veterans show a range of reactions to the deployment relative to their personal life.

Turning points

Google "turning point" coupled with "Iraq" and a host of newspaper articles and editorials emerge. A cursory content analysis of those hits shows writers speculating about major events that might change the direction of the war. However, no popular articles examine how the war might be a turning point for individual soldiers particularly by providing them a platform to share their experiences. That is the goal here.

Called "meaning moments," a "crossroads," or a "tipping point," military service influences the lives of men and women in significant ways. The authors of *Geeks and Geezers: How Era, Values, and Defining Moments Shape Leaders* (Bennis and Thomas, 2002) refer to making meaning out of often difficult events such as "crucibles" and how such moments spurs them in new ways. Serving in a war could certainly by considered a crucible experience in the life of an American.

Soldiers responded "yes" or "no" to a question asking whether they considered the current deployment a turning point in their life. Again, this question was asked of soldiers from three different periods—soldiers of Iraq and Kuwait and veterans of Operation Uphold Democracy in Haiti 10 years earlier. The percentages in Chart 9.1 show the distributions. Iraq veterans first differentiate by rank. Their total is comparable to Haiti and Kuwait veterans. Overall, the turning points appear similar. Yet, on closer observation, just more than 75 percent of soldiers in Iraq in the summer of 2004 reported "yes," whereas just less than 70 percent of those from Kuwait reported "yes" and fewer (60 percent) of Haiti veterans reported "yes." There are no outstanding differences by rank.

A follow-up question to the "yeses" among the Iraq and Kuwait veterans asked why it was a turning point in their life.[2] For both groups, four distinct category responses emerged, and there is diversity within these categories. They included (1) personal, social, or both; (2) military; (3) family; and (4) other. People might expect veterans to focus on the negative dimension of their military experience exclusively and collectively. This is not the case. About one-fourth of the Kuwait and about half of the Iraq soldiers identified some positive personal or social turning point associated with their deployment.

Personal and social turning points

In responding to the survey question, soldiers took the opportunity to reflect. In particular, many compared the status of American society with that of Iraq. They linked their individual quality of life, Americans in general, and others around the world. The most common response for veterans involved social comparisons between "American Privilege" and the advantages as a prosperous nation compared to the way of life of other nations. That they acquired a newfound lease on life—no longer taking their privileges for granted. Some typical responses in the words of the soldiers included "By realizing that I am very fortunate to be an American citizen. I appreciate my way of life much more. I will enjoy my life much more" (48-year-old African-American male NCO, on second marriage with one child); "I realize what we have in America that others don't have and how I took it for granted" (22-year-old white male private, single and no children); "It's made me realize how much I am blessed to be an American" (21-year-old white male private, engaged and no children); "It showed me how great America is in comparison to less fortunate nations" (25-year-old African-American male junior officer, on second marriage with one child); and "The deployment has made me enjoy life as an American. Before this deployment I took a lot of stuff for granted" (25-year-old African-American male specialist, married with one child).

Another kind of response had to do with a personal recognition and a socially responsible and "Humanitarian Consciousness-Raising": something we might not typically associate with soldiers but more with American youth traveling to less developed countries for the first time, perhaps on humanitarian missions. Typical responses included "Got to know the needs of others around the world and helping the needy is worth a million to me. So making the military a career to help freedom for people around the world is now my main focus" (34-year-

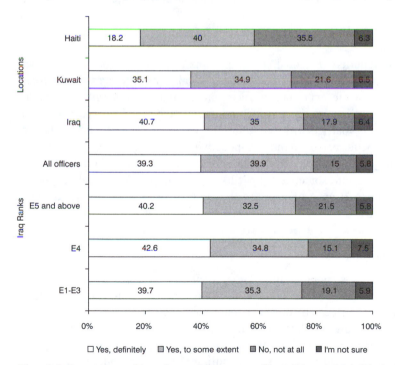

Chart 9.1 Percentages of American soldiers responding to "do you think this deployment is a turning point in your life?" by deployment location and by ranks for Iraq veterans

Note: Bars may not equal 100 percent due to rounding error

old African-American male sergeant, married with one child); "Brings the worlds' realities up front and makes you very aware of what's important" (36-year-old Pacific-Islander male specialist, married with two children); and

> I was born and raised in a third world country, after I moved to the States I became somewhat kind of selfish, but once in Iraq, I looked back into my childhood the way these people live and the things they have to do to feed their children.
>
> > (23-year-old Hispanic-American male specialist, single and no children)

Finally, for many soldiers responding, it simply provided a "Sociological Reality of Another Nation" that they had not considered. A soldier wrote:

> It made me realize how the world is like in a first person point of view, instead of seeing it on TV. It is a big change to me when thinking that I live in a country where you are free and have the luxuries that the United States has.
>
> > (21-year-old white male specialist, declined to report marital status with two children)

Others reported "Personal" turning points in their life—both positive and negative. One wrote, "I am more willing to takes risks to accomplish goals" (22-year-old white male junior officer, single and no children), and another penned, "A little more open to life and unexpected turns" (23-year-old white male sergeant, married with no children). Two others shared: "It has changed me to be a better person, a more responsible man, and I am looking to stay in the military" (21-year-old white male sergeant, single and no children) and "It has turned me into someone I don't like. I'm not the same person anymore" (28-year-old African-American female declined to report her rank, divorced single parent).

Military turning points

The second most popular response for soldiers of Iraq had to do with a "Military" turning point. About one-fourth of soldiers commented on wanting to leave the service. For others it reinforced their resolve to remain in the military. For Kuwait soldiers, about 45 percent list a military turning point, especially having to do with leadership issues. Two soldiers put pen to paper: "It has helped me learn a lot about handling my soldiers and interacting with people during difficult times, making quick decisions, etc. It has greatly impacted my attitude about the Army and my role in the Army" (23-year-old white female junior officer, single); "Seeing how I just got married recently, just got off a nine month deployment and now I'm gone for another six to 12 months, it is really making me try to decide whether to stay in or get out" (23-year-old white male specialist, married with one child); "I feel it has made me a competent and confident leader. I have become proficient in real world aspects of tactical operations" (33-year-old white male captain, married with two children); "Has made me realize my time is worth more than the Army is capable of compensating" (35-year-old white male staff sergeant, married with four children); "It made me hate the Army even more because they won't let me get out when my time is up" (29-year-old African-American female sergeant, married and no children); and:

> It showed me that the Army is a mission first organization. All about numbers, not what do you need to make the mission work, but just how many people was someone in charge of in war times. The Army is not rooted and grounded in moral values. The same units and the same people always make deployments. Support units are always the first in, last out. Dates are given out, ones to leave for a deployment are never right, and then once deployed, dates for leaving are never right.
>
> (22-year-old African-American male sergeant, single with no children)

Family turning points

Similar to the military dimension associated with the turning point, about one-fourth of both Iraq and Kuwait veterans reported "Family" as a turning point for them. A renewed appreciation for their families dominated the responses while some mentioned problems with families such as divorce. Typical responses included "Well, being shot at and mortared every other day, plus having near death experiences and close calls really puts things in perspective. You begin to truly understand what is important in life, family and loved ones" (20-year-old white male private, married for the first time with no children); "Truly shows how important family is and being able to spend time with your children. The work-a-holic ends" (37-year-old white male senior officer, married for the first time with three children); "I have decided that I do not wish to have my son under the care of someone else besides me for a long period of time…my son needs to be with his mother" (28-year-old African-American female sergeant, divorced with one child); "During this deployment, both of my parents died and my wife divorced me. I believe when I get home I will not get too excited over trivial things" (51-year-old white male staff sergeant, divorced with one child); and "My life seems shorter now. I never thought about having a family before" (23-year-old bi-racial male specialist, single with no children).

Other turning points

Last, a catchall category emerged from the soldier comments that I labeled "Other" and emerged from the findings with a small percent of soldiers having responses that fell into this category. Their responses included topics such as spiritual, political, and even physical awakenings. Examples of responses of all three categories included "It made me realize my body will not be able to handle much more injury. A P-2 profile keeps me from progressing" (41-year-old Hispanic male NCO, second marriage and three children); "I don't see the point of being here other than establishing a beachhead for American business interest in the region. We are using force to make peace which is absurd" (23-year-old white male specialist, married with no children); and "It has made me appreciate the glory of God and all that he has given me. Not material things…" (39-year-old African-American male NCO, second marriage with three children).

Turning points for women

Men and women veterans from both the Haiti and Iraq experience the deployment as a turning point in their lives similarly. However, just more than 90 percent of the women experiencing the Kuwait deployment compared to almost 70 percent of the men consider the deployment a turning point. However, when asked how the war is a turning point, all groups experience war as a turning point similarly. In terms of how the experience changed them, the women's ways mirrored their male peers. Examples of the three themes of "Military," "Family," and "Personal Issues" included "[The deployment] helped me learn a lot about handling my soldiers; interacting with people during difficult times, make quick decisions, etc. [The war] impacted my attitude about the Army greatly and my role in the Army" (23-year-old white female junior officer, single); "[I am] getting a divorce and leaving the Army" (25-year-old Hispanic female sergeant with no children); and "To appreciate everything I take for granted; to adapt to different living situations" (35-year-old Other ethnicity female private, separated with two children).

Reenlistment intentions

At this writing, the wars in both Afghanistan and Iraq have moved into years rather than months. The number of days in Iraq for American soldiers has exceeded the number of days the United States participated in WWII. Regardless of the names and labels of the conflict that have been paraded forth—"The Long War," "The Iraq War," "Global War on Terror," or even "World War IV"—recruitment of service members is an ongoing concern of the U.S. Army. Enlistment for the all-volunteer force ebbs and flows generally and among specific populations of recruits, such as racial/ethnic minorities and in regions of the country. Some members of Congress, such as Charles B. Rangel (Democrat from New York), became concerned enough to call for a wartime draft. The current wars in Iraq and Afghanistan have created contexts for shifts in recruiting standards including allowing moral waivers and raising of the maximum age of first enlistment.

Military recruitment is a complicated matter socially constructed in and around contextual sociopolitical strategic needs, social demographics, and the economic labor market. The question might be "to serve what purpose?" For example, the Pentagon puts forth a particular recruitment goal for a year based on troop strength to meet particular military needs anticipated in the future. In 2005, the U.S. Army estimated needing between 176,400 to 183,000 enlisted soldiers and between 17,500 and 21,500 officers to meet a strength level. This number typically correlates with a number of variables including the demographic pool of people in a particular age range, mental aptitude, education level, physical ability, moral character such as an absence of criminal record, and other requirements such as citizenship status, language ability, and the number of family member dependents for whom the person might be responsible. Notably, only about 50 percent of the American eligible age pool population actually qualifies for military service. In addition, people such as parents, coaches, and other socializing agents and institutions (e.g., financial aid packages of colleges and universities) influence young people's intention to enlist. Further complicating factors include mass media portrayals, assessments of personal risk, and real and perceived opportunities available in the military organization.

The U.S. Army has addressed recruitment shortfalls with some strategies such as enlistment bonuses, novel marketing, aggressive recruitment, and compromising some enlistment restrictions such as weight, age, and criminal record standards. For example, in 2006, the U.S. Army raised the maximum enlistment age from 35 to 40 and then to 42 years of age. An additional factor that connects to troop strength at any given time is the amount of reenlistment— whether service members remain beyond their initial service obligation. With more attrition (leaving military service) after their initial enlistments, there is greater need to recruit more new members.

During relatively peaceful times, the assumption is that new recruits are fairly naïve about the military once they enlist. Once they deploy, particularly for an extended length of time, the variance and length of deployment may create a turning point for the service members and change their attitude about military service, and they might opt out of the military. Research on deployments has shown, however, that reenlistment is as high as or, in some cases, higher among those who deploy than those who do not deploy (Hosek and Totten, 2002). While in Iraq, the division I attached to celebrated achieving a 100 percent reenlistment goal. Leaders recognized that the hostile nature of the deployment, length of time away from home, and the possibility of multiple

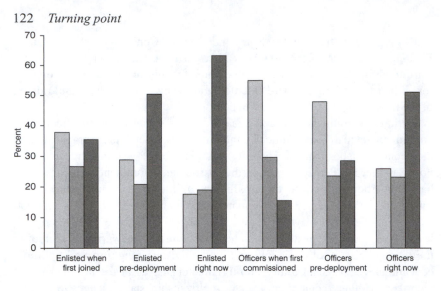

Chart 9.2 Percentage distributions of post-Iraq reenlistment intentions: junior enlisted soldiers and junior officers across three time periods—first joined, pre-deployment to Iraq, and midway through Iraq deployment

Note: Bars may not equal 100 percent due to rounding error

deployments existed and might counter reenlistment in an undesirable way. Those reservations did not bear on the bottom line in the summer of 2004.

I took the topic a step further and asked a series of questions on the survey inviting responses about reenlistment intentions. The questions required that the soldiers respond by thinking retrospectively—considering three points in time: their attitude toward service when they first came into the Army, prior to the present deployment, and now (at the time of the survey), and whether they were leaning toward an Army career, undecided, or leaning toward a civilian career. For some, obviously, the first point in time differs, but the latter two points in time coincide and, at a minimum, there is some distance between the three points.

First-term enlistees and junior officers clearly have the most attitude and behavioral flexibility about their career choices. Two groups appear in the next three tables. The bar chart in Chart 9.2 shows the post-Iraq reenlistment intentions for first-term junior enlisted soldiers (E1 to E4) and first-term officers (lieutenants and captains) at the three points in time. As the story unfolds, we see that among first-term enlisted soldiers from Iraq, upon first coming into the Army, had even distribution among three groups. Most leaned toward a military career (37.9 percent); the fewest were undecided (26.6 percent), and a middle-range group leaned toward a civilian career (35.5 percent). By their pre-deployment to Iraq, a noticeable decrease existed for soldiers leaning toward

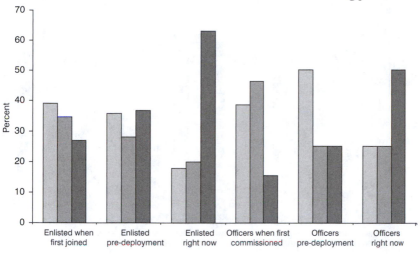

Chart 9.3 Percentage distributions of post-Kuwait reenlistment intentions: junior enlisted soldiers and junior officers across three time periods—first joined, pre-deployment to Kuwait, and end of the Kuwait deployment

Note: Bars may not equal 100 percent due to rounding error

the Army as a career and undecided, with the huge spike among those leaning toward a civilian career. The trend continued to move away from the Army at the time of the survey—6 months into a military deployment.

Among the junior officers, there are greater dramatic differences across the periods. More than 50 percent were reported to be leaning toward a military career when they first came into the Army, about 30 percent were undecided, and a small percent leaned toward a civilian career. By pre-deployment, the Army careerist and undecided moved toward a civilian career, and by the time of the survey, the group had flipped, with more than 50 percent leaning toward a civilian career.

The Kuwait group mirrored the Iraq soldiers with a few exceptions. The bar charts in Chart 9.3 remain fairly even for first enlistment and at pre-deployment. However, at the end of their tour of Kuwait, we see a 50 percent increase over first joined for those leaning toward a civilian career. For officers, there is a similar pattern to Iraq—half leaning toward a civilian career by the end of their deployment to Kuwait.

Finally, looking back over 10 years, American soldiers who had returned from Haiti show the junior enlisted soldiers similar to the Kuwait veterans. For Haiti veteran officers (Chart 9.4), the largest percentage leaned toward an Army career at commissioning only to shift to leaning toward a civilian career after returning from their deployment to Haiti. Notably, not a single junior officer

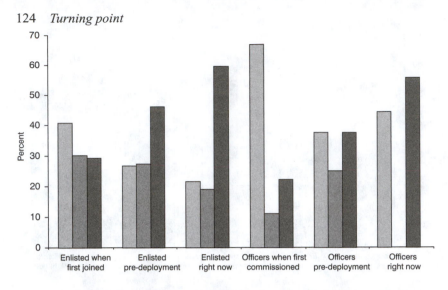

□ Leaning toward army   ▣ Undecided   ■ Leaning toward civilian

Chart 9.4 Percentage distributions of post-Haiti reenlistment intentions: junior enlisted soldiers and junior officers across three time periods—first joined, prior to deployment to Haiti, and two months after returning to U.S.

Note: Bars may not equal 100 percent due to rounding error

was undecided after the tour in Haiti—they leaned either in or out in almost equal numbers. This points to the split among leaders regarding their attitudes toward military operations other than war, such as a police enforcement effort in Haiti; they may either like them or they don't! Overall, the major finding is that the six groups of soldiers following three different military deployments look to be leaning toward civilian careers after initially having leaned toward an Army career and then deploying on a military mission.

Reenlistment intentions for women

Men and women veterans of Haiti had similar orientations when they first came in, just prior to the deployment, and at the time of the survey—1 month after returning from Haiti. Kuwait male veterans distributed evenly, with a third leaning toward civilian careers, a third leaned toward military careers, and a third undecided. Women veterans of Kuwait leaned toward an Army career when they first came in. By the time of the survey, both men and women leaned in greater numbers toward, and planned on, a civilian career but women about 15 percent more than men. Iraq women veterans in greater numbers planned on an Army career compared to men when they came in. By the time of the survey, their reenlistment intentions matched up.

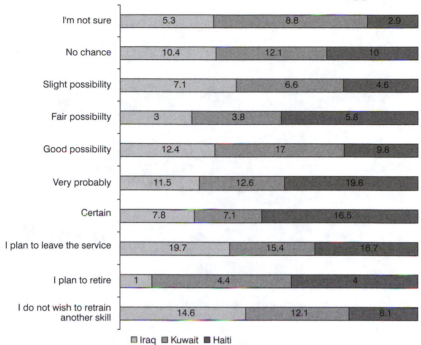

Chart 9.5 Percentage of American soldiers responding to "if you could, would you reenlist for better career opportunities?" by deployment location

Note: Bars may not equal 100 percent due to rounding error

Reenlistment options

Reenlistment intentions are one way to assess how soldiers feel and ultimately might react to their military experiences. Another technique for tapping those intentions are the possible options to keep soldiers in the military (e.g., allowing some job changes to accommodate overcoming any general reservations about their current position).

In particular, the U.S. Army can offer service member reenlist options that might better mesh with their career intentions. Two questions tapped optimal career intentions within the military. The first question concerns better career opportunities. I queried soldiers, "If you could, would you re-enlist for better career opportunities?" followed by a long list of career options. The percentages in Chart 9.5 show a fairly well-distributed group of responses. The largest groups of soldiers planned to leave the service and still others—primarily Iraq and Kuwait soldiers—did not wish to retain another skill. A moderate percentage of soldiers had a possibility of reenlisting for better career opportunities.

Next, the options are somewhat collapsed and more hypothetically radical (Chart 9.6). I asked soldiers, "If you could, which of the following would you

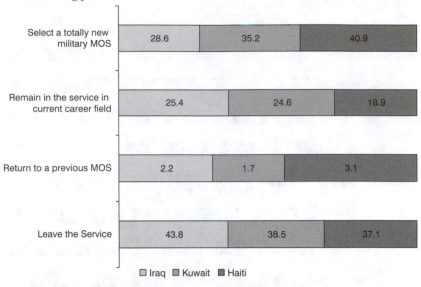

Chart 9.6 Percentage of American soldiers responding to "if you could, which of the following would you choose?" by deployment location

Note: Columns may not equal 100 percent due to rounding error

choose?" They have four different shift options. The responses synchronized well across the three groups. However, more Iraq veterans and a large percentage of Kuwait veterans would opt to leave the service. More Haiti soldiers would opt for selecting a new military specialty, and many would leave the service as well. Notably, reenlistment options did not vary by gender. Similarly, no differences by gender emerged in the hypothetical option of starting over and reenlisting for a new military occupational specialty.

Representing the military to others

A willingness to recommend the military to others is another indicator for tapping how soldiers feel about the Army or at least their experience in the Army. Two questions addressed representing or recommending the military to others. The distributions in Chart 9.7 show that more than 40 percent of two veterans groups would be willing to recommend the service to others. Kuwait soldiers recommended least (about 35.4 percent). Although not shown in the chart, officers were the best advocates for joining the military.

Next, all soldiers responded to a question about their level of agreement with the statement, "I would recommend that others pursue an active duty Army career." The percentage distributions in Chart 9.8 show the responses. The

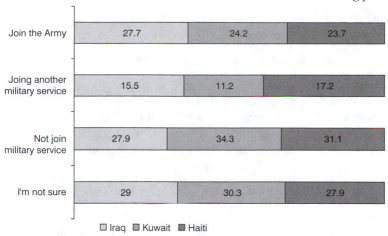

Chart 9.7 Percentage of American soldiers responding to "if you met someone … would you recommend joining?" by deployment location

Note: Columns may not equal 100 percent due to rounding error

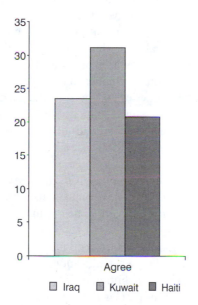

Chart 9.8 Percent of American soldiers agreeing to "I would recommend that others pursue an active duty army career" by deployment location

groups responded somewhat similarly, but more disagreed with the statement. Kuwait veterans agreed slightly more than veterans from the other two military deployments in Haiti and Iraq. No major differences emerged between male and female veterans in recommending the active Army to others. Women serving in Iraq felt more neutral than males. Males reported more positive views about recommending that others pursue an active Army career.

Discussion and conclusion

In this chapter, qualitative and quantitative results revealed some of the future orientations of American veterans who have served real-world Army missions in Haiti, Kuwait, and Iraq. Is military service and a subsequent deployment perceived as a turning point in the lives of soldiers and if so, how? Soldiers responded to questions about their reenlistment intentions and options at three different points in their military tenure. Finally, veterans provided their position on representing the military to others.

First, military service is a major experience in the adult life cycle, even if the tenure is a typical 3-year enlistment. Additionally, a deployment during one's term of enlistment can certainly make the experience more profound. For many, a deployment is a crucible experience. War is a turning point for American soldiers who served in Iraq, but it is also one for veterans of Haiti some 10 years earlier and no doubt for soldiers before them. The turning point seems to be the deployment in general irrespective of locale—Iraq, Haiti, or Kuwait. What the deployment turns on is divergent for soldiers; it could be personal, social, occupational, familial, physical, or spiritual. However, for many young men and women who are likely to have never been out of the United States, especially in a less-developed nation, the global inequities in the world clearly make a mark on them. We can only assume American soldiers in Afghanistan are having similar experiences. Here is an entire subgeneration, a cohort, of Americans learning directly about the have-have not dichotomies of the world. Many assessed their value orientations and reprioritized them. Some considered putting family ahead of professional interests. Finally, many American soldiers probably found what they were looking for in military service—adventure, patriotism, camaraderie, and service. They are now ready to move on to civilian life.

Enlistment in the military is a major concern. In an all-volunteer force, the military obtains members through a market model approach. People make choices about being in the Army. Indeed, a military enlistment decision involves a number of variables including what educational and career opportunities the military might provide. These opportunities include both intrinsic and extrinsic motivations. During the early part of the war in Iraq, American enlistments dropped as the perceptions of opportunities weighted against time away and the potential for mortality and injury salience resulting from deploying to a war. A similar assessment likely existed for those who reenlist during the deployment. They have more experience with war compared to the typical 18-year-old with no military experience thinking about such service.

Overall, when asking about reenlistment, we find much initial optimism when American soldiers first come into the Army. However, once they experience a major deployment, they lean toward civilian careers. Again, this is not exclusive with a war deployment, as a deployment to a peacekeeping mission in Haiti showed a similar result. Future research might consider surveying non-deployed soldiers as well. Another feature of reenlistment involves options within the organization. The U.S. Army might consider offering some soldiers options as a few of them might accept alternative forms of service to remain in uniform or even another form of service without a uniform. The last issue is the degree to which current and former members of the military are advocates for service. The U.S. Army would do well by capitalizing on these committed, cross-cultured, and experienced men and women who now have leadership experience. Peace Corps workers oriented toward internationally oriented careers are a comparison group. One option is to serve as local ambassadors in schools, non-governmental organizations, and corporations in America while on a 6-month to 1-year paid sabbatical. This might provide reflection time to teach and learn from their unique experience. Most members of the military have a family member or trusted family friend who served and acted as role models for them. It appears that about half of the veterans of Haiti and Southwest Asia would serve as these role models. It also suggests that another half may not. A deployment appears to be the turnoff away from service; however, the kind of deployment appears to make little difference. More research is necessary to determine this relationship.

Both the words of soldiers and their collective survey responses presented here highlight the qualitative and quantitative data from American soldiers serving in Iraq, Kuwait, and Haiti. The results feature an assortment of reactions to and within the deployments. Contrary to a singular experience, soldiers have different thematic reactions to deploying and react along a continuum to each of these themes from positive to negative. Consistent with their attitudes and everyday events during a deployment, American soldiers show a multiplicity and range of views rather than a singular mind-set. This chapter has provided American soldiers with an opportunity to voice their experiences in the context of the deployment rather than with a retrospective interpretation of the experiences long after they have returned home. Finally, we learn how different soldiers experience a deployment overseas, in particular how living, working, and interacting with another culture forces a comparison to the insular life of living in America, within the military culture, and away from family.

In the next and last chapter involving empirical data, the focus is on death in the military. For service member fatalities, their friends and loved ones, their community, and the nation, they have paid the ultimate sacrifice. I collected and analyzed a separate set of data on the backgrounds of American service men and women killed in Iraq. Socio-cultural variables are assessed, including the distributions of age, branch of service, race/ethnicity, type of death, gender, rank, and social class during Operation Iraqi Freedom, and comparisons are made of these distributions to the general military population.

10 Death in the American ranks

Class war or equal opportunity

I feel how weak and fruitless must be any word of mine which should attempt to beguile you from the grief of a loss so overwhelming. But I cannot refrain from tendering you the consolation that may be found in the thanks of the Republic they died to save.

From the Letter to Mrs. Bixby by Abraham Lincoln November 21, 1864

One day we opened a playground and gave out toys for the kids. The next day a kid planted an IED that killed a SSG in my troop.

American soldier in Iraq

Introduction

In the previous chapter, I presented survey results highlighting the impact of Army service and a military deployment on the future orientations of American soldiers. Military service and the deployment are a turning point in their lives and meant different things to different soldiers. Queried about their reenlistment intentions and options and their position on representing the military to others, most soldiers reported service in Iraq to be a crucible-type experience for them. This, the final chapter reporting results, is a turn to the ultimate turning point for American soldiers who served in Iraq—death.

Death and serious injury are a relatively normal part of U.S. military life today. For service members and their families in the Army, Air Force, Navy, Marines, and their sister services of the National Guard and reserves, they have paid the ultimate sacrifice. Here I present the social backgrounds of U.S. service men and women fatalities in service to Operation Iraqi Freedom in Iraq.[1] First, a discussion is provided of some history of death in the U.S. ranks followed by a review of past research literature on death in the military. Next, in the bulk of this chapter, I examine sociocultural variables coupled with American service members' deaths in Iraq. They include the distributions of age, branch of service, race/ethnicity, types of death, military occupational specialty (MOS), military rank, home of record and social class, and gender during Operation

Iraqi Freedom. I compare these distributions where appropriate to previous wars, the general military population, and civilian populations.

As the U.S.-led war in Iraq known as Operation Iraqi Freedom (OIF) moves into a sixth year of continuous engagement, the death toll for both service members and civilians from all the principal groups involved continues to climb. Between March 21, 2003 and October 6, 2007 there were 3,807 U.S. military fatalities.

Given the continued war and number of deaths, American political leaders voiced concern about the demographics of the deaths. Major questions any nation needs to ask itself during both peace and war include "Who serves when everyone doesn't?" and "Who dies when everyone doesn't?" For example, flames fanned early in the Iraq war in conjunction with ongoing questions surrounding President George W. Bush's service during the Vietnam War were concerned with class privilege during war. Significant enough were these concerns that Congressman Charles Rangel of New York and South Carolina Senator Fritz Hollings introduced legislation for a reintroduction of the draft.[2] The basic argument is that with an all-volunteer force, minorities—read racial minorities, the poor, and uneducated—disproportionately pay the ultimate sacrifice in military service during times of war for the nation, as they are disproportionately economically conscripted into the service. During war, the arguments hold, they become the "cannon fodder" for the nation's military conflicts. In theory, a draft would eliminate racial and economic disparity and provide a more equitable distribution across the socio-demographics of the nation. An outcome is a burden of war equally shared. With a draft, the military would represent national diversity with men (and presumably women) selected from a cross-section of America's young adults. However, the finding I report here on war fatalities shows death to be an equal-opportunity affair at least among those serving on the ground in Iraq. Once on the ground in Iraq, death among Americans fails to discriminate.

The class bias thesis

The class bias thesis is associated principally with the Vietnam War dating back to James Fallow's 1975 characterization of Vietnam as a "class" war, but it has reverberations back to WWI. It was purportedly first questioned in 1918 by Eugene Debs (Tremoglie, 2003). Applied principally to the Korean and Vietnam wars, the class-bias thesis holds that upper-class men are generally spared not only from fighting but from any participation in the armed forces and that the poor and minorities are overrepresented in the services and among the fatality rates. Research support for the thesis is mixed (Appy, 1993; Bartnett et al., 1992: Badillo and Curry, 1976; Campbell, 2003; Fallows, 1975; 1993; Foust and Bolts, 1991/92; Mayer and Hoult, 1955; Mazur, 1995; Useem, 1980; Willis, 1975; Wilson, 1995). Some research finds members of the nation fairly represented during times of war and among the dead, whereas other research suggests there has been disproportionate representation. More recently, three studies examined the thesis in the post-Vietnam era. Despite numerous service members but small numbers of fatalities relative to previous wars (e.g., Panama and the first Persian Gulf war) and military operations other than war (e.g., Haiti, Somalia, Bosnia), all three studies examined race and fatality and casualty rates and found little-to-no support for the race-bias thesis. I discuss the details for the three studies further.

First, Charles Moskos and John Sibley Butler (1996) examined U.S. combat fatalities for an 18-year period between 1975 and 1993. They found black fatality rates to be 15 percent—underrepresenting their numbers in the military at the same time periods but fairly consistent with their representation in the larger society.

Second, a similar and recent exception was the analysis of the racial distribution of service members both killed (fatalities) and wounded (casualties) in Operation Iraqi Freedom, the U.S. intervention in Iraq (Gifford, 2005). Sociologist Brian Gifford addresses the racial composition of the casualties (service member fatalities or wounded in hostile and non-hostile situations in Iraq) from three perspectives: (1) MIlitary Occupational Sorting (MOS), (2) units and MOS sorting in military contexts, and (3) the battle situation. Using 3,276 wounded and 643 killed U.S. personnel up until April 12, 2004, Gifford found no support for a race bias among African-Americans but with some Hispanic overrepresentation, especially in U.S. Army and Marine units. Moreover, casualties for this group were highest in high-intensity missions such as assault missions.[3]

The third study is a September 2005 United States Government Accountability Office (GAO) report that sought to clarify the status of demographics in the all-volunteer force (United States Government Accountability Office, 2005). In the cover letter of the report, the director of the Defense Capabilities and Management branch of GAO wrote to Senator Ike Skelton and Congressman Charles Rangel. In the letter, he highlights that events such as 9/11 and Operations Enduring Freedom (OEF), Noble Eagle, and Iraqi Freedom and a desire for recruiting high-quality personnel to serve in the military hinder recruitment overall.

Most of the report focused on demographics in general; however, 15 pages of the 155-page report dedicated space to fatalities of OIF and OEF. The major findings reveal male, junior enlisted personnel in the active Army and Marine Corps to be overrepresented among the dead. Whites were slightly overrepresented and African-Americans slightly underrepresented. A novel and new finding was the socioeconomic status of a subset of reserve service members killed or wounded. The majority came from middle socioeconomic status communities. The findings suggested there is no class bias but there is some racial/ethnic disparity.

Beyond the simple fatality counts given by the popular media, the previously noted studies and others reviewed and referenced in the body of this chapter provide some background and comparative knowledge to place the experience of fatalities in Iraq in a sociological context for those service members who paid the ultimate sacrifice for their nation in Iraq. The remaining chapter begins with a brief history of death in the U.S. military. Next, the socio-demographics of death in the military are presented from all U.S. personnel who died ($n = 3,807$) in OIF between March 19, 2003 and October 6, 2007—1,669 days from the start date to the end date with the end date included—roughly two to three per day. The time equals 4 years, 6 months, and 24 days. The days are convertible to other time units, such as 144,201,600 seconds; 2,403,360 minutes; 40,056 hours; or 238 weeks (rounded down).[4]

A brief history of death in the American military

Millions of people have died in war, and the supreme sacrifice of those in uniform has been a major consequence of American wars though our 200-plus-year history. The major events listed in Table 10.1 features the total number of deaths for principal wars and selected U.S. military engagements. More than 1 million American service members have died in military campaigns. More Americans died in the Civil War than any other war (the numbers for the Confederacy are not included). When combining the deaths of World War I, World War II, and the conflicts in Korea and Vietnam, the twentieth century was the deadliest century for Americans, with the highest fatalities for any century (Caplow and Hicks, 2002). Yet, since the U.S. involvement in Vietnam, the number of U.S. deaths is modest compared with the previous 150 years, making military service less hazardous than many other occupations. During the latter period, organizational responses to death in the ranks have broadened and deepened, with more benefits and entitlements going to the beneficiary survivors of U.S. service members (Bartone and Ender, 1994).

The end of the twentieth century proved one of the safest periods to be an American soldier. The probability of death on active duty under hostile conditions was the lowest ever. Less than 1 percent of military deaths between 1980 and 2000 resulted from hostile actions.[5] Most military deaths after Vietnam and prior to Afghanistan and Iraq occurred in peacetime, resulting from training accidents such as helicopter crashes during humanitarian and disaster relief efforts. Accidental deaths, the leading cause of death of U.S. service personnel, happen while service members are vacationing or driving into the office. Other causes of death, in addition to training accidents, include homicide, illness, suicide, and terrorist attacks. Some deaths of American service personnel remain undetermined at this writing, and some are missing in action (MIA).

Approximately 229 hostile action deaths of U.S. military active-duty personnel occurred since 1980, with 33,316 deaths occurring between 1980 and 2000.[6] Accidental deaths were the leading cause of death and represented more than half of all deaths for a given year. The second largest number of deaths per

Table 10.1 Worldwide American military fatalities by principal wars and military engagements other than war, 1775–1996

War/Conflict/Operation/Incident	Total Deaths*
Revolutionary War (1775–1783)	4,435
War of 1812 (1812–1815)	2,260
Mexican War (1846–1848)	13,283
Civil War (1861–1865 representing Union Forces Only)	364,511
Spanish-American War (1898–1902)	2,446
World War I (1917–1918)	116,516
World War II (1941–1946)	405,399
Korean War (1950–1953)	36,516
Vietnam Conflict (1964–1973)	58,198
Iranian Hostage Rescue Mission (April 25, 1980)	8
Lebanon Peacekeeping (1982–1984)	265
Urgent Fury, Grenada (1983)	19
Gander, Newfoundland air crash disaster (1985 soldiers returning from a peacekeeping mission in the Sinai)	248
Just Cause, Panama (1989)	23
Desert Shield/Storm, Persian Gulf War (1990–1991)	383
Restore Hope, Somalia (1992–1994)	43
Uphold Democracy, Haiti (1994–1996)	4
Total	1,004,557

Source: Adapted from the U.S. Department of Defense, 2007
Note: *Includes both hostile and non-hostile deaths

100,000 military personnel resulted from illnesses, followed closely by self-inflicted deaths. Self-inflicted deaths, homicides, and pending/undetermined deaths accounted for the remaining and fewest per 100,000 deaths for the same period. All non-hostile military deaths had been on a slight decline for 22 years; however, the size of the military population had been steadily decreasing as well. Accidental deaths had dramatically reduced since 1980, by just less than half. All of these numbers and sources of death require closer monitoring as those individuals who have died in service deserve social justice and the collective perception of what happens in the military impacts recruitment and other national security matters.

Military personnel deaths vary by service. The U.S. Army had the highest number of deaths and was the largest of the four services during the twentieth century. The Marines had the fewest. However, the Marines often accounted for the largest number of deaths per 100,000, suffering 233.9 deaths per 100,000 in 1984 following the bombing of the Marine barracks in Lebanon the previous year. In their demographic analysis of 14 years of causes of death among U.S. military personnel, researchers found that the young (17–24), male, white, lower-ranked enlisted Marines suffered the highest rates of accidental (unintentional deaths) (Helmkamp and Kennedy, 1996).

The least likely to suffer an accidental death were older than 35, non-black or white, female naval officers. For diseases, black, male, senior noncommissioned officers (NCOs) older than 35 years of age in the Army had the highest rates. Young, female, non-black or exclusively white Marines had the lowest rate. For suicides, the numbers distributed rather equally except for males and enlisted service members having higher rates. The lowest rates for suicide were female naval officers who were non-black or white. Finally, the highest homicide rates in the U.S. military between 1980 and 1993 were for young, black, female, junior enlisted Marines. The lowest rates of homicides were for older, non-black or white Air Force officers. Of special noteworthiness was the reverse trend for homicide and suicide rates among males and females. Suicide rates in the military were higher for males than for females; however, homicide rates were higher for females than for males. This latter rate was also higher than for civilian females for the same period.

Clearly, the risk of injury or death remains a major demand of the military lifestyle in both peace and war. Social research on death in the military, however, has continued quietly.[7] The U.S. military has established and refined elaborate support systems to manage death in the ranks (U.S. Army Memorial Affairs and Casualty Operations Center, 2003). In the years prior to 9/11, research on Notification NCOs, Casualty Notification Officers, Casualty Assistance Officers (CAOs), mortuary workers, and a host of other rituals and organizational responses involving death in the military, described the process of casualty operations (see Ender, Bartone, and Kolditz, 2003; McCarroll et al., 2002). A good deal of knowledge about mass fatality experiences emerged out of research following the 1985 Gander, Newfoundland, Canada air disaster in which a chartered airline crashed and burned during takeoff carrying U.S. service members home to Fort Campbell, Kentucky from a 6-month peacekeeping mission in the Sinai.

More recently, new books are emerging in the aftermath of Operation Iraqi Freedom. Notably among them are *Soldier Dead*, a meticulous study of the recovering of service member remains and the process of recovery, identification, return, burial, and how the nation, community, and individuals remember and memorialize the dead (Sledge, 2005). Another book titled *The Remains of War* deals with the POW/MIA-body politics of the Vietnam and the post-Vietnam "wars" (Hawley, 2005). Finally, a recent book titled *Shane Comes Home* detailed the life and post-death life of the first person killed in Operation Iraqi Freedom—Marine 1LT Therrel Shane Childers—his immediate and extended family, the community, and the casualty assistance team that responded to his death (Buck, 2005). It is a compelling ethnographic of sorts that accounts as well as tributes; the book somewhat foreshadows the emerging e-memorializations of those killed in Iraq and Afghanistan that pepper the Internet.

Deaths in Operation Iraqi Freedom

Before beginning the analysis of the socio-demographics of American service members who died in support of OIF, it is important to recognize and respect the thousands of others that have died in the Southwest Asian centered Global War on Terrorism.

Operation Enduring Freedom

OEF is the official name given to the U.S. military response to the September 11, 2001 terrorist attacks on U.S. soil in New York and Washington, DC and over the skies of Pennsylvania. OEF is typically referred to as the war in Afghanistan, but it actually has three locales: Afghanistan, the Philippines, and Africa. Begun on October 7, 2001, it is an ongoing effort. At this writing, at least 1 service member has died in Djibouti and 10 in the Philippines. Numerous service members from countries around the world have died in support of OEF.[8] For the American forces in and around Afghanistan, the Republic of the Philippines, Southwest Asia (not Iraq), Africa, and other locations at the end of 2006, there had been 351 fatalities and 1,062 wounded. Most of the deaths were hostility-related involving a range of demographics but with the larger percentages comprising 25- to 30-year-olds, whites, males, junior enlisted, and active-duty service members.

Others in Operation Iraqi Freedom

In 2003, the official White House web site noted that "nearly 50" nations were a part of the Coalition Forces. However, not all of those nations provided military support. At the end of December 2006, 17 nations reported service members having died while in support of OIF.[9] One British soldier is Sergeant Graham Hesketh. Born in Liverpool, England on 1 December, 1971, he grew up in Runcorn in Cheshire. He died from injuries sustained from a roadside IED in Basra City in southern Iraq. He was engaged to a soldier also serving in Iraq, and he is the father of two children, a 7-year-old daughter and a 3-year-old son.

Similarly, international contractors comprise a significant feature of those participating in Operation Iraqi Freedom. A partial list of contractor deaths includes 42 countries with 377 deaths at the end of December 2006—147 American.[10] One typical death was Rudy Mesa, a 56-year-old retired police officer from Maxwell, California who was in Iraq working for Dyncorp

International helping train Iraqi police officers and was killed by an IED on May 9, 2006 (Liscano, 2006).

Journalists are another group of outsiders in Iraq in large numbers. The not-for-profit Reporters without Borders for Press Freedom (2007), a media watchdog organization, reported 139 journalists killed in Iraq at the end of December 2006 since the beginning of the war. Most of the victims had been Iraqi journalists (Balmar, 2007). One Iraqi journalist was Jassim Al Qais, of *Al Siyada*, an Iraqi daily paper. He and his son were shot to death on 22 June, 2005, as they traveled on a road near Baghdad, Iraq (Reporters without Borders for Press Freedom, 2007).

Estimates of the number of Iraqis killed since the beginning of the war vary considerably from as low as 52,000 to 600,000.[11] A *New York Times* story lists four major sources of estimates of Iraqi deaths (Cox, 2007). The lowest number is 52,000 Iraqi deaths between March 2003 and December 2006 from the *Iraq Body Count*.[12] For example, Faliha Ahmed Hassan was a women's organization leader reported as killed by gunfire on either 27 or 28 October, 2006, in Hawija, Iraq. Two news sources—*CNN* and *Kuwait News Agency KUNA*—are listed as references. Next, the *New York Times* article cites an off-the-cuff remark by the Iraqi Minister of Health reporting 150,000 deaths in Iraq since the war began. A mortality study undertaken by Johns Hopkins University and Al Mustansiriya University in Baghdad, with the assistance of researchers at the Massachusetts Institute of Technology, estimated approximately 600,000 deaths between March 2003 and December 2006 (Burnham et al., 2006). They predicted in an earlier study that between March 2003 and October 2004 approximately 100,000 killed (Roberts et al., 2004). Finally, the web site *iCasualties.org* (White, 2007) estimates 26,002 military, police, and civilian Iraqi deaths in an 8-month period from April to December 2006 based on Iraqi government sources. The point of providing these sources is to acknowledge attempts to account for deaths of the many others in and around Iraq. The debates on the death count will likely continue long after the war has ended.

Non-governmental organizations (NGO) are another group working in Iraq. Again, this is a difficult number to ascertain. Numerous groups assisted in Iraq—some as small as two or three people, especially at the local level, such as the *Iraqi Red Crescent Society*. The NGO Coordination Committee in Iraq (2007) estimated in October 2006 that 81 aid workers were killed in Iraq since March 2003.

By the end of December 2006, 22,057 American service members had been wounded in Iraq owing to hostile action. One argument for the large number of wounded is that war has become less lethal—a larger proportion of people survive wounds in Iraq that would have been fatal in previous wars because of instantaneous communications, swifter transports, and medical advancements both in the field and in the rear (Gawande, 2004). Their socio-demographics look similar to those dead reported in more detail below. Terry Rodgers might represent the typical wounded American service member having served in Iraq. He is a 21-year-old, white male and from an upper-working-class background in Rockville, Maryland. He suffered a broken femur, broken jaw and cheekbone, significant muscle blown away from his right calf, deafness in the right ear, and partial blindness in his right eye (Carlson, 2005). The wounded include civilian government workers as well. An atypical example is Sarah Latona. A 42-year-old Army and Air Force Exchange Service employee at the time; she was wounded on October 9, 2004, by a roadside IED in Iraq while she was driving a bus to Kuwait to transport stock for the post exchange (PX) (Barr, 2005). She is the first recipient of the Defense Medal of Freedom—the civilian equivalent of the military's Purple Heart.

American service member deaths in Iraq

By Christmas Day 2006, U.S. military deaths in Iraq exceeded the 2,973 who died in the terrorist attacks on September 11, 2001. The number of deaths quickly exceeded 3,000 by the beginning of 2007. Among the military deaths are seven Department of Defense (DOD), Department of Air Force, and Department of Army civilians killed in Iraq. Analyzed here are the fatality data from March 19, 2003 through October 7, 2007 ($n = 3,807$) along socio-demographic characteristics to include age, military branch, MOS, race, type of death, rank, home of record and social class, and gender. The dataset originates from a primary source—the *Department of Defense Personnel & Procurement Statistics* website (U.S. Department of Defense, 2007).

The files at the DOD web site are publicly available and viewable in various formats including tables, pdf, and Excel spreadsheet files. For analytical purposes, I converted the master Excel spreadsheet file and uploaded it into a statistical database. There were numerous omissions, misspellings, and other syntax errors in the official data source. Prior to conversion, I scrubbed the data for these errors by using sources on the Internet at the time. For example, if a hometown was missing, I Googled the service member's full name and located at least two independent sources to verify the appropriate hometown. Organizations with web sites at the time that were useful included iraqwarheroes. com; fallenheroesmemorial.com; icasualties.org; iraqwar-memorial.com; cnn. com; legacy.com, and militarycity.com, among others. Numerous newspapers around the country carry online obituaries about many service members, and many provided exceptional and detailed obituaries and follow-up stories with family members and friends—especially hometown newspapers of the next of kin. Specific posts and units have web sites commemorating the fallen service member. For example, the Association of Graduates at the United States Military Academy at West Point maintains an elaborate, intimate, and detailed web site of remembrances of graduates who have died in support of the GWOT at aogusma.org.[13]

The official DOD file provides unique information compared to the many web sites listed above, such as race and MOS. Most of the web sites were user-friendly and relied on the same demographic data that I use. The web sites were usually updated daily and provided colorful, up-to-date graphics of most of the topics I cover. I write here in the past tense, but I anticipate that such web sites will remain updated and expanded and become normative in American society to commemorate and memorialize people who have died. However, unlike the other web sites that provide primarily univariate statistics; the data below were examined for bivariate and comparative purposes. The data below represent a broader research tradition along with some historical perspective on the variables under scrutiny including age, branch of service, MOS, rank, type of death, hometown, and gender. Finally, the study of social class is an additional and historically novel variable in the present study. Overall, the findings are consistent with the book's overall theme: The diversity of service member fatalities in Iraq is consistent with the other forms of diversity studied in the previous chapters. Death in the ranks in Iraq is an equal-opportunity experience. While some groups are more or less overrepresented, the American military fatalities in Iraq look similar to the military, America, and in some ways, similar to fatalities of past American wars.

Social demography of American fatalities and Operation Iraqi Freedom

Age

Young people have long made the ultimate sacrifice during times of war. Iraq is no exception. For 3,807 service members who died supporting OIF, the overall average (mean) age is 26. In the first Persian Gulf War, the mean age was 26.7. In Vietnam, the mean age was 22.6. Nineteen is the popular modal death age from the Vietnam War. However, the most common single age at death was actually 20. For Iraq, the modal death was 21 years of age (12.9 percent) followed by 20 (11 percent) and 22 (10.1 percent). No other ages have double-digit percentages. In terms of age, Iraq is much like Vietnam.

Deaths differ, however, in range of ages. For the 3,807 deaths, the youngest were 18 ($n = 30$; .8 percent) and 19 ($n = 219$; 5.8 percent) years of age. The two eldest are 59 years of age—a range of 41 years between the youngest and eldest fatalities. The median death age is 24 (the age in the middle from youngest to oldest). Twenty-two service members 50 years old and older died in Iraq. What accounts somewhat for much of the range and the higher average age is the number of reserve and National Guard service members who served in Iraq: They are typically older.

Mean age deaths differed by service component: National Guard was 30.3, reserves 29, and active duty 25.1. There was also greater deviation in ages within the Guard and reserves compared to the active component. For example, the Guard and reserve were more likely to have troops killed in their 50s and had a higher percentage of service members killed who were older than 40. The Guard and reserve introduce a broader range of ages in service and death in Iraq.

Note that deaths in Afghanistan were of older service members—a mean age of 29—but this was probably attributed to the SF and helicopter pilots, both of which tend to be older; Special Forces (SF) tend to be senior NCOs, and pilots tend to be warrant officers, first coming up through the junior enlisted ranks.

Branch of service

The branches of the U.S. military have traditionally shared the burden of American wars. For example, between 1941 and 1946, there were 405,399 U.S. deaths in WWII (Beebe and De Bakey, 1952). Of those, the U.S. Army had 302,268 hostile and non-hostile (disease, suicide, etc.) deaths, or 75 percent of deaths were Army, and the remaining 25 percent were from the Marines and Navy, as the Air Force did not formally exist as a branch of the military until 1947.

The U.S. Army and Marines continued to share the major burden of the war in Iraq. Of the 3,807 deaths, 71.3 percent (n = 2,715) were Army, and 25.4 percent (n =968) were Marines. For comparisons, the Army comprised 44.9 percent of the total U.S. armed forces in 2007. The USMC comprised 10.3 percent of the total force. The Navy had 84 fatalities (2.2 percent) and the Air Force 40 (1.1 percent). The Navy comprised 20.4 percent of the total military force, and the Air Force comprised 22.5 percent of the total force in 2007.

The active duty military—members of the armed forces full-time in uniform during peace and wartime—comprised the majority of deaths (81 percent). The U.S. active duty represented roughly 63 percent of the total force in 2007. However, significant components of the reserve and National Guard—citizen service members—have died as well: 7.5 and 11.5 percents, respectively. The U.S. reserve component of the military comprised roughly 17 of the total force available to the nation, and the U.S. National Guard comprised roughly 20 percent of the total U.S. force. Various representations exist across services, but the Army is paying a larger burden to the war, including among fatalities.

Military occupational specialty

The MOS is a system of codes used in categorizing career fields in the U.S. armed forces. Essentially, the codes, usually numeric and alphabetic combinations, are not unlike U.S. Department of Labor Dictionary of Occupational Titles (DOT) used to categorize civilian jobs. Examples might be 613.462–014 for Soaking-Pit Operator or 700.684.014 for Bracelet Maker. U.S. Army recruiting web sites list more than 150 jobs or career fields for entry-level service members; technically, there are considerably more.

During WWI, WWII, Korea, and Vietnam, the rates of death of the various arms of the military varied primarily because of the operational occupations they entailed. Essentially, your job often defined your mortality salience. In previous wars, combat specialties were by design the closest to danger, followed by combat support and then combat service support. The tactical environment in Iraq is slightly different from other wars, placing everyone in the military theater of operation in a significant degree of danger—granting that some provinces of Iraq were relatively more dangerous than others. Some level of danger also linked to quantity and quality of being inside or outside the FOB, again, often defined by MOS.

Among the 3,807 who died in support of Operation Iraqi Freedom, there were more than 322 MOS occupational codes listed. Among them, 181 had two or more deaths listed. Many had no MOS identified. The largest number were 11B (pronounced "eleven bravo")—Army Infantryman ($n = 804$).[14] Overall, these numbers are, however, consistent with the American Infantry Divisions in WWII, where riflemen comprised roughly 35 percent of those killed, wounded, and missing (Beebe and De Bakey, 1952:42). American Iraq deaths reflect WWII, although far fewer in number.

Military rank

The military enlisted-to-officer percentage in the U.S. armed forces is 85 percent to 15 percent, respectively. This percentage can vary some by branch of service (Segal and Segal, 2004). In OIF, the largest number of deaths occurred at the junior enlisted levels—E4 ($n = 1,109$) followed by sergeants (E5; $n = 753$) and E3 ($n = 727$) (U.S. Department of Defense, 2007).[15] Junior enlisted accounted for the largest number percentage of deaths (52.9 percent) followed by NCOs (37.7 percent), officers (7.9 percent), and warrant officers (1.5 percent). Officers comprised 5.4 percent of all killed, wounded, and missing in WWII (Beebe and De Bakey, 1952:42). For comparison, the enlisted in WWII and OIF are similarly overrepresented among the dead.

Race and ethnicity

Race and ethnicity remain one of the most contentious topics regarding equity among Americans in general and the war in Iraq more specifically. The data reported here on race/ethnic representation is consistent with that found by Gifford (2005) 2 years into the war. That is, race and ethnicity are fairly equally distributed among fatalities and wounded with the exception of some overrepresentation of whites and Hispanics.

In American society, whites comprised the majority (75.1 percent) in 2000. As of December 2004, whites comprised 67 percent of the total military force, including active duty, reserve, and National Guard,[16] and they represented 74.6 percent (n = 2,839) of the fatalities in Iraq as of October 6, 2007. Hispanics comprised 12.5 of the U.S. population in 2000, 9 percent of the total U.S. military force, and accounted for 10.8 percent of the fatalities in Iraq. Blacks comprised 12.3 of the U.S. population in 2000, 17 percent of the total military, and accounted for 9.4 percent (n = 357) of the American soldier fatalities of Iraq.

Other groups including Asian Americans, Pacific Islanders, American Indians, and Alaskan Natives total 4 percent of the total military force. Collectively, they totaled 4.6 percent of the U.S. population with the largest group, Asian Americans, encompassing 3.8 percent of the U.S. population at the time. They collectively accounted for 3.7 percent (n = 139) of the military fatalities. Although the multi-racial/ethnic category (two or more races) is currently not available for military personnel socio-demographics, the U.S. Census as of 2000 did include this category: 2.4 percent of the population (almost 7,000,000 Americans) checked the category. The category is included for fatalities in Iraq. Among the dead Americans having served in OIF, 1.5 percent (n = 59) were listed as multi-racial/ethnic.

Data on racial/ethnic categories of Americans killed in previous military operations is available (United States Government Accountability Office, 2005:116). Comparatively, white deaths have increased slightly from Korea (80 percent) to Vietnam (86 percent) and then decreased with the Persian Gulf War (76 percent) and OIF (74.2 percent). African-Americans deaths rose and fell: Korea (8 percent) to Vietnam (12 percent), the Persian Gulf War (17 percent), and OIF (9.7 percent). Hispanics have increased from Korea (2 percent) and Vietnam (1 percent) to the Persian Gulf War (4 percent) and OIF (11 percent). All other groups remain in the 1-percent range (United States Government Accountability Office, 2005:116).[17] Whites and Hispanics are certainly higher today; however, across history, whites have died in lower numbers. American minorities are integrating more fully into American society and so too are their numbers among the dead, reflecting their societal representations and acculturations. Minorities are historically paying an increased burden in American wars, paying the ultimate sacrifice for their citizenship as Americans.

Race and ethnic deaths have become more diverse in the military. This social fact points to an increasingly diverse military with service members in all ranks and branches representing the mosaic of races in the United States and the relational declining significance of race and ethnicity in the U.S. military.

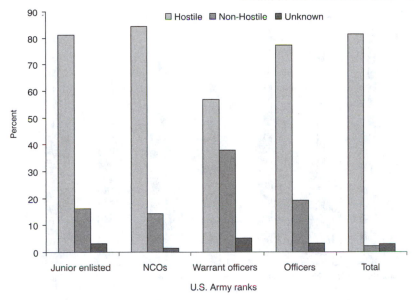

Chart 10.1 Percentage distribution of types of American service member deaths in OIF by ranks (*n* = 3,807)

Source: Adapted from U.S. Department of Defense. 2007

Note: Bars may not equal 100 percent due to rounding error

Types of death

Deaths in wars occur through both hostile actions such as combat and being killed or wounded by a range of weapons originating with the enemy or through friendly fire. Similarly, non-hostile deaths occur in war zones as well, including diseases, natural causes, traffic accidents, homicides, accidental discharges of weapons, and suicides among other causes. Again, in WWII, the U.S. Army experienced 302,268 deaths. Of those, 210,343 were official battle deaths, including those who died as POWs. Non-battle deaths accounted for 65,219 deaths, of which 14,243 were reported as "disease"-related and another 50,976 from "injuries." Injury in these cases included "…homicides, suicides, executions, and drownings…" among aircraft and other accidents and diseases (Beebe and De Bakey, 1952:20–21). Almost one-fourth (22 percent) of the U.S. Army deaths in WWII were non-battle-related.

In Iraq, by October 2007, hostile and non-hostile deaths looked similar to WWII. The distributions in Chart 10.1 show percentage comparisons of hostile and non-hostile deaths for service members (*n* = 3,807) who served in OIF by their ranks. A third category of "unknown" exists, as many deaths were still under investigation (pending) amid the fog of war where cause of death can be less than clear. More than 80 percent of the deaths were categorized as hostile. Non-hostile deaths accounted for 16.2 percent and "unknowns" just

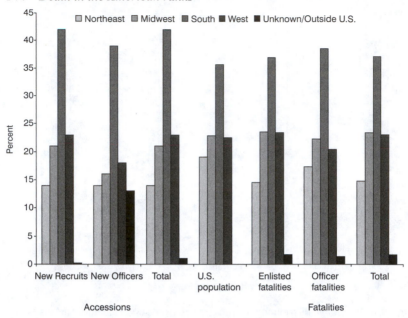

Chart 10.2 Percentage distribution of U.S. regional of accessions (2002), U.S. population (2000), and OIF fatalities (til October 6, 2007) for enlisted, officer, and total service members (*n* = 3,807).

Source: Adapted from Segal and Segal, 2004

Note: Bars may not equal 100 percent due to rounding error

less than 3 percent. The Department of Defense did provide information on the non-hostile deaths in OIF—as of October 6, 2007. Among them, 434 involved accidents, 69 illnesses related, 18 homicides, 128 self-inflicted (suicides), seven undetermined, and 45 pending (U.S. Department of Defense, 2007).

Home of record, region of country, and population size

Many of the footnotes listed previously have web sites that provide a distribution of the fatalities in Iraq by state of residence. None, however, at the time gave comparisons to provide perspective on the deaths and their representation to other factors—most important, the accessions of service members. The data in Chart 10.2 show the United States's regional distribution of military accessions of new military recruits and new officers in the U.S. military in 2002 (Segal and Segal, 2004),[18] the U.S. population in 2000 (U.S. Census Bureau. 2001b), and OIF fatalities serving between 2003 to 2006.

Overall, the data show no outstanding differences between the groups. The deaths of service members in OIF by the four regions of the country represent service member accessions controlling for both enlisted and officer accessions

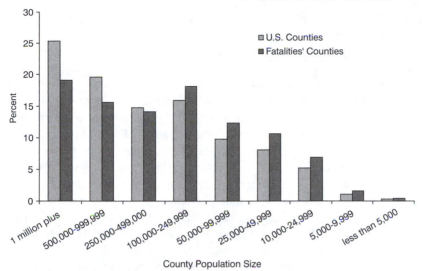

Chart 10.3 Percentage distribution of U.S. county population size (July 2001) and OIF service member fatalities' by county home of record (n = 3,807)

Source: Adapted from U.S. Census Bureau, 2001a

Note: Bars may not equal 100 percent due to rounding error

(United States Government Accountability Office, 2005:122).[19] For the most part, American service members by region reflect representations when they came into the Army. Southern enlisted service member fatalities are less than accessions, made up, however, by Midwestern fatalities. Officer fatalities are higher than accessions. However, this is likely because of a high number of "unknowns" or outside the U.S. accession origins that changed once they came into service.

The data in Chart 10.3 present a distribution of nine U.S. population sizes from July 2001 and OIF service member fatalities by county home of record (n = 3,807) (U.S. Census Bureau, 2001a). There is a shift in underrepresentation of fatalities between the three largest population sizes toward overrepresentation in the six smaller population sizes—again pointing to some rural overrepresentation among fatalities.

Social class

As any student of an introductory sociology course can tell you, social class in the United States is a complicated measure. There is trifling agreement on what it is and how it is measured. It has both objective and subjective dimensions. Income, education, occupation and occupational prestige, father's occupation, and neighborhood are all objective elements of social class. Likewise, people's subjective perception of *social class*—what they believe their social class to be—varies. What people perceive as reality does not necessarily jive with the objective reality of their social class background. However, it is important to gauge social class.

The home of record information of service members is measurable via the socioeconomic class of American service member fatalities who died serving in support of OIF. Researchers at the GAO (2005) conducted a socioeconomic analysis of 482 reservists who died in both OIF and OEF as of May 28, 2005. They found 13 percent from high estimated socioeconomic status, 58 percent from medium, and 29 percent from low; their median income of $44,500 roughly matched the $44,300 of the United States at the time.[20]

As a proxy for social class, I conducted a similar analysis as the GAO study. I assigned the yearly medium household income for counties in the United States in 2003 to the U.S. service member fatalities associated with OIF based on their home of record.[21] For example, the wealthiest median household income in the United States in 2003 by county was Douglas County, Colorado, at $92,732. The poorest was Buffalo County, South Dakota, at $17,003. The median household income in the United States in 2003 was $45,016 and $46,326 in 2006.

Next, the U.S. Census Bureau aggregates the incomes into manageable categories for analysis and comparison. The Census uses quintile categories: five categories where in 2005 dollars the lowest fifth earns $18,499 or less; second fifth earns $18,500 to $34,737; middle fifth earns $34,738 to $55,330; fourth fifth earns $55,331 to $88,029; and the highest fifth earns $88,030 to $157,175 (U.S. Census Bureau. 2007a).[22]

These categories correspond roughly to what sociologists would classify as "The Underclass," "The Working Poor," "The Working Class," "The Lower Middle Class," and "The Upper Middle Class" (Cherlin, 2005; Henslin, 2005; Rose, 2000; Thompson and Hickey, 2005). The underclass household typically might lack a high school diploma, adults are chronically unemployed or part-time employed, rely on some form of government assistance, and likely rent their home. Their nutritional diet is poor.

The working poor have some high school education and are typically laborers or service workers, perhaps working multiple part-time jobs. They, too, rent their home and have a poor nutritional diet.

The working class household has adult high school graduates, and the adults are employed in factory-type work, craftwork, clerical, or some other low-end service job. They, too, rent although some might own their home.

The lower middle class has a high school diploma and some college, perhaps vocational training. They are semi-professionals, service industry managers, and lower level leaders. They may link to unions. Their standard of living is higher than the workers, and they own a modest home.

The upper middle class are graduates of the nation's colleges and universities and may have some graduate education. They are the leadership of institutions in medicine, education, and corporate America. They are professionals who lead and supervise the people of the other classes in varied fields.

Finally, the "5 Percent Club" are the nation's elites. They own the means of production and control the major institutions and organizations in society. They are graduates of the elite universities and own multiple homes. Their incomes are $158,000 and higher in 2005 dollars.

There are roughly 3,066 counties in the U.S. including Alaska and Hawaii. Louisiana refers to counties as parishes and Alaska as boroughs. Some states have city-counties (Virginia). In the dataset of OIF service member fatalities, there are roughly 1,000 named counties. Many names represent multiple counties such as various Orange countries located in California, New York, Florida, and Texas and different Marion counties in Florida, Illinois, Indiana, Kentucky, Mississippi, Oregon, and West Virginia. Among the fatalities, 69 (1.8 percent) had cities as their home of record that fall into more than one county such as Columbus, Ohio and Austin, Texas. The latter are not included in the analysis. Additionally, 63 (1.7 percent) fatalities had cities outside the United States as their home of records, such as Western American Samoa and Puerto

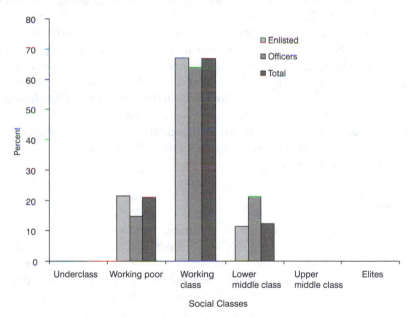

Chart 10.4 Percentage distribution of socio-economic class backgrounds of OIF fatalities by rank of service members

Sources: Adapted from U.S. Census Bureau, 2007a and Thompson, and Hickey, 2005

Note: Bars may not equal 100 percent due to rounding error

Rico. These places have no median household incomes available and so, too, are excluded from the analysis.

The data on the household incomes of the home of record of the counties of the service member fatalities in support of Operation Iraq Freedom yielded 3,675 valid cases. The minimum income was $20,520 to the highest income at $92,732, a $72,212 range. The median (and modal) income was $41,486—just less than $5,000 less than the median income for the United States ($46,326). The mean income is $42,987. The data in Chart 10.4 show the distributions of OIF American service member fatalities across the six different socioeconomic classes controlling for enlisted service members and officers.

No service members had homes of record in counties where the median incomes represent the underclass or the elites. Concomitantly, only two service members (both enlisted) had homes of record in counties were the median income represented the upper middle class. Overall, the largest group (two-thirds of the majority; 66.8 percent) of service members had home of records in working-class counties with median incomes between $34,738 and $55,330. The working poor with median household incomes between $18,500 and $34,737 represented the next largest group (20.9 percent).

Finally, the lower-middle class, with median household incomes between $55,331 and $88,029, represented just more than 12 (12.2 percent). Controlling for military rank, in this case, enlisted service members versus officers yields no change. The majority of officers have more formal education than enlisted service members; generally, they have at least a 4-year baccalaureate degree, placing them educationally and economically in the middle class. However, there was only a 7-percent change from the working poor to lower middle class for officers of which officers listed as their home of record. Essentially, service members fatalities of Iraq are highly representative of family backgrounds of the working class and working poor of America—certainly not the underclass or the upper middle class.

Sex and gender

Women serve and women die in the military. As of October 6, 2007, 3,807 American fatalities resulted in OIF—84 of them women (2.2 percent of all the deaths). A closer examination reveals few significant differences, but the percentages conflate because of the small numbers of women. Female deaths were more likely to be from the Army than men, and women suffered more non-hostile and unknown deaths (35.7 percent) than men (18.1 percent). For example, the eldest female death was a 47-year-old U.S. Army soldier named Major Gloria Dean Davis from St. Louis, Missouri. Her death in Iraq was reported as a suicide. The women did not represent every state, with most coming from Illinois ($n = 8$) and California ($n = 7$). The largest single percentage MOS of females killed were 88M—Motor Transport Operators—

essentially, MPs; military police ($n = 9$) and truck drivers ($n = 9$), followed by the Quartermaster branch including 92Ys (Supply Specialists; $n = 5$) and 92As (Automated Logistical Specialists; $n = 5$). The women who died are more likely to be women of color: 39.3 percent versus 25.1 percent for men. Hispanic women died in a higher proportion than their representation in the Army, while blacks died in a lower proportion. Women who died were similar to men in age (both close to 26 years), rank, and socioeconomic background.

Discussion and conclusion

In this the final chapter presenting some empirical data, the focus is on death in the military. Service member deaths in Iraq anchor in the broader literature on the class bias thesis. The major focus of the chapter assessed sociocultural variables connected with American service members' fatalities connected to OIF. The overall finding shows equal opportunity in death in Iraq. Death does not discriminate overwhelming against any particular group. Service members have an equitable probability of being a fatality in service to OIF if one is in-country. As Williams and Smith reflected of casualties in WWII, "War is a special province of chance, and the gods of luck rise to full stature on the field of battle" (1949:83). While some individuals in particular social categories are more prone to death, such as young people and men, just as many are likely to escape harm's way.

Groups representing all social characteristics have been killed in Iraq from U.S. service members to non-American troops, civilian government workers, civilian contractors from the United States and other nations, NGO representatives, and certainly Iraqis. Young American service members were overrepresented among those killed, looking much like Vietnam. However, older service members have died as well, more akin to the first Gulf War and WWII. There is an overrepresentation of active-duty Army and Marines and, within both, the infantrymen. However, reserve and National Guard and service members from other branches of the armed forces died as well. Likewise, junior enlisted service members are overrepresented among the dead. In terms of race and ethnicity, the numbers are in fair proportion to the numbers in previous wars, the services in general, and the society, respectively. Whites have been overrepresented among service members killed in wars. Similarly, whites have died in larger numbers during peacetime in more recent years. In recent wars, American minorities have fluctuated in paying the ultimate sacrifice in increased numbers. Those numbers will likely continue to fluctuate as the nation and the military become more equitable in their treatment of all American peoples. Race and ethnicity, more than any other social institution, have shown a declining significance.

Hostile deaths in Iraq dominated. Nevertheless, large numbers of non-hostile accidents reflect the deprivation of the WWII context and the subsequent pattern of death. Service members' fatalities in Iraq look much like where enlisted service members and officers come from in the United States. The military is a mostly working-class organization, with most service members coming from working-class backgrounds, including officers who climbed the economic social mobility ladder through military service. There does appear to be a high concentration of service members from working poor backgrounds among fatalities in Iraq. The social class backgrounds of service members helps to understand representations across the larger Army, military, and American society. Finally, while female service members died in Iraq, American men were paying a disproportionate burden of service in OIF. Yet, there is limited public discussion that the Global War on Terror is primarily a male war.

U.S. Army Specialist Erik W. Hayes typifies the American fatality in Iraq. Born on November 14, 1980, he grew up in Harney, Maryland. According to one web site, he played Agent Mulder in a Christmas play. He attended a small high school in Blue Ridge Summit, Pennsylvania, and after high school graduation worked as a laborer before he joined the active duty Army 5 days before the September 11, 2001 attacks (Hare 2004). He was assigned to the 2nd Battalion, 2nd Infantry, 1st Infantry Division, based in Vilseck, Germany. His MOS was an 11C, pronounced "Eleven Charlie"—essentially an Indirect Fire Infantryman. On November 29, 2004—2 weeks after his twenty-fourth birthday—in Al Miqdadihay, Iraq, an IED detonated near his military vehicle and killed him. He was young, white, male, and single and from a working-class background. Described as concerned about others, Erik genuinely lived to serve, showed ambition, and looked to the military to provide money for college. Had he lived longer he may have been a veterinarian, a medical technician, or a Sergeant Major.

11 Conclusion

Soldiers, minds, and American society

> I personally don't see why we are asked to do these surveys. Is it because someone cares what goes through a soldier's mind or is it that they want to have statistical data for our gossip happy media? I doubt whoever puts out this survey will take a look, a real honest look, at these surveys with the best interest in mind *for the soldiers*.
>
> (25-year-old African-American male E4, married with one child)

This quotation returns to an American soldier who completed a survey in Iraq. He is a harsh critic. I have, however, met his concerns. I am optimistic that this book answers the proverbial mail put forth in his comments—the best interest of the soldiers. I am curious and concerned about what goes on in the mind of soldiers. The preceding pages provide an honest look into the experience of soldiers, for soldiers, and from the perspective of the soldiers. Truth is certainly in the best interest of the soldiers.

This book sought to fulfill three purposes: to represent the collective experiences of American soldiers in Iraq from their perspective, to serve as a vehicle to broader audiences to educate them about war from the perspective of the American soldier and, finally, to provide insights into the relative diversity of American soldiers today. Overall, the findings concomitantly both confirm and contravene traditional knowledge about American soldiers. In addition, the findings subvert some dominant belief systems about American soldiers in war and in general. In this chapter, I conclude with the more salient findings from the study, air some limitations of the findings, share some broader observations of the current generation of service members and a personal statement on the war, and return to the diversity theme at the intersection of the armed forces and society.

After introducing the three study groups of U.S. Army soldiers, Chapter Two begins the book with an examination of boredom in Iraq. Sociologists studying soldiers in war have long identified boredom as a social reality of war. The boredom factor and its five constituent elements—isolation, cultural deprivation, privacy, utilization, and spatio-temporal reality—provides a window to view their experience. Mundane boredom remains a salient factor for American soldiers. Soldiers in Iraq in 2004 had much in common with veterans of previous wars dating back to WWII. Yet, there are some nuanced differences as well. The novelty of Iraq is too much privacy, and the Creeping Bedouin syndrome of the first Persian Gulf War has metamorphosed into a *Groundhog Day*-like experience in Iraq—essentially, a creeping banality. In addition to an increase in privacy, isolation has changed. An electronic inclusiveness connected soldiers in Iraq to the world. In this information-rich environment, soldiers are over-stimulated. Meaning is degraded. Information becomes noisy and confusing. Soldiers initially experience overload rather than boredom, but ultimately they are left bored. Further, soldiers experience boredom differently across Iraq.

A tradition of social psychological elements continues to be salient for American soldiers in Iraq. The elements include perceptions of war preparation, satisfaction, morale, and day-to-day experiences. Similar to boredom, soldiers share similar levels of each dimension with their peers of the past, but they differ some today as well. Many soldiers reported preparation, morale, and satisfaction as both high and low. Similarly, soldiers differed on the length of their workday. Senior-ranked soldiers worked longer days and generally had a more positive experience than the enlisted. What should fascinate the reader, however, is that individual soldiers believed their personal morale and preparation to be better than others such as military units and the larger Army in Iraq. This belies findings of earlier generations of soldiers and relative deprivation. American soldiers from previous wars thought others to be better off than they—that they were not as well off. This perception has reversed today: Individual soldiers believe they are better off than the whole.

The next few chapters compared and contrasted the attitudes of soldiers toward U.S. -specific American domestic and broader social issues and showed that soldiers are both politically oriented and politically diverse. Their divergences are along the liberal-conservative continuum we would expect for civilians as well as with some decisive orientations. Overall, no singular attitude prevails. There is no "military mind" on matters associated with domestic and social issues.

Turning to foreign policy issues, American soldiers, while diverse, are oriented toward the United States. Soldiers are nationalistic. Charlie Moskos referred to this orientation among Vietnam era soldiers as a latent ideology (Moskos, 1970). On the one hand, they fought for their primary group—their battle buddies—but country still mattered, and it continues to matter today. The "Duty, Honor, Country" triad is prevalent today, but country is perhaps more complicated than in past wars. In addition to the Americentric perspective of American soldiers, they also have both an expanded view of defense and what it means to be American. Essentially, they are trans-cultural. This means their attitudes place America first. In this sense, they are less global compared to their civilian peers. Nevertheless, they do have an orientation beyond U.S. borders that ties to American sensibilities. They are concurrently willing to go overseas, but it must be on behalf of America—suggesting a slightly paradoxical "international-isolationism" among American service members today.

Continuing this complex view of American soldiers, the findings reported in the later chapters provide a host of thematic responses to the experiences of American soldiers. In particular, American soldiers in Iraq vacillated between being dependent and independent actors. While not completely McDonaldized, neither were they fully innovative or autonomous. They traverse the cusp between being McSoldiers and innovative professionals. Officers experienced and practiced more innovation. Soldiers shared examples of irrationality from the personal to their unit to the most public, including how their experiences were treated in the broadcast media—an institution they seemingly despise, yet consume conspicuously. They likewise adapted and found their creative muse in the deprived environment of Iraq. Notably, they overcame broader structural problems of too few troops on the ground in Iraq and limited resources, such as inadequate armor, by using individual and small unit-level creativity. They had divergent experiences on and off the Forward Operation Base (FOB). Life on the FOB reflected the more traditional view of military life—a McDonaldized experience—limited in creativity, autonomy, and spontaneity. Off the FOB, on missions and patrols and working with Iraqis, they experienced various moments of innovative professionalism, as reflected in the words of American officers in Iraq.

One of the most compelling changes associated with Iraq is the shared experiences of American men and women soldiers. Like racial and ethnic minorities, women have integrated well into the U.S. military and are performing alongside their male counterparts in Iraq in unprecedented ways. The next war may not warrant an exclusive book or chapter focused on gender differences during the war. On the topics covered, male and female soldiers in Iraq shared more similarities than differences. Yet while women have acculturated more than less into the Army, they do maintain some distinct qualities—but perhaps no more than racial and ethnic minorities. However, their unique gender features have structural implications. For example, women worked less than men and took more time off. While this might certainly reflect leadership and roles, it may also reflect less burnout and greater self-pacing preservation. Further, female soldiers seem more oriented and partial to working with foreign nationals compared to their male counterparts. This is an important and noteworthy distinction as the new counterinsurgency tactics demand for greater and more holistic orientations toward others (U.S. Army Marine Corps, 2007). This finding speaks to the necessity of increased opportunities for women in the military now and in the future on par with their roles in the larger civilian society. For the sake of national security, we cannot afford to discriminate based on gender ideology, especially in an era of an all-volunteer force.

For American soldiers and their circle of others significant to them, Iraq is the most communicated war in American history. The home and war fronts telephonically, electronically, and digitally link in unprecedented ways, and the two fronts spill into each other like never before. American soldiers desire and use the most modern modes of communication. Soldiers and a host of others affiliated with them communicate with a trove of communication media. The new media and gadgetry do not, however, displace the traditional forms of communication of packages and snail mail. Rather they are simply but immediately adding them into their communication repertoires. In just more than a decade, e-mail went from a novelty in communication in Haiti to the standard in Kuwait and Iraq. Soldiers today e-mail home daily. Officers have greater satisfaction with communication media usage, but rank connects with access and availability. More should continue to be made of this inequity potential. A communication gap may emerge in forward-deployed contexts in the future. At a minimum, communication during war is here to stay.

The last two chapters examined the implications of war deployments for American soldiers, the U.S. Army, and the nation. Experiencing a war is a crucible experience for anyone. For American soldiers, many die in war. Many suffer lifelong physical injuries, from military career-limiting to career-ending. Many suffer permanent physical and mental scarring. Others suffer from mental traumas that impede on their daily lives long after the war has ended. The current wars in Iraq and Afghanistan have seen no shortage of physical or mental casualties of war. A larger group includes an ever-broader group that experiences war as a turning point in their life. Still another group experiences a deployment in stride and continues in their lives unabated. From the findings here, clearly Iraq is a turning point in the lives of many American soldiers prior to their completing their tours in Iraq. Deployments in general appear to be turning points in a soldier's enlistment. Thousands leave the Army every year. Perhaps the Army is fulfilling a promise of service, adventure, and experience that young American women and men are seeking. For others, the war in Iraq has soured their view of the military. Irrespective, there is no single mind-set associated with these soldiers and veterans. Running parallel to their larger views of the profession, soldiers have identified a range of healthy responses to their wartime experience—including family, work, and an orientation on American culture in general.

Finally, an analysis of U.S. military fatalities in Iraq showed little to no support for the class bias thesis. Working- and lower-middle-class Americans certainly serve, fight, and die at the behest of the upper middle class and elites. However, thousands, perhaps millions, climbed the military mobility ladder from the working class into the middle class—relatively unattainable elsewhere in American society (Smith, 2007). For those in the air over Iraq and those on the ground, death appears to be an equal-opportunity experience characterized more by random unluckiness than any specific social characteristic. The fatalities have not approached the 58,226 American fatalities connected to the Vietnam War; however, they do account for the largest loss of service member life since the end of those hostilities in May 1975. Some groups, such as men and Marines, have died in disproportionate numbers; yet, all types of service members from across the mosaic of the military experience have been a fatality in Iraq.

Limitations and delimitations

Like all research, this study suffers some limitations and delimitations. Limitations are those boundaries researchers have little to no control over; delimitations are boundaries the researcher imposes on the study. Time and location limit the study. First, the findings are constrained by the ongoing war in Iraq. The U.S. military at this writing continues to be heavily involved in Iraq. The so-called surge of forces in 2007 sent both greater numbers of American troops into Iraq compared to previous years and injected them deeper into communities rather than being isolated on FOBs. With the surge came a modest reduction in insurgent attacks as 2007 drew to a close; however, the year proved the most deadly to date for American forces. The context of the deployment has perhaps changed from year to year, and increasingly American troops are returning for second and third tours of duty—a certain impact on attitudes. It is unclear whether the subsequent deployments and changes in perspective would have an impact on the findings. Another limitation of this study is one point in time. For sure, soldiers finding significance in the military experience today self-select in, and others self-select out. As time goes on, perhaps the majority in the middle likely reflect the soldiers depicted in this book. Nevertheless, is the war more boring the second and third time in Iraq? Is it more or less McDonaldized? How do attitudes toward domestic and social issues change, if at all? Is Iraq more or less a turning point? How do multiple deployments change a soldier? Is each deployment unique? Do men and women have different experiences during their second and third deployments? Is morale higher or lower on second, third, and even fourth tours? Do attitudes change toward the military? Thus, the results reported here certainly represent the American soldiers of Haiti and less so Kuwait. However, the findings should not be over-generalized to the entire war in Iraq or beyond a single deployment.

Another limitation is a focus on the active Army in Iraq. Gaining access to soldiers is difficult enough, and I recognized that permissions to gain access to units would be difficult. Thus, no reservists, Marines, air(wo)men, or sailors in Iraq completed the survey (although the majority of the small sample of Kuwait soldiers were from the National Guard, and the fatality data represented all branches and services). Consequently, any generalizing (other than the fatality data) beyond the active Army should be cautionary. Additionally, no Coalition Forces members such as Poles, Spaniards, Estonians, Brits, or Australians, among others, completed the surveys. While I did observe and interact with these troops, I did not interact enough to draw any significant conclusions. Again, permissions to survey these countries would have been difficult. Thus, this study is limited to the American Army.

Finally, my ability to travel throughout Iraq was greatly constrained. While I had no limitations placed on my movements by anyone in Iraq, gaining transportation would have been difficult for a number of reasons. Foremost, Iraq remained exceptionally dangerous and deadly for travel between FOBs and to and from the Green Zone in Baghdad. I could not travel on the ground without significant escorts. Helicopter travel was an option, but most seats on flights had advanced reservations for troop movement and changed readily. Securing a patrol on my behalf would place American forces in jeopardy—a situation I did not want to take responsibility for. When I did travel, which I did occasionally, I usually traveled with units as an unobtrusive passenger on an already preplanned mission. When I traveled as part of an official party, a bodyguard was always assigned to me (I was by choice an unarmed noncombatant although I am qualified in the use of some military automatic weapons). Consequently, the surveys, as noted in the introductory chapter, received a widespread distribution across Baghdad and other parts of Iraq, with an exceptionally high response rate. On the contrary, my observations were delimited to the summer months, a large military FOB in Baghdad, Iraq with a great deal of amenities and accoutrements (not the so-called Green Zone), and a few FOBs and the countryside surrounding Baghdad.

Another delimitation I imposed on the study is the number of topics included in the study. Many topics are of interest to military sociologists but not covered in the study. First, the survey covered 22 pages and required approximately 45 minutes to complete—a large amount of time valuable to troops. Consequently, I omitted many topics. In addition, having only a few months in-country limited my observations. As a result, I focused on specific topics. Further, too few observations limited significant conclusions. A few worthwhile sociological topics for future analysis include racial/ethnic issues, severe stress and other psychological problems such as posttraumatic stress syndrome; matters of death, dying, and grief; combat; political topics; economic issues for soldiers; leadership concerns; sexual or gender harassment; rapes; soldier-family issues; interactions with homosexual soldiers; religious matters; concerns of reservists and the National Guard; civilian-military interactions including international contractors; cross-national comparison; deviance in combat and on the FOB; human rights issues; and finally, interactions between Iraqis and American soldiers.[1] These themes are certainly salient features of the Iraq deployment and warrant further study.

Despite these shortcomings, the descriptions provided here are unique and rare. Few studies have captured a large number of soldier experiences during a war. Journalists and practitioners provide non-empirical observations—in most cases lacking grounding in past research and lacking a systematic analysis. The efforts reported here are inspired and anchored in previous and recent research especially studies of war including *The American Soldier* series (Stouffer et al., 1949: vol 1); Roger Little's (1965) research during Korea; Charles Moskos's (1970) work during Vietnam; David Segal on peacekeeping missions (Segal et al., 1984); John Wattendorf (1992) during the first Persian Gulf War; and an array of singular works by mostly uniformed scholars back to WWII and up through the current wars in Afghanistan and Iraq (Wong et al., 2003; Wong and Gerras, 2006). Before turning to diversity and inclusiveness at the intersection of the armed forces and society, I could not allow this book to end without two generation observations: one public, dealing with the current generation of service members and the other more private, my personal view of the war in Iraq.

The greatest sub-generation

Many are referring to the current generation of service members serving in Iraq and Afghanistan, indeed those serving in the post-9/11 military, as the new "greatest generation" (Robbins, 2007; Webb and Hagel, 2007). This is a comparison to the Greatest Generation made popular by journalist Tom Brokaw in 1998 with a book of the same name. The term refers to a cohort of Americans who fought (served) in World War II and those who maintained the home-front. More broadly, they are a cohort born between 1901 and 1924 and known as the "G.I. Generation" (Strauss and Howe, 1992). I first heard of a comparison between today's soldiers and the Greatest Generation made by a colonel in Iraq. We were walking to the dining facility together for lunch. He convinced me that such a frame would increase some positive affect—for both troops and the American public—and amid the throng of soldiers quietly eating their lunch in Iraq, I wholeheartedly agreed with him.

I continue to think about his comment. I have, however, tempered my agreement and concluded that the warranting of such a label would apply only to a portion, indeed a minority, of the present generation, not the entire cohort. I would label them the greatest sub-generation. By adopting the sub prefix, I do not mean to imply something secondary, junior, or subordinate to the larger generation. I simply mean something smaller, a select group of the larger generation. Only a extraordinarily small percentage of post-9/11 American soldiers and their families burdened themselves by serving in the wars in Afghanistan and Iraq. This would include a handful of "others," including contractors and other Americans (and their families) who "served" in this war in a consistent and sustained manner. The remainder of Americans—the masses—appear unaffected by Iraq. This is not to say Americans do not possess opinions or positions about the war. Rather, their personal life world and their life-course continue unabated with a minimum of disruption through national service obligations or volunteerism or sacrifice related to the wars. Further, few national leaders inspired service. Many more do support the troops in both rhetoric and action. The collective nation after 9/11 was encouraged to continue their lives as business as usual, to avoid forsaking their habits.

In contrast, many Americans have run counter to the constructed norm of business as usual. In an ironic twist, a counter-culture has emerged and prevailed. They share a feeling of a higher calling, and it has emerged among a cross-section of Americans—to either serve in the military or serve those serving in the military. Pat Tillman and his brother Kevin are perhaps the best representatives of the counter-culture (Tillman, 2008). They sacrificed highly traditional American values such as wealth, material gain, fame, progress, individualism (and one ultimately his life) for service. I suspect many soldiers, their immediate and extended families, and others are loath to characterize their experiences as counter to the larger culture. However, the shear minority of their status and the quality of their commitment qualifies them as a group with values, beliefs, and behaviors in opposition to the broader culture and norms. For those who have shared some of their time and energy on behalf of service members, either through not-for-profit-type organizations established to assist soldiers, Iraqis, or others impacted by the war, in some consistent, long-term, and methodical manner, to include protesting against it, you are a part of the counter-culture or on the periphery of it. Overall, your numbers are miniscule in comparison to the greatest generation that made collective and epic sacrifices for the war effort and were completely endorsed and inspired by leaders at multiple levels. Few today have interrupted their lives in major ways to serve "the greater good" (put into quotes to highlight the relative status of good). Granted, the label of greatest sub-generation is perhaps premature. It may be too early to determine the legacy of an entire generation. They are busy fulfilling their legacy. They need more history. We will have to wait and see and reassess. For now, an entire generation has certainly not mobilized for the "greater good" or rather been inspired to mobilize to bring peace and prosperity to Afghanistan or Iraq—certainly not within the U.S. borders.

What America lacks is a favorable response to a national mobilization for war. The best and brightest are needed to be inspired to win the war on terror, if indeed enough terror actually exists to wage an outright war against it. Further, more effort is required to bring the elements of democracy to the regions that are not politicized. These would include equality, liberty, and humanitarianism, among other American ideals. Had we done this, the nation would have been able to produce enough armored HMMWV's as we produced cargo ships during WWII (Kearns Goodwin, 2007). Finally, research in universities to understand aspects of the war and various constituents would be more pervasive.

Recruitment would not be a problem. Anthropologists and psychologists would not be fretting over the role of their disciplines in war. Other nations would scramble to stand shoulder to shoulder with us.

Personal statement on the war in Iraq

I remain opposed to the war in Iraq in theory but believe that in practice the U.S. cannot abandon Iraq at this point. Foremost, I am opposed to the initial Wolfowitz Bush Doctrine that provided the rational for preemptive interventions. I believe the leadership misled the nation about the activities of Saddam Hussein, constructing them to fit a larger agenda, all of which led to the U.S. -led invasion of Iraq. Saddam Hussein certainly committed crimes against humanity and needed an arrest from and for those crimes. Unfortunately, we had evidence for years of crimes against humanity and did little. The international community had a responsibility to take diplomatic action to remove him from power many years ago and failed. Had we done so, additional atrocities may not have occurred. Today, I am thankful a tyrant is out of power. I heard a handful of stories while in Iraq from Iraqis about the atrocities he and co-conspirators committed and a trial ultimately confirmed. Such stories coupled with forensic evidence of mass graves reinforce my ongoing concerns (Simons, 2006).

I certainly do not think we owe an entire campaign to the lives of the service members who died there. I do not think anyone is so naïve to base U.S. foreign policy on the lives of soldiers who are fatalities of a war. They are not around to speak for themselves. They accomplished their mission regardless of the broader political outcomes. They will never die in vain because they served. It is irresponsible to redirect the politics of the war to their experience. But I do think the *Groundhog Day* (Ramis, 1993) observations of soldiers over the course of years is a compelling story: Change is slow, and progress sometimes reverses over the course of 12 months in Iraq. One wonders about progress after 5 or even 10 years. As some change has been incremental, we should be asking ourselves whether our current policy is working. If Americans continue to be injured or killed and billions of dollars are both spent and misappropriated, should we reconsider such a campaign?

Diversity in the military and civil-military fusion

Diversity is a major focus of this book. The U.S. military today is more inclusive than ever before but continues systematic discrimination of select groups. Diversity emerged out of the analysis of the empirical data from American soldiers serving in Haiti, Kuwait, and Iraq. The theme of diversity manifested in similarity and difference among American soldiers with specificity to the context of the all-volunteer force and at the junction of civilian and military life. Diversity provides a window to compare and contrast various groups and social topics that military sociologists have been keen on for almost 100 years.

The findings from Army soldiers deployed to Iraq shows two types of diversity—social diversity and diversity of mind. American soldiers in Iraq represent a range of social categories. Racial and ethnic groups, social class, religious affiliation (Banerjee, 2007), and regions of the country are all in relative proportion to their representations in the U.S. society. Highly apparent are women as well—not in comparison to the larger society but in proportion to the Army and it terms of what they do.

Prior to Iraq, the U.S. Army required men and women to be between 17 and 34 years of age, a U.S. citizen or resident alien, a high school graduate or equivalent, have limited familial dependents, be physically fit, not openly homosexual, and possess a minimal number of law violations. Similar to past wars, where Americans gained relatively greater citizenship status through military service, usually because of (wo)manpower shortfalls and those minorities exercising a willingness to serve, the first war of the twenty-first century for Americans in Afghanistan and Iraq continue this trend. People deviating from the traditional seven characteristics—male, white, fit, young, Christian, working class, and straight—are acculturating and finding full citizenship status in the organization. Army recruiting shortfalls resulted after the first wave of patriotic enlistees inspired by 9/11 events, forcing the Army to subsequently soften some of the enlistment social criteria. The upper age limit lifted from 34 to 42. Greater numbers of enlistees closer to the lower limits for moral, physical, educational, and familial criteria are accepted. Soldiers with physical anomalies—resulting from their deployment—are increasingly remaining in service (Kenen, 2007). Yet, other groups, ironically in both subtle and extreme ends of these criteria, continue to be systematically discriminated against, including women in specific combat arms MOSs and openly gay and lesbian service members. In spite of these latter systematic "isms," the Army represents the American population in specific areas. Many have proven themselves worthy of full Army culture citizenship, especially women.

Alongside social diversity is diversity in mind. American soldiers are not drones of one mind when it comes to a number of social psychological characteristics. Indeed, social research reported elsewhere shows military affiliation matters less than political affiliation for soldiers and future soldiers (Rohall and Ender, 2007; Rohall et al., 2006). Essentially, in the post-9/11 world, American soldiers and future soldiers look more like their civilian peers than their fellow soldiers. Soldiers responding to the surveys in Iraq likewise show a multitude of attitudes, perceptions, opinions, and orientations.

I have long been a advocate for universal national service in America as advocated by the late Charlie Moskos (1988). I believe it would provide an energetic labor force to right many of the social ills we suffer from, instill civic responsibility and pride, and correct the proportional representation—the diversity needed of a military representing the peoples of the nation. However, the research reported here suggests I rethink at least the last argument for universal national service. The AVF, while not yet fully inclusive, is diverse on many levels.

The U.S. is far from a total civil-military fusion. There is considerable narrowing of the distance between the two areas. The findings reported here point more toward a fourth wave in civil-military relations in the United States. Again, not a closure of the delta between the civilian and military, rather it is increased convergence and civilianization of military life with not only increased social representation but attitudinal representation as well.[2] If the trend is to continue, the AVF needs to increase access for more American constituent groups. Further, it is necessary to continue to give them a voice and measure their socio-demographics and perspectives. At the intersection of the armed forces and society, we should always know who serves when everyone does not and, within the military, who dies when everyone does not.

Appendices

Appendix 4.1. Domestic social issue statements

Statements

Bussing children in order to achieve school integration

Using any budget surpluses to reduce the national debt rather than to reduce taxes

Relaxing environmental regulations to stimulate economic growth

Providing tuition tax credits to parents who send children to private or parochial schools

Leaving abortion decisions to women and their doctors

Encouraging mothers to stay at home with their children rather than working outside the home

Permitting prayer in public schools

Reducing the defense budget in order to increase the federal education budget

Barring homosexuals from teaching in public schools

Barring homosexuals from serving in the military

Easing restrictions on the construction of nuclear power plants

Redistributing income from the wealthy to the poor through taxation and subsidies

Banning the death penalty

Placing stringent controls on the sale of handguns

Appendix 4.2. Moral issues and value statements

Statements

The decline of traditional values is contributing to the breakdown of our society.

Through leading by example, the military could help American society become more moral.

The world is changing, and we should adjust our view of what is moral and immoral behavior to fit these changes.

Civilian society would be better off if it adopted more of the military's values and customs.

American society would have fewer problems if people took God's will more seriously.

All Americans should be willing to give up their lives to defend our country.

Appendix 5.1. Attitude statements toward foreign issues

Statements
It's much more difficult to work with foreign nationals than with the people of the United States.
You can trust foreign nationals as much as you can trust people from the United States.
Most people from most countries are pretty much alike.
I like to travel.
I look forward to new experiences.
I like to try foreign foods.

Appendix 5.2. Attitude statements toward roles and missions

Statements
Peacekeeping force
Guerilla war
Limited conventional war
Large conventional war
Tactical nuclear war
A war in which tactical chemical weapons are used
A war in which tactical biological weapons are used
Strategic nuclear war
Humanitarian assistance after a domestic disaster
Restoration of order after a domestic disturbance or riot
Overseas humanitarian assistance
Other: _____

Appendix 5.3. Attitudes toward types of military operations other than war

Statements
Combat the flow of illegal drugs into the U.S.
Provide humanitarian relief in the U.S
Provide humanitarian relief outside the U.S.
Be part of a United Nations peacekeeping force.
Maintain a military presence in overseas areas of vital interest to the U.S. in order to prevent problems.
Provide training to U.S. federal, state, and municipal employees.
Provide training to foreign federal, state and municipal employees.
Other: _____

Appendix 5.4. Attitude statements toward peacekeeping

Statements

A soldier who is well trained in basic military skills requires additional training for peacekeeping.

Soldiers can be effective in a peacekeeping role even if they cannot use force except in self-defense.

Peacekeeping duty is boring.

A peacekeeping force should be impartial in a conflict situation.

Soldiers on peacekeeping duty should be unarmed.

The primary mission of peacekeepers is to contain or reduce conflict without the use of force.

Peacekeeping operations are appropriate missions for my unit.

Peacekeeping assignments help a soldier's career.

Peacekeeping operations are hardest on soldiers with families.

A professional soldier is able to perform peacekeeping missions and war-fighting missions equally effectively.

Peacekeeping missions should be performed by civilians rather than by soldiers.

Peacekeeping missions should be performed by military police rather than by infantry.

Reservists can perform peacekeeping missions as well as regular military personnel.

Other _____

Appendix 6.1. Elements of McDonaldization (and one non-McDonaldized dimension—creativity) and open-ended questions asked of American soldiers in Iraq

Dimension	Question
Efficiency	What tasks seem to get done quickly and efficiently in your unit, but not necessarily to the best possible quality? Regarding your job, what do you do quickly and efficiently, but know you could do more thoroughly (e.g. if you had more time)?
Control	Do the rules of Operation Iraqi Freedom II (OIFII) make you feel too restricted in any way? If so, explain the particulars and how and why they make you (or the buddies in your unit) feel overly constrained.
Predictability	Are coalition forces too predictable for the enemy to assess as it plans its attacks? Does your unit do things in repetitive patterns that seem overly predictable, making enemy's planning of attacks relatively easy? Do you do things in your job—which are observable to the enemy—in a predictable or fairly consistent manner? Explain your thoughts about how predictable coalition forces or your unit or you are in OIF.
Quantification	Are there any statistics or numbers that you feel get too much attention in Iraq? For example, the news reports are beginning to compare casualties in both sides for given skirmishes and battles.
Irrationality	What are the most unreasonable things that the chain-of-command has asked you or your unit to do? How did you (or your unit) respond to those requests?
Creativity	Does your unit creatively adjust what they do to better accomplish the mission? Cite examples of creativity to illustrate how you feel about this—whether (or the lack thereof) it impacts the mission.

Notes

1 Introduction: American soldiers

1 For a discussion of values in sociology, see D.A. Snow, "1998 PSA presidential address: the value of sociology," *Sociological Perspectives, 42*(1), 1999, 1–22.

2 That effort was successful. We helped construct and institute survey projects that expanded on the handful of narrowly focused political polls administered in Iraq up until the summer of 2004. I worked directly with two Iraqi research centers—the *Independent Institute for Administrative and Civil Society Studies* and the ASHARQ: Center for Polls & Marketing Research. Two sociological studies have emerged from the survey data thus far: D.L.L. Schnack, *A case for the separation of hearts and minds: an analysis of Iraqi attitudes and perceptions in Baghdad,* Unpublished thesis. Boston, MA: Boston College, 2006, and S. Carlton-Ford, M.G. Ender, and A. Tabatabai, 2008, "Iraqi adolescents: Self-Regard, self-derogation, and perceived threat in war, *The Journal of Adolescence,* 31, 2008, 53–75. Others have picked up the research lacunae in Iraq, and are now working directly with the Iraqis. See R. Inglehart, M. Moaddel, and M. Tessler, "Xenophobia and in-group solidarity in Iraq: a natural experiment on the impact of insecurity," *Perspectives on Politics, 4*(3), 2006, 495–505.

3 Two special published issues of *Sociological Focus* appeared on the Sociology of the Iraq War. Issues include November 39(4), 2006 and February 40,(1), 2007.

4 For an interesting discussion of citizenship and military service see J. Burk, "The changing moral contract for military service," in A.J. Bacevich (ed.), *The Long War: A New History of US National Security Policy Since World War II,* (NY: Columbia University Press), 2007, pp. 405–455

5 I had originally been in a position to travel to Haiti. However, political negotiations resolved, and President Bill Clinton brought the troops home earlier than expected, requiring a suspension of our site visit. Further, since soldiers were anticipating reconnecting with their families and taking a well-deserved vacation, we opted to wait until a degree of normalcy had returned to the division before we would survey and conduct individual and group interviews with soldiers.

6 D. Soyini Madison contrasts "deep hanging out" and ethnographic methods on a loose continuum in *Critical Ethnography: Methods, Ethics, and Performance,* Thousand Oaks, CA: Sage Publications, 2005, pp. 17–19.

2 Creeping banality: the boredom factor and American soldiers

1 The next question might be how then does one avoid boredom?" P. Conrad, "It's boring: notes on the meanings of boredom in everyday life," *Qualitative Sociology,*

20(4), 1997, pp. 465–475. Goffman would say the use of "aways"—games to occupy ourselves. See E. Goffman, *Behavior in Public Places: Notes on the Social Organization of Gatherings*. New York: Free Press of Glencoe, 1963, pp. 33–42.

2　There were roughly 100 Forward Operating Bases in Iraq in 2004. See L. Wong and S. Gerras, *CU @ the FOB: How the Forward Operating Base is Changing the Life of Combat soldiers,* Carlisle, PA: Strategic Studies Institute, 2006, p. 1.

3　D.H. Petraeus, "Letter to families of the 101st, from General Petraeus," Online, Available HTTP:<http://screamingeagles-327thvietnam.com/general_petraeus. htm>, (Retrieved September 18, 2006), no date. This was a published letter to military families of the 101st Airborne Division at Fort Campbell, Kentucky. MG Petraeus served as the division commander of the 101st at the time and was a major general (two stars).

4　There had been occasional curfews during nightfall, and this creates some control on time in Iraq between day and night activities.

5　For an excellent comparison of the ground combat experiences of US soldiers during the twentieth century, see P.S. Kindsvatter, *American Soldiers: Ground Combat in the World Wars, Korea, and Vietnam,* Lawrence, KS: University of Kansas Press, 2003.

6　See the eyewitness story written by D. Hoffmeyer, "Mosul attack kills 24, wounds 64." *Richmond Times-Dispatch* (December 21), Online, Available HTTP: <http://www.timesdispatch.com/cva/ric/times_dispatch.html> (accessed December 24, 2004), 2004. The reporter embedded with a unit and lived on the FOB.

7　For an interesting discussion of American soldier and German civilian population convergence in post-WWII Germany see M. Höhn, *GIs and Fräuleins: The German-American Encounter in 1950s West Germany,* Chapel Hill, NC: University of North Carolina Press, 2002.

8　This remains an area of ongoing interest, and others I have written individually or in collaboration on this topic across a number of military deployments. See M.G. Ender, "G.I. phone home: the use of telecommunications by the soldiers of Operation Just Cause," *Armed Forces & Society, 21*(3), 1995, pp. 335–334; M.G. Ender, "E-mail to Somalia: new communication media between home and war fronts," J.E. Behar (ed.), *Mapping Cyberspace: Social Research on the Electronic Frontier,* Oakdale, NY: Dowling College Press, Dowling Studies in the Humanities and the Social Sciences, 1997, pp. 27–52; ; M.G. Ender, "The postmodern military: soldiering, new media, and the post-cold war," *Journal for the Study of Peace and Conflict,* (1997–1998 Annual Edition), 1998, pp. 50–58; M.G. Ender, "Divergences in traditional and new communication media use among Army families," in E. Ouellet (ed.), *New Directions in Military Sociology* (de Sitter Publications), 2005, 255–295; M.G. Ender and D.R. Segal, "V(E)-mail to the foxhole: isolation, (tele) communication, and forward deployed soldiers," *Journal of Political and Military Sociology, 24*(1), 1996, pp. 83–104; M.G. Ender and D.R. Segal, "Cyber-soldiering: race, class, gender and new media use in the military," in B. Ebo (ed.), *Cyberghetto or Cybertopia: Race, Class, and Gender on the Internet,* Westport CT: Praeger Publishers, 1998, pp. 65–82; and W.R. Schumm, D.B. Bell, M.G. Ender, and R.E. Rice, "Expectations, use, and evaluations of communications media among deployed peacekeepers," *Armed Forces & Society, 30*(4), 2004, pp. 649–662.

3　Troop morale: the social psychology of American soldiers

1　Some argue that the most productive period for the field of social psychology dates to World War II and the studies of American soldiers. See W.H. Sewell, "Some reflections on the golden age of interdisciplinary social psychology," *Social Psychology Quarterly, 52*(2), 1998, pp. 88–97.

2 Response categories included a five-point scale from "Not at All," "Not Well," "Moderately," "Well," to "Very Well" prepared.
3 In previous wars, people in the rear were known as REMFs—Rear echelon mother fuckers. The new combat environment diminishes the "combat environment" in the country; soldiers back at the home base, be it the US, Germany, or Italy, are busily involved with the forward-deployed units.
4 The large number features those soldiers having 3 or more days off and with no deployment to Haiti.
5 Responses asked them to rate morale at five points on a scale from "Very Low," "Low," "Moderately," "High," to "Very High."
6 For a critical examination of the relationship between soldier morale and public support for the war in Iraq see A. Klein, "The Morale Myth," *Washington Monthly* (May), 2006, Online. Available HTTP: <http://www.washingtonmonthly.com/ features/2006/0605.klein.html> (accessed July 1, 2007).

4   Fusion and fissure: American soldier attitudes toward social issues

1 When sociologists study attitudes, we are usually referring to some favorable or unfavorable position or positive or negative evaluation on a particular object. The object can be almost anything—a person, a place, a thing, or an idea. Attitudes can be thought of as perspectives, positions, an outlook, thoughts, feelings, approaches, a standpoint, an opinion, a way of thinking, a party line, a disposition, a posture, or a frame of reference. The idea is to get persons to share their internal attitude about something out in the world. In addition to simply having an attitude, attitudes have strength as well. Attitudes can be extreme, intense, and important, or weak. Thus, we often ask people their attitudes along some type of continuum or scaled response category. Further, but very importantly, attitudes are linked in a chain process involving beliefs, attitudes, and ultimately behavior. The meaning here is that an attitude is usually based on a foundation of beliefs about the way the world works. For those interested in the practical or usefulness of attitudes, you should recognize that attitudes do have action potential at some point. For example, in the simplest form—a person might believe that democrats (or republicans, independents, greens, etc.) have the best interest of the nation at heart, may develop a positive attitude toward a democratic presidential candidate, and take action and vote for the candidate—belief, attitude, and ultimately action are linked. See H. Schuman, "Attitudes, beliefs, and behavior," In K.S. Cook, G.A. Fine, and J.S. House (eds.), *Sociological Perspectives on Social Psychology,* Needham Heights, MA: Allyn & Bacon, 1995, pp. 68–89.
2 Established in 1998, the seven U.S. Army values include loyalty, duty, respect, selfless service, honor, integrity, and personal courage. See U.S. Army Training and Doctrine Command: Office of the Chief of Public Affairs, *Army Values,* Online. Available HTTP: <http://www.tradoc.army.mil/pao/ArmyValues/ArmyValues. htm> (accessed November 6, 2006), undated. For discussions comparing and contrasting Army and American society values see R. Hajjar and M. G. Ender, "Harnessing the power of culture and diversity for organizational performance," in D. Crandall. (ed.), *Leadership Lessons from West Point,* San Francisco, CA: Jossey-Bass, 2007, pp. 313–337.
3 Response categories ranged from "Agree Strongly," "Agree Somewhat," "Disagree Somewhat," to "Disagree Strongly" and a "No opinion."
4 Note that this gap is wider than for barring homosexuals from teaching in public schools (16.1 percent).

5 For a novel example of civilians becoming militarized, see J. Bleifuss, "Disasters: natural and social: Eric Klinenberg discusses the militarization of social services and what will be missing from any national conversations about poverty," *In These Times,* (September 26), Online, Available HTTP: <http://ww.inthesetimes.com/site/main/article/2330/> (accessed November 6, 2006), 2005. For an example of the military becoming civilianized, see A. MacGinnis, "Downtown Fort Belvoir: Army post in Fairfax County gets a taste of off-post living with its own town center," *Washington Post,* (October 22), 2006, p. C01.

6 For an excellent discussion of the masculine dominated culture of the Cold War military, see M.W. Segal, "The nature of work and family linkages: a theoretical perspective," 1989, pp. 3–36. This finding requires further analysis in the post–Cold War era controlling for gender, education, and marital status.

5   Over there: Americn soldier attitudes toward foreign issues

1 A classic sociological axiom from W.I. Thomas and D.S. Thomas, *The Child in America,* New York: Knopf, 1928.

2 The responses to the attitudes toward foreign issues scale is six-items based on a five-point Likert scale from "Strongly Agree," "Agree," "Neither Agree or Disagree," to "Disagree" and "Strongly Disagree" (Appendix 5.1).

3 The attitudes toward likely future roles and missions the U.S. military might be involved in the next 10 years are an 11–item scale plus an "other" category (Appendix 5.2). Responses deal mostly with both conventional military missions as well as military type missions other than war. Response categories are on a five-point scale from "Very Unlikely," "Somewhat Unlikely," "Neither Unlikely or Likely," to "Somewhat Likely," and "Very Likely."

4 The next scale asks soldiers to respond to military type missions other than conventional warfare that they would support (see Appendix 5.3). Statements include fighting a war on drugs to providing training to foreign nations. Responses range on a five-point Likert-type scale from "Definitely Would," Probably Would," "Not Sure," to "Probably Would Not" and "Definitely Would Not."

5 This scale asks soldiers about their attitudes toward peacekeeping (see Appendix 5.4). The scale statements range from soldiers requiring additional training for peacekeeping to boredom associated with peacekeeping to reservists performing peacekeeping missions as well as regular military personnel. It has 13 statements plus an "other" category.

6   McSoldiers: human tools or innovative professionals

1 Wong follows this statement in the next paragraph using a food preparation example in the spirit of McDonaldization to illustrate this point. "To use a culinary example, *cooks* are quite adept at carrying out a recipe. While there is a small degree of artistic license that goes into preparing a meal, the recipe drives the direction—not the cook. *Chefs,* on the other hand, look at the ingredients available to them and create a meal. The success of the meal comes from the creativity of the chef—not the recipe. In a large hierarchical Army, many "cooks" are needed—leaders who can be counted on to follow doctrine competently in their part of the hierarchy. But the environment of the Objective Force calls for "chefs"—leaders capable of operating outside of established doctrine and existing hierarchy" See L. Wong, *Stifled Innovation? Developing Tomorrow's Leaders Today,* Carlisle, PA: Strategic Studies Institute, 2002, p. 3.

2 See Headquarters, Department of the Army, *The Army Training and Leader Development Panel Officer Study Report to the Army,* Online, Available HTTP: <http://www.Army.mil/atld>, (accessed October 9, 2006), 2001. The report uses four study groups, surveyed and interviewed, of 13,500 leaders and spouses in the U.S. Army. We reviewed this report and located many practices illustrative of McDonaldization.

3 In a brief to senior leaders, Charles Moskos notes that "Hajji" is more a term of endearment rather than a stigmatizing term. "Hajji" refers to a Muslim who adheres to one of the five pillars of Islam—a Hajj or pilgrimage to Mecca once in one's life if it is affordable. See C. Moskos, *American Military Interaction with Locals in OIF/OEF: Preliminary Draft,* Electronic—mail communication with Generals Peter Pace, John Abizaid, James Jones, and Peter Schoomaker (March 7), Unpublished document, 2006. Available from the author.

7 Real G. I. Janes: American female soldiers in war

1 Some examples of compelling articles include A. Paulson, "The new veterans among US: women," *Christian Science Monitor,* (November 10, 2006), Online, Available HTTP: <http://www.csmonitor.com> (accessed December 2, 2006), 2006; E. Solaro, "Lionesses of Iraq," *Seattle Weekly,* (October 6, 2004), Online, Available HTTP: <http://www.seatleweekly.com>, (accessed December 2, 2006), 2006; K. Semple, "A captain's journey from hope to just getting her unit home," *New York Times* (November 19), 2006, p. 1. One noteworthy book is E. Solaro, *Women in the Line of Fire: What You Should Know about Women in the Military* Emeryville, CA: Seal Press, 2006.

2 Sixteen participants did not report their gender.

3 Eleven participants did not report their gender.

4 Fifteen participants did not report their gender.

5 See D.L. Leal, "American public opinion toward the military: differences by race, gender, and class?," *Armed Forces & Society, 32*(1), 2005, pp. 123–138. Leal cites and reviews other literature pointing to women being consistently more tolerant of social policies benefiting the underprivileged and opposing violence through the latter part of the twentieth century.

8 Baghdad calling: soldier communications with other fronts

1 I was first interviewed about research and publications on the use of electronic-mail for mediating communication between deployed soldiers and their family members and the implications of communication during the American peacemaking mission in Bosnia. See N. Hudson, "E-mail from Bosnia: a new can of worms," *Army Times.* (December 11), 1995b, p. 27. A similar story appeared in the *Navy Times.* See Neff Hudson, "Advantages over snail mail," *Navy Times.* (December 11), 1995a, p. 26. Other stories include N. Hudson, "Pentagon plugs Bosnia into the internet," *Army Times,* (December 25), 1995c, p. 14 and "Special report, military gets wired: internet connections puts world at service members fingertips," *Army Times,* (October 2), 1995d, pp. 14–18.

2 See I. Wielawski, "For troops, home can be too close," *New York Times,* Science Section, (March 15), Online, Available HTTP: <http://www.nytimes.com/2005/03/15/health/psychology/15fami.html> (accessed October 9, 2007), 2005. I interviewed for this story about research on the human dimensions of real- and lag-time interpersonal communication media devices used by American military service members in Iraq and their military families around the world

and the social implications for well-being, information overload, morale, and notifications of deaths and serious injuries. The reporter shared with me that the inspiration for the story came from her own experiences of being the wife of an embedded *Los Angeles Times* reporter, with troops in Iraq. She found the experience of communicating with her "deployed" husband and with the children and their significant others fascinating and curious and wanted a better understanding of the phenomena for military families.

3 This chapter does not focus on mass media. Indeed, I did not ask soldiers about their uses of mass media while in Iraq. The chapter deals with soldier attitudes toward mass media as a serendipitous finding. Vietnam clearly became the first TV war, and Army families surely used this media to learn about what was happening in Vietnam. Live television broadcasting from the war front also began during the 1980s. The Persian Gulf War was the first "Live TV War" broadcast world-wide. Two studies report on the uses and gratifications associated with the mass media. The following studies deal with mass media, the public, soldiers, and war: D.R. Segal, "Communication about the military: people and media in the flow of information," *Communication Research*, 2(1), 1975, pp. 68–78; D. Kellner, *The Persian Gulf TV War,* Boulder, CO: Westview Press, 1992; M.G. Ender, K. Campbell, T. Davis, and P. Michaelis, "Greedy media: army families, embedded reporting, and the war in Iraq," *Sociological Focus*, 40(1), 2007, pp. 48–71; and M.G. Ender and D.R. Segal, "V(e)-mail to the foxhole: isolation, (tele)communication, and forward deployed soldiers," *Journal of Political and Military Sociology*, 24(1), 1996, pp. 83–104.

4 *Over There* ran for 13 weeks on the American cable television program F/X in 2005. *Over There,* [TV program] F/X, created by Gerolmo, C. and Saloman, M., Online. Available HTTP: <http://www.imdb.com/title/tt0446241/> (accessed August 30, 2006), 2005. Created by C. Gerolmo and M. Saloman, *Over There,* Online, Available HTTP: <http://www.imdb.com/title/tt0446241/>, (accessed August 30, 2006), 2005.

5 For a review of Iraq related films see M.G. Ender, *Essay on Film Documentaries about Iraq, Iraqis, War, and Soldiers.* Peace, War, and Social Conflict Newsletter (July), 2007, pp. 10–11.

6 See *Heartbreak Ridge,* [Film] Directed by Clint Eastwood. USA: Jay Weston Productions, 1986. The actual incident involved a friendly fire incident where a U.S. Navy ship off the Coast of Grenada was shelling a position of U.S. Army paratroopers. As the radios between the two did not share a frequency; a thoughtful soldier called Fort Bragg, North Carolina where a call was patched through to the Pentagon and Army and Navy members communicated a message to the ship to stop shelling friendly forces. The story is published in C. Doe, "Grenada: will its lessons be taught?," *Army Times,* (November 5), 1984, p. 34. See also R. Marshall, "Battlefield communications: technology's challenge," *Defense & Foreign Affairs,* (October), 1986, p. 26.

7 MP3 players and iPods are the Walkmans of today.

9 Turning point: Iraq as a change agent for American soldiers

1 For the most recent research on social status attainment among veterans see I. Smith, *The World War II Veteran Advantage?: A Lifetime Cross-Sectional Study of Social Status Attainment,* Unpublished doctoral dissertation, College Park, MD: University of Maryland, 2007.

2 I did not ask Haiti veterans to explain why their deployment was a turning point in their life.

10 Death in the American ranks: class war or equal opportunity

1 "Died in Iraq" can have varied meanings. The military refers to casualties—meaning those both injured and killed. I refer to fatalities and use it interchangeably with deaths to cover American soldiers who died in service to OIF. Further, many soldiers did not actually die in Iraq, but they certainly died from incidents that occurred in Iraq and may have died in en route to medical care. About 95 percent of the incidents occurred in Iraq according to official reports. Other incidents occurred in Kuwait ($n = 37$) and a small list of other countries. For example, 59-year-old, SFC William D. Chaney died in Landstuhl, Germany. From Schaumburg, Illinois, an Army National Guardsman and Vietnam veteran, he died from medical complications associated with an intestinal infection following surgery. Similarly, SFC Ruben J. Villa Jr. died in Dubai, United Arab Emirates, while supporting OIF. His cause of death is non-hostile. Also of note is that almost 95 percent of deaths of soldiers occurred in Iraq. The remaining 5 percent of soldiers died in other countries or en route to another country. Those countries included Kuwait, Germany, Qatar, Bahrain, and the United States among others.

2 See Charles Rangel point in Forum, "Should the draft be reinstated," *Newsweek* (December 29/January 5), 2004, pp. 101–102. The forum includes both pro and con positions by policy influencers.

3 Others have studied a correlate to the class bias thesis. Known as the Casualty Hypothesis, here the argument holds that Americans tend to be supportive of wars until a critical mass of deaths or a small number of highly publicized deaths reduce their belligerence support. The research findings on the casualty hypothesis are mixed. See J. Burk, "Public support for peacekeeping in Lebanon and Somalia: assessing the casualties hypothesis," *Political Science Quarterly* 114, 1999, pp. 53–79.

4 There is no specific reason for stopping in October 2007. Unfortunately, the war continues, and more significantly, casualties among all groups—civilian, military, American, Iraqi, and other occupations and nations continue. However, there appears some progress as 2007 closes—violence and casualty numbers are down for all groups, although 2007 has more American troops killed than in any previous year. Bush Administration officials linked the decline in violence and casualties to the so-called "surge" of adding an additional 30,000 American forces beginning in the winter and spring of 2007.

5 See Department of Defense, *Personnel and Military Casualty Statistics,* Online. Available HTTP: <http://siadapp.dmdc.osd.mil/personnel/MMIDHOME.HTM> (accessed September 11, 2008), 2008. Hostile action deaths does not include terrorist attacks for this same period, of which there were 438, including 234 Marines killed in Lebanon in 1983.

6 Ibid.

7 There is also a good deal of psychological research dealing with death and dying in the military. For example, see J. E. McCarroll, R. J. Ursano, C. S. Fullerton, G. L. Oates, W. L. Ventis, H. Friedman, G. L. Shean, and K. M. Wright, "Gruesomeness, emotional attachment, and personal threat: dimensions of the anticipated stress of body recovery," *Journal of Traumatic Stress*, 8(2), 1995, pp. 343–349; J. E. McCarroll, R.J. Ursano, C.S. Fullerton, X. Liu, A. Lundy, "Effects of exposure to death in a war mortuary on posttraumatic stress disorder symptoms of intrusion and avoidance," *Journal of Nervous & Mental Disease*, 189(1), 2001, pp. 44–48; J. E. McCarroll, R. J. Ursano, C. S. Fullerton, X. Liu, and A. Lundy, "Somatic symptoms in Gulf War mortuary workers," *Psychosomatic Medicine,* 64, 2002, pp. 29–33.

8　The countries and their fatalities included the following at the time: from Australia (1), Canada (44), Denmark (3), France (9), Germany (18), Italy (9), the Netherlands (4), Norway (1), Portugal (1), Romania (4), Spain (19), Sweden (2), and the United Kingdom (44). These data come from a Web site named *iCasuaties.org.* See M. White, *iCasualties.org,* Online, Available HTTP: <http://icasualties.org/ oif/Methodology.aspx>, (accessed January 2, 2007), 2007. The Web site mission states: "…to document coalition casualties for Operation Iraqi Freedom and Operation Enduring Freedom. We attempt to be up to date, precise, accurate and reliable." The data are compiled from a number of sources including press releases from the Department of Defense, Central Command, the Multinational Forces Iraq and the British Ministry of Defense, Web sites, and news stories.

9　Ibid. These countries and their fatalities at the time included the United Kingdom (127), Italy (33), Poland (18), Ukraine (18), Bulgaria (13), Spain (11), Denmark (6), El Salvador (5), Slovenia (4), Latvia (3), with Romania, Thailand, Australia, the Netherlands, and Estonia 2 each and Kazakhstan and Hungary 1 each.

10　Ibid. However, a *Reuters* news service article reports a much higher number, 647, based on claims for death benefits had been made between March 1, 2003, and Sept. 30, 2006— U.S. Department of Labor requires an insurance policy taken out for U.S. government contractors and subcontractors working outside the United States and covered under the 1941 Defense Base Act. See B. Debusmann, "In Iraq, contractor deaths near 650, legal fog thickens," *Reuters.com* (October 10), Online, Available HTTP: <http://today.reuters.com/News/CrisesArticle.aspx?storyId=N10275842> (accessed January 2, 2006), 2006. See the Defense Base Act, Defensebaseact.com, Online, Available HTTP: <http://www.defensebaseact.com/>, (accessed January 2, 2007), 2007.

11　One other group of outsiders of sorts are Iraqi interpreters working with Coalition Forces. Known affectionately as "terps," one inquiry reported 257 fatalities between March 2003 through 2006. See J. Milliman and G. Chon, "Lost in translation: Iraq's injured 'terps," *The Wall Street Journal* (January 18), 2007, p. A1.

12　Iraq Body Count, *Iraq Body Count,* Online, Available HTTP: <http://www. iraqbodycount.org/>, (accessed January 2, 2007), 2007. They stipulate the primary source of their methodology as "we put accuracy above speed and do not update the data base until we have located and cross-checked two or more independent approved news sources for the same incident."

13　The use of the internet to memorialize these service members in unprecedented in U.S. history and marks a turning point in the sociology of death and may expand the space of future static memorials and monuments to the fallen. It is altering how we interact with the dead and those connected to the dead. For example, the Vietnam Memorial is certainly interactive in terms of visitors leaving mementos and other artifacts and taking away pencil etchings on paper of names engraved on the wall. Any memorials to soldiers who died in Afghanistan and Iraq will need to account for the plethora of individual and group memorials, remembrances, and other forms now spanning the globe via the internet. Problems may emerge. For example see I. Urbina, "In online mourning, don't speak ill of the dead," *The New York Times* (November 5), Online, Available HTTP: <http://www.nytimes.com>, (accessed January 2, 2007), 2006..

14　The next largest included 0311 Marine (Rifleman) Infantry ($n = 307$); 19D Army Cavalry Scout ($n = 132$); 21B Army Combat Engineer (n = 123); 19K Armor Crewmember ($n = 121$); 13B Cannon Crewmember ($n = 94$); 88M Transportation ($n = 87$); 11A Infantry Officer ($n = 68$); 31B Military Police ($n = 50$); and 91W Ordnance Branch ($n = 50$). Individual MOS deaths included a 45B—Small Arms Repairman; two 44Bs—Metal Workers; a 68E—Dental Specialist; a 92S—Shower/

Laundry and Clothing Repair Specialist; a 92W—Water Treatment Specialist; a 27A—JAG Corps Attorney; a 56A—Chaplain; a 63F Prosthodontist (specialized dentist); a 67F—Optometrist, two 920As—Property Accounting Technicians; and 24 92Gs—Food Service Specialists, among many others.

15 There appear to be some data entry problems with the official data of fatalities. The acronym ranks are correct but the alpha-numerical ranks do match in many cases. In some cases, the rank may be one rank higher or lower. This can be explained by differing designations by service or it could be a posthumous promotion. However, in some cases the ranks do not match by a wide margin. In these instances, I sought out two sources through the Internet to verify the rank. In all cases, the acronym rank was correct and the alphanumeric rank was incorrect.

16 For another comparison, Whites made up 71 percent of civilian work force in 2003. Blacks (11 percent), Hispanics (11 percent), Asian American/Pacific Islander (5 percent), American Indian/Alaskan Native (<1 percent) and Other/Unknown (1 percent) comprised the remaining civilian work force.

17 It is notable that 8 percent of the deaths in Korea were listed as "Other/Multiple race/Unknown."

18 The distributions of states are based on a standard classification of four regions used by the U.S. Census Bureau: North East (CT, ME, MA, NH, NJ, NY, PA, RI, and VT); Midwest (IL, IN, IA, KS, MI, MN, MO, NE, ND, OH, SD, and WI); South (AL, AR, DE, DC, FL, GA, KY, LA, MD, MS, NC, OK, SC, TN, TX, VA, and WV); and West (AK, AZ, CA, CO, HI, ID, MT, NV, NM, OR, UT, WA, and WY). The distributions are only for active-duty service members.

19 It should be noted that the home of record of soldiers may not be the best indicator of their background. It may reflect either their current address or some other address where they either lived previously or lived when they initially came into the military.

20 Using zip codes from the home of record, a problem noted above earlier, the study also failed to describe the justification for the three categories other than the "… software partitions the U.S. into market segments with unique socioeconomic characteristics."

21 Median income involves dividing households evenly from lowest to highest. The household in the middle is the median, with half of all the households above the median and the same number below the median. I used the 2004 estimates for median household income from the U.S. Census Bureau—created and maintained in the Small Area Income and Poverty Estimates (SAIPE) program. See U.S. Census Bureau, *Small Area Income and Poverty Estimates (SAIPE),* Online, Available HTTP: <http://www.census.gov/hhes/www/saipe/>, (accessed January 7, 2007), 2007b.

22 Note there is another category of the top 5 percent of American households earning more than $157,175 a year.

11   Conclusion: soldiers, minds, and American society

1 For example, just more than one-third of American soldiers and Marines in Iraq agreed that torture be allowed against insurgents. Office of the Surgeon and Office of the Surgeon General, *Mental Health Advisory Team (MHAT-III): Operation Iraqi Freedom 04–06 REPORT,* Multi-National Force Iraq: Baghdad, Iraq and United States Army Medical Command: Washington, DC (May 29), Online, Available HTTP: <http://www.medicine.army.mil/reports/mhat/mhat.html> (accessed September 11, 2008), 2006. See also Office of the Suroeon, 20066.

2 David Segal made a similar argument projecting into the 1990s, and John Allen Williams makes a similar argument for social representation. He states that the AVF is working better than most would have predicted—perhaps as a result of increased representation and diversity. See D.R. Segal, *Recruiting for Uncle Sam: Citizenship and Military Manpower Policy,* Lawrence, KS: University of Kansas Press, 1989 and J.A. Williams, *Anticipated and unanticipated consequences of the creation of the total force.* Paper presented at the McCormick Tribune Foundation Conference, Wheaton, IL (October 12), 2007.

Bibliography

American Association of University Professors, *Books for Understanding Iraq*. Online. Available HTTP: <http://aaupnet.org/news/bfu/iraq/list.html> (accessed January 27, 2007), 2006.

Applewhite, L.W., Furukawa, T.P., Segal, D.R. and Segal, M.W., "Lightfighters in the Desert," in D.R. Segal and M.W. Segal (eds.) *Peacekeepers and the Wives: American Participation in the Multinational Force and Observers,* Westport, CT: Greenwood, pp. 95–108, 1993.

Applewhite, L.W. and Segal, D.R., "Telephone use by peacekeeping troops in the Sinai," *Armed Forces & Society,* 17:117–26, 1990.

Appy, C., *Working-Class War,* Chapel Hill, NC: University of North Carolina Press, 1993.

Aspin, L., *Direct Ground Combat Definition and Assignment Rule* [memorandum], Washington, DC: The Office of the Secretary of Defense (January 13), 1994.

Associated Press., "Rumsfeld inquisitor not one to bite his tongue," December 8. Online. Available HTTP: <http://www.msnbc.msn.com/id/6679801/> (accessed September 11, 2006), 2004.

Avant, D. and Lebovic, J., "US military attitudes toward post-Cold War missions," *Armed Forces & Society,* 27(1):37–57, 2000.

Avellar, R., "Service men send living letters back home" *New York World Telegram,* February 16, 1942, p. 3, 1942.

Bachman, J.G., Freedman-Doan, P. Segal, D.R. and O'Malley, P.M., "Distinctive military attitudes among US enlistees, 1976–1997: self-selection versus socialization," *Armed Forces & Society,* 26:561–86, 2000.

Back to the Future [Film] Directed by Robert Zemeckis. USA: Amblin Entertainment, 1985.

Badillo, G. and Curry, G.D., "The social incidence of Vietnam casualties," *Armed Forces & Society,* 2:397–406, 1976.

Balmar, C., "Group cites 81 killings of journalists," *New York Times,* January 1, p. A10, 2007.

Banerjee, N., "Use of Wiccan symbol on veterans' headstones is approved," *New York Times,* April 24. Online. Available HTTP: <http://www.nytimes.com/> (accessed April 24, 2007), 2007.

Barr, S., "'Ordinary women' wounded in Iraq awarded defense Medal of Freedom," *Washington Post,* April 4, p. B02, 2005.

Bartnett, A., Stanley, T. and Shore, M., "America's Vietnam casualties: victims of a class war?" *Operations Research,* 40(5):856–66, 1992.

Bartone, P.T. and Adler, A.B., "Cohesion over time in a peacekeeping medical task force," *Military Psychology,* 11(1):85–107, 1999.

Bartone, P.T., Adler, A.B. and Vaitkus, M.A., "Dimensions of psychological stress in peacekeeping missions," *Military Medicine,* 163(9):587–93, 1998.

Bartone, P.T. and Ender, M.G., "Organizational responses to death in the military," *Death Studies* 18:25–40, 1994.

Beebe, G.W. and De Bakey, M.E., *Battle Casualties: Incidence, Mortality, and Logistical Considerations,* Springfield, IL: Charles C. Thomas, 1952.

Bell, D.B., Schumm, W.R., Scott, B. and Ender, M.G., "The desert FAX: calling home from Somalia," *Armed Forces & Society*, 25(3):509–21, 1999.

Bell, D.B. and Teitelbaum, J., "Operation Restore Hope: preliminary results of a survey of army spouses at Fort Drum, New York," paper presented at the Biennial International Conference of the Inter-University Seminar on Armed Forces and Society, Baltimore, MD, October, 1993.

Bennis, W.G. and Thomas, R.J., *Geeks and Geezers: How Era, Values, and Defining Moments Shape Leaders,* Cambridge, MA: Harvard Business School Press, 2002.

Bleifuss, J., "*Disasters: Natural and Social*: Eric Klinenberg discusses the militarization of social services and what will be missing from any national conversations about poverty," *In These Times,* September 26. Online. Available HTTP: <http://ww.inthesetimes.com/site/main/article/2330/> (accessed November 6, 2006), 2005.

Booth, B., Segal, M.W., Bell, D.B. with Martin, J.A., Ender, M.G., Rohall, D.E. and Nelson, J., *What We Know about Army Families: 2007 Update,* Alexandria, VA: U.S. Army Family and Morale, Welfare and Recreation Command, 2007.

Bowling, K.L., Firestone, J.M. and Harris, R.J. "Analyzing questions that cannot be asked of respondents who cannot respond," *Armed Forces & Society,* 31(3):411–37, 2005.

Britt, T.W. and Dickinson, J.M., "Morale during military operations: a positive psychology approach," in T.W. Britt, C.A. Castro and A.B. Adler (eds.) *Military Life: The Psychology of Serving in Peace and Conflict,* Vol 1, Westport, CT: Praeger Security International, pp. 157–84, 2006.

Bryman, A., "McDonald's as a Disneyized institution," *American Behavioral Scientist,* 47(2):154–68, 2003.

Buck, R., *Shane Comes Home,* New York: HarperCollins, 2005.

Burk, J., "Public support for peacekeeping in Lebanon and Somalia: assessing the casualties hypothesis," *Political Science Quarterly,* 114:53–79, 1999.

—"The changing moral contract for military service," in A.J. Bacevich (ed.) *The Long War: A New History of US National Security Policy Since World War II,* New York: Columbia University Press, pp. 405–55, 2007.

Burke, P.J., *Contemporary Social Psychological Theories,* Palo Alto, CA: Stanford University Press, 2006.

Burnham, G., Doocy, S., Dzeng, E., Lafta, R. and Roberts, L., *The human cost of the war in Iraq: a mortality study, 2002–2006,* Baltimore, MD: Johns Hopkins University. Online. Available HTTP: <http://web.mit.edu/cis/human-cost-war-101106.pdf> (accessed January 2, 2007), 2006.

Caforio, G., "Military officer education," in G. Caforio (ed.) *Handbook of the Sociology of the Military,* New York: Kluwer Academic/Plenum Publishers, pp. 255–78, 2003.

Campbell, A., "Class bias, elite bias, and no bias: Who served and died in Vietnam?" paper presented at the Annual Meetings of the Eastern Sociological Society Meetings, Philadelphia, PA, March, 2003.

Campbell, D.A., *Women at War with America: Private Lives in a Patriotic Era,* Cambridge, MA: Harvard University Press, 1984.

Caplow, T. and Hicks, L., *Systems of War and Peace,* Lanham, MD: University Press of America, 2002.

Carlson, P., "Talking wounded: Terry Rodgers came back from Iraq a changed man, and not just because of the bomb," *Washington Post,* August 10, p. C01, 2005.

Carlton-Ford, S., Ender, M.G. and Tabatabai, A., "Iraqi adolescents: self-regard, self-derogation, and perceived threat in war," *The Journal of Adolescence,* 31:53–75, 2008.

Carroll, M.H. and Clark, M.D., "Men's acquaintance rape scripts: a comparison between a regional university and a military academy," *Sex Roles,* 55:469–80, 2006.

Charlton, J. and Hertz, R., "Guarding against boredom: security specialists in the US Air Force," *Journal of Contemporary Ethnography,* 18(3):299–326, 1989.

Cherlin, A.J., *Public & Private Families,* Boston, MA: McGraw Hill, 2005.

Chiarelli, P.W. and Michaelis, P.R., "Winning the peace: the requirement for full-spectrum operations," *Military Review* (July-August):4–17, 2005.

Cockerham, W.C., "The military institution," in L.T. Reynolds and N.J. Herman-Kinney (eds.) *The Handbook of Symbolic Interaction,* Walnut Creek, CA: AltaMira, pp. 491–510, 2003.

Conrad, P., "It's boring: notes on the meanings of boredom in everyday life," *Qualitative Sociology,* 20(4):465–75, 1997.

Cox, A., "Estimates of Iraqi civilian deaths," *New York Times,* January 1. Online. Available HTTP: <http://www.nytimes.com/2007/01/01/us/01deathsbox.html> (accessed January 1, 2007), 2007.

Cresciani, G., "Captivity in Australia: the case of Italian prisoners of war, 1940–1947" *Studi Emigrazione/Etudes Migrations,* 26:195–220, 1989.

Cronan, T.A., Conway, T.L. and Kaszas, S.L., "Starting to smoke in the navy: when, where and why," *Social Science & Medicine,* 33(12):1349–53, 1991.

Dansby, M.R., Stewart, J.B. and Webb, S.C. (eds.), *Managing Diversity in the Military: Research Perspectives from the Defense Equal Opportunity Management Institute,* New Brunswick, NJ: Transaction Publishers, 2001.

Datta, A., "MacDonaldization of gender in urban India: a tentative exploration," *Gender, Technology and Development,* 9(1):125–35, 2005.

Debusmann, B. "In Iraq, contractor deaths near 650, legal fog thickens," *Reuters,* October 10. Online. Available HTTP: <http://today.reuters.com/News/CrisesArticle. aspx?storyId=N10275842> (accessed January 2, 2006), 2006.

Dechter, A.R. and Elder, G.H. Jr., "World War II mobilization in men's work lives: continuity or disruption for the middle class," *American Journal of Sociology,* 110(3):761–93, 2004.

Defense Base Act, *Defensebaseact.com.* Online. Available HTTP: <http://www. defensebaseact.com/> (accessed January 2, 2007), 2007.

Department of Defense, *Personnel and Military Casualty Statistics.* Online. Available HTTP: < http://siadapp.dmdc.osd.mil/personnel/MMIDHOME.HTM> (accessed September 11, 2008), 2008.

Department of the Army, *FM 100–23: Peace Operations,* Washington, DC: Headquarters, Department of the Army, 1994.

Department of the Army, *FM 6–22 Army Leadership: Competent, Confident, and Agile.* Washington, DC: Headquarters, Department of the Army, 2006.

Doe, C., "Grenada: will its lessons be taught?" *Army Times,* November 5: p. 34, 1984.

Drane, J., *The McDonaldization of the Church: Consumer Culture and the Church's Future,* Macon, GA: Smyth & Helwys Publishing, 2002.

Dunlap, C.J. Jr., "The origins of the American military coup of 2012," *Parameters,* (Winter):2–20, 1992.

Ender, M.G., "G.I. phone home: the use of telecommunications by the soldiers of Operation Just Cause," *Armed Forces & Society,* 21(3):435–53, 1995.

— "Soldiering toward the information superhighway: the comparison of old and new communication media use during military operations in the post-Cold War era," unpublished dissertation, University of Maryland, 1996.

— "E-mail to Somalia: new communication media between home and war fronts," in Joseph E. Behar (ed.) *Mapping Cyberspace: Social Research on the Electronic Frontier,* Oakdale, NY: Dowling College Press, Dowling Studies in the Humanities and the Social Sciences, pp. 27–52, 1997.

— "The postmodern military: soldiering, new media, and the post-cold war," *Journal for the Study of Peace and Conflict,* (1997–1998 Annual Edition):50–8, 1998.

— "Divergences in traditional and new communication media use among army families," in E. Ouellet (ed.) *New Directions in Military Sociology,* Willowdale, Canada: de Sitter Publications, pp. 255–95, 2005.

— *Essay on film documentaries about Iraq, Iraqis, war, and soldiers,* Peace, War, and Social Conflict Newsletter (July):10–11. Online. Available HTTP: <http://peacewarconflict.org/> (accessed October 1, 2007), 2007.

Ender, M.G., Bartone, P.T. and Kolditz, T.A., "The fallen soldier: death and the US military," in C.D. Bryant (ed.) *Handbook of Death and Dying: The Responses to Death, vol two,* Thousands Oaks, CA, London, and New Delhi: Sage, pp. 544–55, 2003.

Ender, M.G., Campbell, K., Davis, T. and Michaelis, P., "Greedy media: army families, embedded reporting, and the war in Iraq," *Sociological Focus,* 40(1):48–71, 2007.

Ender, M.G. and Segal, D.R., "V(E)-mail to the foxhole: isolation, (tele)communication, and forward deployed soldiers," *Journal of Political and Military Sociology,* 24(1):83–104, 1996.

— "Cyber-soldiering: Race, class, gender and new media use in the military," in B. Ebo (ed.) *Cyberghetto or Cybertopia: Race, Class, and Gender on the Internet,* Westport CT: Praeger Publishers, pp. 65–82, 1998.

Fallows, J., "What did you do in the class war, daddy?" *Washington Monthly,* 7(8):5–20, 1975.

— "Low-class conclusions," *The Atlantic,* 272(2):11–12, 1993.

Feaver, P.D. and Kohn, R.H., "Overview," *Armed Forces & Society* 27:177–82, 2001a.

Feaver, P.D. and Kohn, R.H. (eds.), *Soldiers and Civilians: The Civil-Military Gap and American National Security,* Cambridge, MA and London: MIT Press, 2001b.

Feaver, P.D., Kohn, R.H. and Cohn, L.P., "Introduction" in P.D. Feaver and R.H. Kohn (eds.) *Soldiers and Civilians: The Civil-Military Gap and American National Security,* Cambridge, MA and London: MIT Press, 1–12, 2001.

Firestone, J.M. and Harris, R.J., "Sexual harassment in the US military: individual and environmental contexts," *Armed Forces & Society* 21:25–43, 1994.

— "Changes in patterns of sexual harassment in the US military: a comparison of the 1988 and 1995 DoD surveys," *Armed Forces & Society* 25:613–32, 1999.

1st Cavalry Division, *Command Climate Survey,* Inspector General Office, Fort Hood, TX (unpublished data sources provided to the author), 2004.

Fleming, J.H. and Scott, B.A., "The cost of confession: the Persian Gulf War POW tapes in historical and theoretical perspective, *Contemporary Social Psychology,* 15(4):127–38, 1991.

Forgas, L. and Meyer, D.M., "Tobacco use habits of naval personnel during Desert Storm," *Military Medicine,* 16(13):165–8, 1996.

Forum, "Should the draft be reinstated," *Newsweek,* December 29, 2003/January 5, pp. 101–2, 2004.

Foust, B. and Bolts, H., "Age, ethnicity, and class in the Viet Nam war: evidence from the casualty file," *Viet Nam Generation Newsletter* 3, 4 (December-January):22–31, 1991/92.

Friedl, V.L., *Women in the United States Military, 1901–1995: A Research Guide and Annotated Bibliography,* Westport, CT: Greenwood Press, 1996.

Friedman, T.L. *The World is Flat: A Brief History of the Twenty-First Century,* updated and expanded edition, New York: Farrar, Straus, & Giroux, 2006.

Frolova, I., "'I'm alive, mom!': Information service to families of soldiers sent to war areas," *Moscow News,* 42(3549), October 18: p. 2, 1992.

Gawande, A. "Notes of a surgeon: casualties of war—military care for the wounded from Iraq and Afghanistan," *The New England Journal of Medicine,* 351(24):2471–5. Online. Available HTTP: <http://content.nejm.org/cgi/content/full/351/24/2471> (accessed September 18, 2006), 2004.

Gehler, C.P., *Agile Leaders, Agile Institutions: Educating Adaptive and Innovative Leaders for Today and Tomorrow,* Carlisle, PA: Strategic Studies Institute, 2005.

General Social Survey, *General Social Survey.* Online. Available HTTP: <http://www.norc.org/GSS+Website/> (accessed October 1, 2007), 2007.

Gifford, B., "Combat casualties and race: what can we learn from the 2003–2004 Iraq conflict?" *Armed Forces & Society,* 31(2):201–25, 2005.

Gifford, R.K., Jackson, J.N. and Deshazo, K.B., *Observations of a human dimensions research team in Somalia during Operation Restore Hope,* paper presented at the Biennial International Conference of the Inter-University Seminar on Armed Forces and Society, Baltimore, MD, October, 1993.

Glicksohn, J., Ben-Shalom, U. and Lazar, M., "Elements of unacceptable risk taking in combat units: an exercise in offender profiling," *Journal of Research in Personality,* 38(3):203–15, 2004.

Goffman, E., *Behavior in Public Places: Notes on the Social Organization of Gatherings,* New York: Free Press of Glencoe, 1963.

Gravino, K.S., Segal, D.R., Segal, M.W. and Waldman, R.J., "The evolution of peacekeeping as a military mission," in D.R. Segal and M.W. Segal (eds.) *Peacekeepers and their Wives: American Participation in the Multinational Force and Observers,* Westport, CT and London: Greenwood Press, pp. 1–14, 1993a.

— "The history of multinational peacekeeping," in D.R. Segal and M.W. Segal (eds.) *Peacekeepers and their Wives: American Participation in the Multinational Force and Observers,* Westport, CT and London: Greenwood Press, pp. 15–26, 1993b.

Greene, R.A., "Soldiers' books show Iraq's front line," *BBC News,* January 13. Online. Available HTTP: <http://news.bbc.co.uk/2/hi/americas/4602958.stm> (accessed January 27, 2007), 2006.

Hajjar, R. and Ender, M.G., "McDonaldization in the U.S. army: a threat to the profession," in D.M. Snider and L.J. Matthews (eds.) *The Future of the Army Profession* (2nd ed), Boston, MA: McGraw Hill Custom Publishing, pp. 515–30, 2005.

— "Harnessing the power of culture and diversity for organizational performance," in D. Crandall (ed.) *Leadership Lessons from West Point,* San Francisco, CA: Jossey-Bass, pp. 313–37, 2007.

Hampson, R., "In this war, troops get a rousing welcome home," *USA Today*, July 2, p. 1, 2008.

Hare, M.G., "Mother recalls Thurmont soldier as caring brother," *The Baltimore Sun,* December 3. Online. Available HTTP: <http://www.baltimoresun.com/news/nationworld/iraq/bal-hayes120304,0,2822802.story?coll=bal-iraq-headlines> (accessed January 14, 2007), 2004.

Harrell, M.C., Beckett, M.K., Chien, C.S. and Sollinger, J.M., *The Status of Gender Integration in the Military: Analysis of Selected Occupations,* Santa Monica, CA: RAND, 2002.

Harrell, M.C. and Miller, L.L., *New Opportunities for Military Women: Effects on Readiness, Cohesion, and Morale,* Santa Monica, CA: RAND, 1997.

Harrell, M.C., Castaneda, L.W., Schirmer, P., Hallmark, B.W., Kavanagh, J., Gershwin, D. and Steinberg, P., *Assessing the Assignment Policy for Army Women,* Washington, DC: RAND, 2007.

Harris, J., Rothberg, J.M., Segal, D.R. and Segal, M.W., "Paratroopers in the desert," in D.R. Segal and M.W. Segal (eds.) *Peacekeepers and their Wives: American Participation in the Multinational Force and Observers,* Westport, CT and London: Greenwood Press, pp. 81–94, 1993.

Harris, J.J. and Segal, D.R., "Observations from the Sinai: boredom as a peacekeeping irritant," *Armed Forces & Society,* 11:235–48, 1985.

Hartley, D., "The 'McDonaldization' of higher education: food for thought?" *Oxford Review of Education,* 21(4):409–23, 1995.

Hawley, T.M., *The Remains of War: Bodies, Politics, and the Search for American Soldiers Unaccounted for in Southeast Asia,* Durham, NC: Duke University Press, 2005.

Hayes, D. and Wynyard, R. (eds.), *The McDonaldization of Higher Education,* Westport, CT: Bergin & Garvey, 2002.

Headquarters, Department of the Army, *The Army Training and Leader Development Panel Officer Study Report to the Army,* Online, Available HTTP: <http://www.Army.mil/atld> (accessed October 9, 2006), 2001.

Heartbreak Ridge, [Film] Directed by Clint Eastwood. USA: Jay Weston Productions, 1986.

Heggie, B., "Service men on wax," *Coronet* (August):140–3, 1942.

Helmkamp, J.C. and Kennedy, R.D., "Causes of death among US military personnel: a 14–year summary, 1980–1993," *Military Medicine,* 161:311–7, 1996.

Henslin, J.M., *Sociology: A Down-to-Earth Approach,* 7th ed, Boston, MA: Allyn & Bacon, 2005.

Higate, P. and Cameron, A., "Reflexivity and researching the military," *Armed Forces & Society,* 32(2):219–33, 2006.

Hoffmeyer, D., "Mosul attack kills 24, wounds 64," *Richmond Times-Dispatch,* December 21. Online. Available HTTP: <http://www.timesdispatch.com/cva/ric/times_dispatch.html> (accessed December 24, 2004), 2004.

Höhn, M., *GIs and Fräuleins: The German-American Encounter in 1950s West Germany,* Chapel Hill, NC: University of North Carolina Press, 2002.

Holm, J., *Women in the Military: An Unfinished Revolution,* revised ed, Novato, CA: Presidio, 1992.

Holsti, O.R., "Of chasms and convergences: attitudes and beliefs of civilians and military elites at the start of the new millennium," in P.D. Feaver and R.H. Kohn (eds.) *Soldiers and Civilians: The Civil-Military Gap and American National Security,* Cambridge, MA and London: MIT Press, pp. 15–100, 2001.

Hong, Y.G., "Encounter with modernity: the "McDonaldization" and "charismatization" of Korean mega churches" *International Review of Mission,* 92(365):239–56, 2003.

Hosek, J., Kavanagh, J. and Miller, L., *How Deployments Affect Service Members,* Santa Monica, CA: RAND Corporation, 2006.

Hosek, J. and Totten, M., *Serving Away from Home: How Deployments Influence Reenlistment,* Santa Monica, CA: RAND Corporation, 2002.

Hosek, S.D., Tiemeyer, P., Kilburn, R., Strong, D.A., Ducksworth, S. and Ray, R., *Minority and Gender Differences in Officer Career Progression,* Santa Monica, CA: RAND, 2001.

House, J.S., "The three faces of social psychology," *Sociometry,* 40:161–77, 1977.

Hovland, C.I., Lumsdaine, A.A. and Sheffield, F.D., *Experiments in Mass Communication,* Princeton, NJ: Princeton University Press, 1949.

Hudson, N., "Advantages over snail mail," *Navy Times,* December 11, p. 26, 1995a.

— "E-mail from Bosnia: a new can of worms," *Army Times,* December 11, p. 27, 1995b.

— "Pentagon plugs Bosnia into the internet," *Army Times,* December 25, p. 14, 1995c.

— "Special report, military gets wired: internet connections puts world at service members fingertips," *Army Times,* October 2, pp. 14–18, 1995d.

Illouz, E. and Nicholas, J. "Global habitus, local stratification, and symbolic struggles over identity," *American Behavioral Scientist,* 47(2):201–30, 2003.

Inglehart, R., Moaddel, M. and Tessler, M., "Xenophobia and in-group solidarity in Iraq: a natural experiment on the impact of insecurity," *Perspectives on Politics,* 4(3):495–505, 2006.

Ingraham, L.H., "The Nam" and "the world": heroin use by US army enlisted men in Vietnam," *Psychiatry,* 37(2):114–28, 1974.

Inskeep, S., "A shelf full of books chronicle Iraq policy, strategy," *NPR Radio,* October 24. Online (transcripts). Available HTTP: <http://www.npr.org/templates/story/story.php?storyID=6271029> (accessed January 27, 2007), 2006.

Iraq Body Count, *Iraq Body Count.* Online. Available HTTP: <http://www.iraqbodycount.org/> (accessed January 2, 2007), 2007.

Iskra, D., Trainor, S., Leithauser, M. and Segal, M.W., "Women's participation in armed forces cross-nationally: expanding Segal's model," *Current Sociology,* 50(5): 771–97, 2002.

It's a Wonderful Life [Film] Directed by Frank Capra. USA: Liberty Films, 1946

Janis, I.L., "Morale attitudes of combat flying personnel in the Air Corps," in S.A. Stouffer, E.A. Lumsdaine, M.H. Lumsdaine, R.M. Williams, Jr., M.B. Smith, I.L. Janis, S.A. Star and L.S. Cottrell, Jr. (eds.) *Volume II. The American Solder: Combat and Its Aftermath,* Princeton, NJ: Princeton University Press, pp. 324–61, 1949.

Jarhead, [Film] Directed by Sam Mendes. USA: Universal Pictures, 2005.

Jowers, K., "'Voice-mail' in service for Desert Shield," *Army Times,* December 3, pp. 62–3, 1991.

Kearns Goodwin, J., "Unmobilized for war," *Boston Globe,* April 6. Online. Available HTTP: <http://www.boston.com/> (accessed April 6, 2007), 2007.

Kellner, D., *The Persian Gulf TV War,* Boulder, CO: Westview Press, 1992.

Kemmesies, U.E., "What do hamburgers and drug care have in common: some unorthodox remarks on the McDonaldization and rationality of drug care," *Journal of Drug Issues,* 32(2):689–709, 2002.

Kenen, J., "For some amputees, future is in the US army," *Reuters,* November 7. Online. Available HTTP: <http://today.reuters.com/> (accessed November 7, 2007), 2007.

Kindsvatter, P.S., *American Soldiers: Ground Combat in the World Wars, Korea, and Vietnam,* Lawrence, KS: University of Kansas Press, 2003.

Klapp, O., *Overload and Boredom: Essays on the Quality of Life in the Information Society,* New York: Greenwood Press, 1986.

Klein, A., "The morale myth," *Washington Monthly,* May. Online. Available HTTP: <http://www.washingtonmonthly.com/features/2006/0605.klein.html> (accessed July 1, 2007), 2006.

Knickerbocker, B., "Soldier blogs bring the front line to the folks at home," *Christian Science Monitor.* Online. Available HTTP: <http://www.csmonitor.com/2005/0419/p01s05–ussc.html> (accessed August 30, 2006), 2005.

Kroupa, E.A., "Use of mass media by US army personnel," *Journal of Broadcasting*, 17(3):309–20, 1973.

Kurashina, Y. "Cyber military community: the emergence of computer-mediated military spouse networks," paper presented at the Department of Defense Quality of Life and Technology Symposium, Washington, DC, February, 2000.

Leal, D.L., "American public opinion toward the military: differences by race, gender, and class?" *Armed Forces & Society,* 32(1):123–38, 2005.

Liscano, M., "Rudy Mesa," *Austin American-Statesman.* Online. Available HTTP: <http://www.statesman.com/> (accessed January 2, 2007), 2006.

Litoff, J.B. and Smith, D.C., "'Will he get my letter?' popular portrayals of mail and morale during World War II," *Journal of Popular Culture*, 23(4):21–43, 1990.

Little, R., "Buddy relations and combat performance," in M. Janowitz (ed.) *The New Military,* New York: Russell Sage Foundation, pp. 194–224, 1965.

Lyons, G.M., "The military mind," *Bulletin of the Atomic Scientists* (November):19–21, 1963.

McCarroll, J.E., Ursano, R.J., Fullerton, C.S., Liu, X. and Lundy, A., "Effects of exposure to death in a war mortuary on posttraumatic stress disorder symptoms of intrusion and avoidance," *Journal of Nervous & Mental Disease*, 189(1):44–8, 2001.

— "Somatic symptoms in Gulf War mortuary workers," *Psychosomatic Medicine,* 64:29–33, 2002.

McCarroll, J.E., Ursano, R.J., Fullerton, C.S., Oates, G.L., Ventis, W.L., Friedman, H., Shean, G.L. and Wright, K.M., "Gruesomeness, emotional attachment, and personal threat: Dimensions of the anticipated stress of body recovery," *Journal of Traumatic Stress*, 8(2):343–9, 1995.

McDonaldization.com, *McDonaldization*. Online. Available HTTP: <http://www. mcdonaldization.com> (accessed July 25, 2006), 2006.

MacGinnis, A., "Downtown Fort Belvoir: army post in Fairfax County gets a taste of off-post living with its own town center," *Washington Post,* October 22, p. C01, 2006.

McLaughlin, A., "E-mail and tv: lifelines for military spouses," *Christian Science Monitor*, March 27, p. 1, 2003.

MacLean, A., "Lessons from the cold war: military service and college education," *Sociology of Education,* 78(3):250–66, 2005a.

— "The varieties of veteran experience: Cold War military service and the life course," Dissertation Abstracts International, A: The Humanities and Social Sciences, 65(8), 3175–A, 2005b.

Madison, D.S., *Critical Ethnography: Methods, Ethics, and Performance,* Thousand Oaks, CA: Sage Publications, 2005.

Marshall, R., "Battlefield communications: technology's challenge," *Defense & Foreign Affairs,* (October):26, 1986.

Matthews, M.D., Ender, M.G., Laurence, J. and Rohall, D.E., "Role of group affiliation and gender attitudes toward women in the military," *Military Psychology,* forthcoming.

Matthews, M.D., Ender, M.G. and Rohall, D.E., "Student attitudes toward women in the military by institution type," paper presented at the Annual Meeting of the American Psychological Association, Honolulu, HI, July, 2004.

Mathews, T. et al., "Letters in the sand," *Newsweek,* November 19, pp. 26–32, 1990.

Mayer, A.J. and Hoult, T.F. "Social stratification and combat survival," *Social Forces* 34:155–9, 1955.

Mazur, A., "Was Vietnam a class war?" *Armed Forces & Society,* 3:455–9, 1995.

Memmott, C., "Iraq war hits home in 300–plus books," *USA Today,* March 20. Online. Available HTTP: <http://www.usatoday.com/life/books/news/2005–03–20–oraq-books_x.htm> (accessed January 27, 2007), 2005.

Miller, L.L., "Do soldiers hate peacekeeping?: the case of preventive diplomacy operations in Macedonia," *Armed Forces & Society,* 23(3):415–50, 1997.

Miller, L.L. and Moskos, C.C., "Humanitarianism or warriors?: race, gender, and combat status in Operation Restore Hope," *Armed Forces & Society,* 21(4):615–37, 1995.

Milliman, J. and Chon, G., "Lost in translation: Iraq's injured 'terps,'" *The Wall Street Journal,* January 18, p. A1, 2007.

Mok, K.H., "The cost of managerialism: the implications for the 'McDonaldization' of higher education in Hong Kong," *Journal of Higher Education Policy & Management,* 21(1):117–28, 1999.

Moore, B., *To Serve my Country, To Serve my Race: The Story of the Only African American WACs Stationed Overseas during World War II,* New York and London: New York University Press, 1996.

— *Serving Our Country: Japanese Women in the Military during World War II,* New Brunswick, NJ: Rutgers University Press, 2003.

Moskos, C.C., *The American Enlisted Man,* New York: Russell Sage Foundation, 1970.

— "UN peacekeepers: the constabulary ethic and military professionalism," *Armed Forces & Society,* 1:338–401, 1975.

— "The military," *Annual Review of Sociology,* 2:55–77, 1976.

— *A Call to Civic Service: National Service for Country and Community,* New York: The Free Press, 1988.

— "American military interaction with locals in OIF/OEF: preliminary draft." E-mail (communication with Generals Peter Pace, John Abizaid, James Jones, and Peter Schoomaker) (March 7), 2006.

Moskos, C.C. and Butler, J.S., *Be All That You Can Be: Black Leadership and Racial Integration the Army Way,* New York: Twentieth Century Fund, 1996.

Moskos, C.C. and Miller, L., "December 2003 sociological survey on Operation Iraqi Freedom," unpublished memo (prepared for General John P. Abizaid, Central Command Commander), Northwestern University, Evanston, IL, 2004.

Moskos, C.C. and Wood, F.R. (eds), *The Military: More than Just a Job?* Washington, DC: Pergamon-Brassey's, 1988.

Musheno, M. and Ross, S.M., *Deployed: The New American Citizen Soldiers,* Ann Arbor, MI: University of Michigan Press, 2008.

Nelson, T.S., *For Love of Country: Confronting Rape and Sexual Harassment in the US Military,* Binghamton, NY: The Haworth Press, 2002.

NGO Coordination Committee in Iraq, "81 aid workers have been killed in Iraq since 2003," *NCCI Web Site.* Online. Available HTTP: <http://www.ncciraq.org/> (accessed January 2, 2007), 2007.

Nguyen, A., "Technology offers lifeline for troops," *Cherry Hill Courier Post,* (November 27) Online. Available HTTP: <http://www.courierpostonline.com/apps/pbcs.dll/frontpage> (accessed November 30, 2005), 2005.

Office of the Surgeon and Office of the Surgeon General, *Mental Health Advisory Team (MHAT-III): Operation Iraqi Freedom 04–06 REPORT,* Multi-National Force Iraq: Baghdad, Iraq and United States Army Medical Command: Washington, DC (May 29). Online. Available HTTP: <http://www.medicine.army.mil/reports/mhat/mhat.html> (accessed September 11, 2008), 2006a.

Office of the Surgeon and Office of the Surgeon General, *Mental Health Advisory Team (MHAT) IV: Operation Iraqi Freedom 05–07,* Multi-National Force Iraq: Baghdad, Iraq and United States Army Medical Command: Washington, DC (November 17). Online. Available HTTP: <http://www.medicine.army.mil/reports/mhat/mhat.html> (accessed 11, 2008), 2006b.

Office of the Under Secretary of Defense, Personnel and Readiness, *Population Representation in the Military Services.* Online. Available HTTP: <http://humrro03.securesites.net/poprep/poprep05/index.html> (accessed September 9, 2008), 2007. (see p. 186 *Over There,* [TV program]).

Over There, [TV program] F/X, created by Gerolmo, C. and Saloman, M., Online. Available HTTP: <http://www.imdb.com/title/tt0446241/> (accessed August 30, 2006), 2005.

Paul, E., "Kiss the sun (A song for Pat Tillman)" American Jukebox Fables, (CD) Philo, 2005.

Paulson, A., "The new veterans among U.S.: women," *Christian Science Monitor,* November 10, 2006. Online. Available HTTP: <http://www.csmonitor.com> (accessed December 2, 2006), 2006.

Peggy Sue Got Married [Film] Dir. by Francis Ford Coppola. Delphi V Productions, 1986.

186 *Bibliography*

Petraeus, D.H., "Letter to families of the 101st, from General Petraeus." Online. Available HTTP: <http://screamingeagles-327thvietnam.com/general_petraeus. htm> (accessed September 18, 2006), undated.

Pierce, P.F., "Monitoring the health of Persian Gulf War veteran women," *Military Medicine,* 170(5):349–54, 2005.

—— "Retention of air force women serving during Desert Shield and Desert Storm," *Military Psychology,* 10(3):195–213, 1998.

Quinn, B., "The McDonaldization of Academic Libraries," *College & Research Libraries,* 61(3):248–61, 2000.

Ramis, H. (director), *Groundhog Day,* [film] Columbia Pictures Inc., 1993.

Redmon, J. (2004) "Mosul attack kills 24; wounds 64: local reporter on scene," *Richmond Times-Dispatch,* December 21. Online. Available HTTP: <http://www. timesdispatch.com> (accessed July 31, 2006), 2004.

Reed, B.J. and Segal, D.R., "The impact of multiple deployments on soldiers' peacekeeping attitudes, morale, and retention," *Armed Forces & Society,* 27(1):57–78, 2000.

Reporters Without Borders for Press Freedom, "Press freedom barometer" Online. Available HTTP: <http://www.rsf.org/killed_2005.php3?id_article=14201> (accessed January 2, 2007), 2007.

Ricks, T.E., "Colonel Dunlap's coup," *The Atlantic Online* (January). Online. Available HTTP: <http://www.theatlantic.com/politics/defense/coldunl.htm> (accessed October 23, 2007), 1993.

—— "The widening gap between the military and society," *The Atlantic Monthly,* July. Online. Available HTTP: <http://www.theatlantic.com/issues/97jul/milisoc.htm> (accessed October 23, 2007), 1997.

Rikhye, I.J., Harbottle, M. and Egge, B., *The Thin Blue Line,* New Haven, CT: Yale University Press, 1974.

Ritzer, G., "The McDonaldization of society," *Journal of American Culture,* 6:100–7, 1983.

—— *McDonaldization: The Reader,* Thousand Oaks, CA: Pine Forge Press, 2002.

—— *The McDonaldization of Society: Revised New Century Edition,* Thousand Oaks, CA: Sage and Pine Forge Press, 2004.

Ritzer, G. and Stillman, T., "The modern Las Vegas-casino hotel: the paradigmatic new means of consumption," *M@n@gement,* 4(3):83–99, 2001a.

—— "The postmodern ballpark as a leisure setting: enchantment and simulated de-McDonaldization," *Leisure Studies,* 23:99–113, 2001b.

Ritzer, G. and Walczak, D., "Rationalization and the deprofessionalization of physicians," *Social Forces,* 67(1):1–22, 1988.

Robbins, E.L., "Gifts of thanks for the troops," *Washington Post,* November 11, p. B07, 2007.

Roberts, L., Lafta, R., Garfield, R., Khudhairi, J. and Burnham, G., "Mortality before and after the 2003 invasion of Iraq: a cluster survey," *The Lancet,* October 29, pp. 1–8. Online. Available HTTP: <http://www.zmag.org/lancet.pdf> (accessed January 2, 2007), 2004.

Rohall, D.E. and Ender, M.G., "Race, gender, and class: attitudes toward the war in Iraq and President Bush among military personnel," *Race, Gender & Class,* 14(3–4):99–116, 2007.

Rohall, D.E., Ender, M.G., and Matthews, M.D., "The effects of military affiliation, sex, and political affiliation toward the wars in Iraq and Afghanistan," *Armed Forces & Society,* 33(1):59–77, 2006.

Rose, S.J., *Social Stratification in the United States,* New York: The New Press, 2000.

Rosen, L.N., Bliese, P.D., Wright, K.A. and Gifford, R.K., "Gender composition and group cohesion in US army units: a comparison across five studies," *Armed Forces & Society,* 25(3):365–86, 1999.

Rosen, L.N. and Martin, L., "Sexual harassment, cohesion and combat readiness in US army support units," *Armed Forces & Society*, 24:221–44, 1997.

Schnack, D.L.L., "A case for the separation of hearts and minds: an analysis of Iraqi attitudes and perceptions in Baghdad," unpublished thesis, Boston College, 2006.

Schumm, W.R., Bell, D.B., Ender, M.G. and Rice, R.E., "Expectations, use, and evaluations of communications media among deployed peacekeepers," *Armed Forces & Society,* 30(4):649–62, 2004.

Schuman, H., "Attitudes, beliefs, and behavior," in K.S. Cook, G.A. Fine and J.S. House (eds.) *Sociological Perspectives on Social Psychology,* Needham Heights, MA: Allyn & Bacon, pp. 68–89, 1995.

Scott, W.J. and Stanley, S.C. (eds.), *Gays and Lesbians in the Military: Issues, Concerns, and Contrasts,* New York: Walter de Gruyter, Inc, 1994.

Segal, D.R., "Communication about the military: people and media in the flow of information," *Communication Research*, 2(1):68–78, 1975.

— *Recruiting for Uncle Sam: Citizenship and Military Manpower Policy,* Lawrence, KS: University of Kansas Press, 1989.

Segal, D.R., Freedman-Doan, P., Bachman, J.G. and O'Malley, P.M., "Attitudes of entry-level enlisted personnel: pro-military and politically mainstreamed," in P.D. Feaver and R.H. Kohn (eds.) *Soldiers and Civilians: The Civil-Military Gap and American National Security,* Cambridge, MA: MIT Press, pp. 163–212, 2001.

Segal, D.R., Harris, J.J., Rothberg, J.M. and Marlowe, D.H., "Paratroopers as peacekeepers," *Armed Forces & Society,* 10:487–506, 1984.

Segal, D.R., Kinzer, N.S. and Woelfel, J.C., "The concept of citizenship and attitudes toward women in combat," *Sex Roles,* 3(5):469–77, 1977.

Segal, D.R., Reed, B.J. and Rohall, D.E., "Constabulary attitudes of national guard and regular soldiers in the US Army," *Armed Forces & Society,* 24(4):535–48, 1998.

Segal, D.R. and Segal, M.W., "Change in military organization," *Annual Review of Sociology,* 9:151–70, 1983.

Segal, D.R. and Segal, M.W. (eds.), *Peacekeepers and their Wives: American Participation in the Multinational Force and Observers,* Westport, CT: Greenwood, 1993.

— "America's military population," *Population Bulletin,* 59(4): December. Online. Available HTTP: <http://www.prb.org/pdf04/59.4AmericanMilitary.pdf> (accessed October 9, 2007), 2004.

Segal, D.R. and Tiggle, R.B., "Attitudes of citizen-soldiers toward military missions in the post-Cold War world," *Armed Forces & Society,* 23(3):373–90, 1997.

Segal, M.W. "The nature of work and family linkages: a theoretical perspective," in G.L. Bowen and D.K. Orthner (eds.) *The Organization Family: Work and Family in the US Military,* New York: Praeger, pp. 3–36, 1989.

— "Women's military roles cross-nationally: past, present, and future," *Gender and Society,* 9(6):757–75, 1995.

Segal, M.W. and Harris, J.J., *What We Know About Army Families* (Research Report 21), Alexandria, VA: U.S. Army Research Institute for the Behavioral and Social Sciences, 1993.

Semple, K., "A captain's journey from hope to just getting her unit home," *New York Times,* November 19, p. 1, 2006.

Sewell, W.H., "Some reflections on the golden age of interdisciplinary social psychology," *Social Psychology Quarterly,* 52(2):88–97, 1998.

Shanker, T., "All quiet on the home front, and some soldiers are asking why" (Military Memo), *New York Times,* July 24. Online. Available HTTP: <http://www.nytimes. com/2005/07/24/politics/24troops.html> (accessed November 23, 2008), 2005.

Simons, L.M., "Genocide unearthed: forensic investigators are assembling grim evidence of mass murders during Saddam Hussein's regime," *National Geographic*, January, pp. 28–35, 2006.

Sledge, M., *Soldier Dead: How We Recover, Identify, Bury, & Honor Our Military Fallen,* New York: Columbia University Press, 2005.

Smith III, I., "The World War II veteran advantage?: a lifetime cross-sectional study of social status attainment," unpublished dissertation, University of Maryland, 2007.

Snider, D.M., Priest, R.F. and Lewis, F., "The civilian-military gap and professional military education at the pre-commissioning level," *Armed Forces & Society* 27:249–72, 2001.

Snow, D.A., "1998 PSA presidential address: the value of sociology," *Sociological Perspectives,* 42(1):1–22, 1999.

Soeters, J. and van der Meulen, J. (eds.), *Managing Diversity in the Armed Forces: Experiences in Nine Countries,* Tilburg, Netherlands: Tilburg University Press, 1999.

Solaro, E. "Lionesses of Iraq," *Seattle Weekly,* (October 6), Online. Available HTTP: <http://www.seatleweekly.com> (accessed December 2, 2006), 2004.

—— *Women in the Line of Fire: What You Should Know about Women in the Military,* Emeryville, CA: Seal Press, 2006.

Stouffer, S.A. and DeVinney, L.C., "How persona adjustment varied in the Army—Preliminary considerations," in Stouffer, S.A., Suchman, E.A., DeVinney, L.C., Star, S.A. and Williams, R.M. Jr. eds. *The American Soldier: Adjustment during Army Life, Volume 1,* Princeton, NJ: Princeton University Press, pp. 82–104, 1949.

Stouffer, S.A., Guttman, L., Suchman, E.A., Lazersfeld, P.F., Star, S.A. and Clausen, J.A., *Measurement and Prediction,* Princeton, NJ: Princeton University Press, 1950.

Stouffer, S.A., Lumsdaine, E.A., Lumsdaine, M.H., Williams, R.M. Jr., Smith, M.B., Janis, I.L., Star, S.A. and Cottrell, L.S. Jr., *Volume II. The American Solder: Combat and Its Aftermath,* Princeton, NJ: Princeton University Press, 1949.

Stouffer, S.A., Suchman, E.A., DeVinney, L.C., Star, S.A. and Williams, R.M. Jr., *Volume I. The American Soldier: Adjustment during Army Life,* Princeton, NJ: Princeton University Press, 1949.

Strauss, W. and Howe, N., *Generations: The History of America's Future, 1584 to 2069,* New York: HarperCollins, 1992.

Suid, L., *Guts and Glory: The Making of the American Military Image in Film* (revised and expanded), Lexington, KY: University of Kentucky Press, 2002.

Taylor, K.M.G. and Harding, G., "Teaching, learning, and research in McSchools of pharmacy," *Pharmacy Education,* 2(2):43–9, 2002.

Teachman, J., "Military service during the Vietnam era: were there consequences for subsequent civilian earnings?" *Social Forces,* 83(2):709–30, 2004.

— "Military service in the Vietnam era and educational attainment," *Sociology of Education,* 78(1):50–68, 2005.

Teachman, J. and Tedrow, L.M., "Wages, earnings, and occupational status: did World War II veterans receive a premium?" *Social Science Research,* 33(4):581–605, 2004.

Thomas, W.I. and Thomas, D.S., *The Child in America,* New York: Knopf, 1928.

Thompson, W. and Hickey, J., *Society in Focus,* Boston, MA: Pearson, 2005.

Three Kings [Film] Directed by David O. Russell. USA: Warner Brothers and Village Roadshow Pictures, 1999.

Thund-Her-Struck, *Thund-Her-Struck.* Online. Available HTTP: <http://thundherstruck. com/> (accessed November 2, 2006), 2006.

Tillman, M., *Boots on the Ground by Dusk: My Tribute to Pat Tillman.* New York: Modern Times, 2008.

Time, "Person of the year: the American soldier," *Time,* 162(26), December 29–January 5, pp. 32–104, 2003/2004.

Tremoglie, M., "Rangel is wrong," *FrontpageMagazine.com,* January 9. Online. Available HTTP: <http://frontpagemag.com/Articles/Read.aspx?GUID=BF7A7069–ECF3–438C-9C82–8CEC725DB518> (accessed September 8, 2008), 2003.

US Army G-1 Human Resource Policy, *Army Profile: FY04.* Online. Available HTTP: <http://www.armyg1.army.mil/hr/Demographics.asp> (accessed January 27, 2007), 2007.

US Army Marine Corps, *Counterinsurgency Field Manual.* Chicago, IL: University of Chicago Press, 2007.

US Army Memorial Affairs and Casualty Operations Center, *Army Casualty: Casualty and Memorial Affairs Operations Center.* Online. Available HTTP: <https://www. perscom.army.mil/tagd/cmaoc/cmaoc.htm> (accessed March 19, 2003), 2003.

US Army Surgeon General and HQDA G-1, *Operation Iraqi Freedom (OIF) Mental Health Advisory Team (MHAT) Report,* Washington, DC: US Army Surgeon General and Headquarters, Department of the Army, G-1 (December 16). Online. Available HTTP: <http://www.medicine.army.mil/reports/mhat/mhat.html > (accessed September 11, 2008), 2003.

US Army Training and Doctrine Command: Office of the Chief of Public Affairs (undated) *Army Values.* Online. Available HTTP: <http://www.tradoc.army.mil/pao/ ArmyValues/ArmyValues.htm> (accessed November 6, 2006), undated.

US Census Bureau, *Distribution of Population by County Population Size: July 1, 2001.* Online. Available HTTP: <http://www.census.gov/popest/gallery/graphs/CO-distpop.html> (accessed January 27, 2007), 2001a.

— *Population Change and Distribution, 1990 to 2000.* Online. Available HTTP: <http:// www.census.gov/prod/2001pubs/c2kbr01–2.pdf> (accessed January 27, 2007), 2001b.

— *Percent Distribution of Households, by Selected Characteristics Within Income Quintile and Top 5 Percent in 2004.* Online. Available HTTP: <http://pubdb3.census. gov/macro/032005/hhinc/new05_000.htm> (accessed January 13, 2007), 2007a.

— *Small Area Income and Poverty Estimates (SAIPE).* Online. Available HTTP: <http:// www.census.gov/hhes/www/saipe/> (accessed January 7, 2007), 2007b.

US Department of Defense, *Military Casualty Information*. Online. Available HTTP: <http://siadapp.dior.whs.mil/personnel/CASUALTY/castop.htm> (accessed January 2, 2007), 2007.

United States Government Accountability Office, *Military Personnel: Reporting Additional Servicemember Demographics Could Enhance Congressional Oversight* (GAO-05–952), Washington, DC: GAO, 2005.

US Department of Veterans Affairs, *Center for Women Veterans*. Online. Available HTTP: <http://www1.va.gov/womenvet/> (accessed October 9, 2006), 2006.

Urbina, I., "In online mourning, don't speak ill of the dead," *The New York Times,* November 5. Online. Available HTTP: <http://www.nytimes.com> (accessed January 2, 2007), 2006.

Useem, M., "The educational and military experience of young men during the Vietnam era: non-linear effects of parental social class," *Journal of Political and Military Sociology,* 8:15–29, 1980.

von Clausewitz, C., *On War,* New York: Penguin Books, 1832/1968.

Wallace, J.C., Vodanovich, S.J. and Restino, B.M., "Predicting cognitive failures from boredom proneness and daytime sleepiness scores: an investigation within military and undergraduate samples," *Personality & Individual Differences,* 34(4):635–44, 2003.

Wattendorf, J.M., "The American soldier in a prewar desert environment: observations from Desert Shield," *Social Science Quarterly,* 73(2):276–95, 1992.

Webb, J. and Hagel, C., "A post-Iraq G.I. Bill," *New York Times,* November 9, Op-Ed contributors. Online. Available HTTP: <http://www.nytimes.com/2007/11/09/opinion/09webb.html> (accessed November 9, 2007), 2007.

Weber, M., *Economy and Society*, Totowa, NJ: Bedminster, 1921/1968.

Weinstein, L. and White, C.C. (eds.), *Wives & Warriors: Women and the Military in the United States and Canada,* Westport, CT: Bergin & Garvey, 1997.

Wenger, W.V., "The Los Angeles riots: a battalion commander's perspective," *Infantry*, (January/February), pp. 13–16, 1994.

Westover, J.G., *The United States Army in the Korean Conflict: Combat Support in Korea*, Washington, DC: Combat Forces Press, 1955.

White, M., *iCasualties.org*. Online. Available HTTP: <http://icasualties.org/oif/Methodology.aspx> (accessed January 2, 2007), 2007.

Wielawski, I., "For troops, home can be too close," *New York Times*, Science Section, March 15. Online. Available HTTP: <http://www.nytimes.com/2005/03/15/health/psychology/15fami.html> (accessed October 9, 2007), 2005.

Wilcox, C., "Race, gender, and support for women in the military," *Social Science Quarterly*, 73(2):310–23, 1992.

Williams, J.A., "Anticipated and unanticipated consequences of the creation of the total force," paper presented at the McCormick Tribune Foundation Conference, Wheaton, IL, October 2007, 2007.

Williams, R.M. Jr. and Smith, M.B., "General characteristics of ground combat," in Stouffer, S.A., Lumsdaine, E.A., Lumsdaine, M.H., Williams, R.M. Jr., Smith, M.B., Janis, I.L., Star, S.A. and Cottrell, L.S. Jr., eds. *Volume II. The American Solder: Combat and Its Aftermath,* Princeton, NJ: Princeton University Press, pp. 59–104, 1949.

Willis, J., "Variations in state casualty rates in World War II and the Vietnam war," *Social Problems,* 22:558–68, 1975.

Wilson, B.A., *Military Women Veterans: Yesterday, Today, Tomorrow.* Online. Available HTTP: <http://userpages.aug.com/captbarb/> (accessed January 28, 2007), 2006.

Wilson, T.C., "Vietnam-era military service: a test of the class-bias thesis," *Armed Forces & Society,* 21(3):461–72, 1995.

Women in Military Service for America Memorial, *Women in Military Service for America Memorial.* Online. Available HTTP: <http://www.womensmemorial.org/> (accessed October 9, 2006), 2006.

Wong, L., *Stifled Innovation? Developing Tomorrow's Leaders Today,* Carlisle, PA: Strategic Studies Institute, 2002.

— *Developing Adaptive Leaders: The Crucible Experience of Operation Iraqi Freedom,* Carlisle, PA: Strategic Studies Institute, 2004.

Wong, L. and Gerras, S., *CU @ the FOB: How the Forward Operating Base is Changing the Life of Combat Soldiers,* Carlisle, PA: Strategic Studies Institute, 2006.

Wong, L., Kolditz, T.A., Millen, R.A. and Potter, T.M., *Why They Fight: Combat Motivation in the Iraq War,* Carlisle, PA: Strategic Studies Institute, 2003.

Woodruff, T., Kelty, R. and Segal, D.R., "Propensity to serve and motivation to enlist among American combat soldiers," *Armed Forces & Society*, 32(3):353–66, 2006.

Wright, J.P., Carter, D.E. and Cullen, F.T., "A life-course analysis of military service in Vietnam," *Journal of Research in Crime and Delinquency,* 42(1):55–83, 2005.

Zeigler, S.L. and Gunderson, G.G., *Moving Beyond G.I. Jane: Women and the US Military,* Lanham, MD: University Press of America, Inc., 2005.

Zweigenhaft, R.L. and Domhoff, G.W., *Diversity in the Power Elite: How it Happened, Why it Matters,* Lanham, MD: Rowman & Littlefield, 2006.

Index